# SON *of a* MIDNIGHT LAND

# ATZ KILCHER

## SON *of a* MIDNIGHT LAND

*A Memoir in Stories*

**BLACK
STONE**
PUBLISHING

Copyright © 2018 by Atz Kilcher
Published in 2018 by Blackstone Publishing
Cover photograph by Scott Dickerson
Cover and book design by Kathryn Galloway English

Printed in the United States of America

First edition: 2018
ISBN 978-1-4708-6018-9
Biography & Autobiography / Personal Memoirs

1 3 5 7 9 10 8 6 4 2

CIP data for this book is available
from the Library of Congress

Blackstone Publishing
31 Mistletoe Rd.
Ashland, OR 97520

www.BlackstonePublishing.com

Dedicated to my father, a dreamer of grand
dreams and a teller of tall stories who held us kids
spellbound beside the warmth of the old woodstove in that homestead cabin of long ago.


Dedicated also to my mother, pioneer poet and
writer of dreams and stories, who always believed
that someday I would do the same.

# TABLE *of* CONTENTS

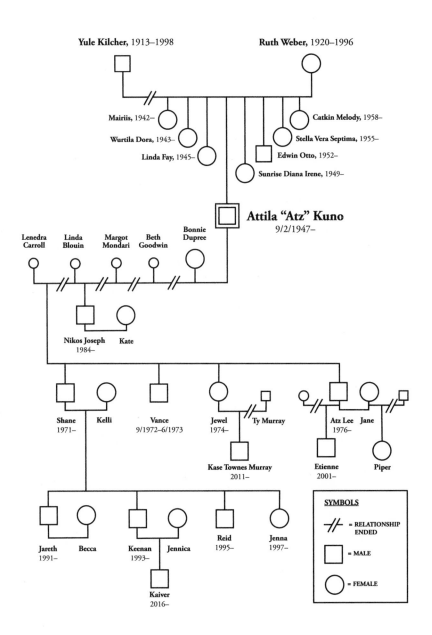

**Yule Kilcher**, 1913–1998    **Ruth Weber**, 1920–1996

Mairiis, 1942–
Wurtila Dora, 1943–
Linda Fay, 1945–
Sunrise Diana Irene, 1949–
Edwin Otto, 1952–
Stella Vera Septima, 1955–
Catkin Melody, 1958–

**Attila "Atz" Kuno**
9/2/1947–

Lenedra Carroll
Linda Blouin
Margot Mondari
Beth Goodwin
Bonnie Dupree

Nikos Joseph 1984–
Kate

Shane 1971–
Kelli
Vance 9/1972–6/1973
Jewel 1974–
Ty Murray
Atz Lee 1976–
Jane

Kase Townes Murray 2011–
Etienne 2001–
Piper

Jareth 1991–
Becca
Keenan 1993–
Jennica
Reid 1995–
Jenna 1997–

Kaiver 2016–

**SYMBOLS**

—//— = RELATIONSHIP ENDED

☐ = MALE

◯ = FEMALE

# KILCHER FAMILY TREE

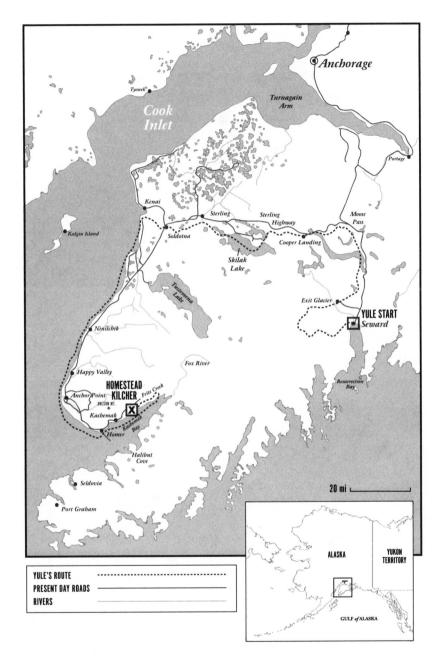

# KENAI PENINSULA, ALASKA

# SURVIVAL LESSONS

# CHAPTER 1

## *Liar*

"You're a damn liar!"

My dear old daddy, quite unknowingly, gave me a valuable gift as I was growing up, a gift that has lasted a lifetime. He used to say (or shout) that I was a "damn liar."

Part of the time you could say it was justified because, well, I was lying. Other times I was telling the truth, but he still called me a damn liar. Hell, he even said it when I was trying to tell him something great I had done, something I hoped would win his approval.

"You're a damn liar."

I can't claim to even begin to know why that was the case (unless I'm lying), but he called me that a lot. He had a real thing about it. I think he had a bit of a suspicious nature. Could be he was struggling with his own inner liar. Who knows?

I also have no idea if I started lying from the get-go, or whether I slowly learned the skill. Was I born with a dishonest soul? All I know is that as I grew, it became more and more a part of my self-image. Somewhere along the line I did become a very good liar, maybe even an expert. If there was ever a contest involving lying, I could give the best of them a run for their money.

Early on, I decided to use this dark gift and make lemonade out of my lemons by capitalizing on it. I decided to become the best liar I could possibly be! I became a storyteller, a spinner of yarns and tall tales. I became an entertainer and learned to embellish, exaggerate, and impress. Why, maybe I'd even write a book someday.

I was determined to make me some sweet lemonade.

One of the first times I wrote a quick song about somebody I hardly knew, I realized I was using that gift. It was for a special occasion, he was a friend of a friend of mine. I took the 10 percent I knew about him and stretched it way out. I exaggerated and made up stuff he'd like to hear. When I sang it for him, he wondered how I had described him so well, as though I had known him for years.

I had the knack.

The other equally important part of my dad's gift to me was that it kept me busy, made my earlier years more interesting. Lying got me into a lot of trouble, and got me out of a lot too. It gave me an identity. And later on, working through my lying issues, unraveling 'em all and trying to change, gave me something to do, kept me focused. If it hadn't been for that, I might have had all kinds of time on my hands for less interesting things like healthy relationships or pursuing spirituality. Plus, there are a whole lot of therapists and authors of self-help books who have benefited greatly from this.

Of course, I might be lying about the whole thing. See, part of me hopes to keep you confused and on your toes so you stop caring what's true and get caught up in the thrill of the ride. And that all goes back to … you guessed it: my childhood, of course.

\* \* \*

Tom Bodett famously described Homer, Alaska, as "the end of the road." But my siblings and I knew that road decades before he arrived.

For us, it was our mile-long dirt driveway at the end of the twelve-mile stretch of gravel to Homer. That was where our homestead sat up at the top of the world. There, overlooking the Kachemak Bay, was where we parked our Jeep and greeted visitors. There was where we learned to trek through waist-deep snow and shin-deep mud to catch the bus. And my sisters' dates would trek to our cabin—a three-mile round-trip that often prevented my sisters from dating the same guy twice.

Those of us eight kids old enough to make the walk to the school bus went to public school. The rest had it easy. They got to lounge around all day cooped up with our stir-crazy mama in that tiny two-room log cabin. The school-aged ones did their lessons; Mama instructed them between her many homestead tasks while dragging and carrying the tiny ones around.

The deciding factor of being able to make it to the school bus was the criteria for being allowed to go to public school, like being tall enough for a ride at the carnival. I could write a book about only what happened along that road over the course of our public-school careers. Imagine encounters with moose, bears, rain, ice, pitch blackness and flashlights, mud and snow, or any combinations thereof. That's the short version.

In the darkest depth of winter, snow was the biggest factor. The oldest took turns breaking trail through sometimes three feet of snow, and deeper through the drifts. It was slow and tough going but we were used to it. Believe me, all that was nothing compared to meeting a half-starved cranky moose unwilling to yield the right of way. It meant breaking a trail around her, now through five or six feet of snow across deadfall logs where you might disappear up to your neck and through almost impenetrable wilderness, canyons, or gullies. Then we had to run the rest of the way to make up for lost time, with one older kid behind cracking the whip to keep the younger ones moving.

My teenaged sisters changing into their non-hick school clothes under a tree, putting on their makeup, fixing their hair, and me trying to keep my Elvis hairdo from getting too messed up under my warm hat might well have been the most challenging part of this whole ordeal. What a kid had to go through just to get a social life. In truth, we would have walked ten miles to get a break from homestead life and see other kids.

My dad worked far away from home a lot in those days. He was elected state senator for our district, which meant he had to spend a few months each winter in our state capital. When he wasn't doing that, he was building houses in Anchorage, several hundred miles away. With only gravel roads back then, he didn't come home much. This meant mom and us kids had to fend for ourselves.

Sometimes we had the deep snow bulldozed, other times we packed it down with our dually jeep, or waited till it was frozen enough to drive on. Sometimes we just waited till spring, whichever was the easiest or came first. Any supplies we would need to supplement our homegrown stuff were brought in ahead of the deep snow, so we were prepared.

Because of her real or imagined heart condition, and probably many factors beyond my scope, my mama seldom got to town during deep snow periods. She left it up to us kids to bring home a few fresh groceries, deliver messages, deliver milk, and check the mail. Of course, we had to do all this over our thirty-minute school lunch period, and on the run. We'd run a half mile uptown with milk to sell, one gallon jug hanging from a throbbing finger, and another one sloshing in a backpack. Then whoever's turn it was that day would return to school with a bunch of mail, packages, and groceries.

Coming from a big homesteading family, we were all good at wolfing food down while on the job or on the run. I was a top athlete in high school. Most Valuable Athlete title 1966, and that's no lie!

We could have lived without the few groceries or checking the mail every day. But my mother couldn't. Why were her baloney, store-bought cheese, and coffee so important? Why was my mama almost obsessive about her mail and newspaper, her crossword puzzles she used to love to drink her coffee by? Well, my greenhorn friend, you obviously know nothing about cabin fever, its causes and cures.

Our mama was already a bit prone toward depression, occasional hysterics, and heart fluttering. But being cooped up in a small cabin in the middle of nowhere, enduring a long, cold, dark winter with not much to do and nowhere to go took its toll. Of course, how tightly wrapped you were going into the winter months determined how much sanity you had left coming out in the spring.

It was always hard for us kids to know exactly whether her mood swings were her nature, her cabin fever, or her and our dad's less-than-perfect and splendidly dysfunctional marriage.

Those marital stresses were replaced by a whole new set when we were left alone to fend for ourselves. I felt less stress when dad was gone, and we all learned to spread his share of the workload early on. But for our mama, his being gone was understandably a big added stress.

We continually watched our mama's pressure gauge and her energy levels. For us kids raised right there in that cabin, those woods with all that snow, it was all we knew. For our dear mama, it was relatively new. The first half of her life was spent in Europe: operas, classical singing, violin lessons, and the best private schools. She had been steeped in culture, history, and modern conveniences.

Yes, she had done incredible things as a young pioneer woman, but cabin fever could slowly infect even the strongest trapper, gold miner, or mountain man. Here was a cultured woman, alone with eight kids, responsible for keeping them safe, healthy, fed, and educated. She was also responsible for the cows and horses and other farm animals. The cabin was small and crowded, with bare light bulbs, drafty floors, leaking ceilings. The cow moose close to the haystack had to be poached when meat was running low. Frozen pipes had to be thawed and water holes for livestock chopped open with an ax.

Us older kids held a lot of responsibility, but she was ultimately responsible for it all. Not another woman's voice or face for miles, or months. No grandparents, no aunts or uncles to lean on or ask for help in this faraway land. The snow just kept getting deeper, the nights longer and darker, the temperature colder, the cabin smaller, and the babies screaming louder.

It was not unusual to come home to no supper, no housework done, and our mama still in her robe. Maybe we'd find her at her altar, her small typewriter, pecking away at a new poem or a short story, with a faraway look in her eyes. Maybe she'd still be in bed, eating the last of her baloney stash, or in the old rocker, rocking the baby while they both cried, or screaming irrationally while wailin' on my seven-year-old brother with her big spatula.

Sooner or later, her cabin fever would become part of the landscape, and just as sure, over time, the effects seeped into who we are today. We tried our best to keep her out of that dark, deep pit. But once she was in it, there was nothing we could do but spread the load, keep going, and wait for the cure to kick in: spring!

Preventing cabin fever was a lot easier than dealing with the effects, or living with it, so we all became certified cabin fever prevention experts. If you talk to any one of us eight kids, we will all agree on one thing: we grew up with the pressure of too much responsibility at too early an age.

For Mama, I was her "little man." What imprinted indelibly on my young mind, soul, and spirit was how, when, and where she told me. It came usually after a fight with my dad. Sometimes there was blood or bruising, sometimes only tears. Sometimes it was when my dad was away and she had the blues real bad and sometimes, even more confusing, he was still home. Sometimes it was when she needed to confide in me, something that only I could understand, the oldest son, a young man. Sometimes it was when she needed my strength physically or emotionally, telling me through sobs never to treat my wife like that, never to make her cry. By then I was already jumping in between my parents to keep my dad away from her. When my role as family clown didn't work, I put on my cape and became the matador.

There were also plenty of ways she let me know I was her special little man. She was the only parent I got praise from for being who I was, my physique, my looks, my voice, my humor. She'd call me her Irish rover, her troubadour, her strong, stalwart son. She praised my guitar playing and songwriting. She once had me flex my muscles with my shirt off and pose while she photographed me. I've long since lost the photo, but I captured the moment forever. I did whatever it took to safeguard that source of nourishment to my fragile self-esteem. And

I cared for my fragile mother and kept my promises to her that may well have begun at my birth.

We came home from school one cabin-feverish day to meet our mama waiting more anxiously than usual for her fix of goodies. There were no greetings, no "how was school today?" Her first words were nervous. "Did I get any mail?" Mail duty had fallen on me that day. Some days she got some, others she didn't, so I thought nothing of telling her I forgot. No big deal. We'd get it tomorrow.

"*How dare you!*" she screamed, and her piercing soprano vibrato and Swiss accent bounced off the logs and turned everyone's heads. I was at full alert! Little man was on duty!

When finally she was able to speak again, she gave me the lesson I've carried all my life: "I would rather you lied and told me there was no mail than tell me you forgot."

Well, I got it. I totally got it! And I ain't forgot it yet.

From then on, I would try to make people happy, truth or lies— whatever it took. As long as my words brought the desired response of smiles and no trouble, that was all I cared about.

It was a big lesson in my survival training. And I cultivated that belief as diligently as my father did the apple trees he transplanted from his homeland.

# CHAPTER 2

## *Lessons and Practice*

My mama and daddy had very different techniques for teaching me to be a bulletproof, skilled, professional liar. Both methods were highly successful. They came at it from different angles and between the two of them, they did a mighty fine job of covering all the bases. They cranked out a well-rounded liar. A son they could both be proud of.

Carrot and stick come to mind, honey and vinegar, reward and punishment. You saw how my mama's honey worked its magic; so very sweet to feel her love, to feel needed as her protector. Well, dessert's over, time for some real food, some roughage, my dad's vinegar cellar.

I don't know if the name B. F. Skinner means anything to you, or the term *behaviorism*. But my dad, like B. F. Skinner, believed in reward and punishment. Mostly punishment. Skinner was also big on punishment—both as a way to extinguish a behavior and as something to avoid when teaching a new behavior.

I went to college for six years and earned a master's degree in social work to learn his name and what his field of psychological research was called. All animal trainers and many parents use his pioneering work. What I realized as I was learning this was that I already knew it, I just didn't know what it was called. We kids were raised by it, and all of our animals lived by it. It was part of life, the way of nature, as basic as food, air, and water.

My dad, without knowing it, was a Skinnerian, a behaviorist. He probably could have taught old B. F. a thing or two. He specialized in the pain and punishment method to eliminate unwanted behaviors. He also rewarded us for the desired results by not hurting us as he had threatened. There was more to it than just the basics though, a little more spice and intrigue. The passing down of pedigreed dysfunction is never a simple matter.

I learned something extra as well, a sort of bonus. I learned to lie. Lying was highly rewarding for me; avoiding pain without having to change my behavior. Brilliant! So lying, making excuses, and rationalizing became a part of my survival technique. If ever my dad rewarded me, other than not hurting me, it was for some extraordinary unbelievable feat. Like cutting three hundred fence posts in one day. Digging half a mile of ditch with a shovel, or removing all the snow from the canyon road with a snow shovel. Oh, to see his face light up with his winning smile. To see that look of love and approval.

Of course, all of that made me an expert at stretching, greatly exaggerating, or plain-out making things up. "Dad, you should have seen that half-ton rock I had to roll out of the ditch," or, "I saw a moose yesterday with a two-hundred-inch rack, but he slipped away." I must say, he raised kids with a hell of a work ethic. One of our favorite pastimes when we get together now as adults is comparing joint ailments, bad backs, and ligament and tendon disorders.

What went wrong? How did someone who hated lying turn me into an expert liar? How did someone who detested anything that even smelled like an excuse end up with a son who was the excuse-making pro? How could this happen to a man who could sniff out a guilty thought before you even thought it? Actually, nothing went wrong even though I used to think so. I used to think he *did* wrong, *went* wrong, *was* wrong, which of course made *me* all wrong. No more! He was great at what he did, though I think the results were not what he intended. I consequently became a pro at what I did.

I doubt I need to go into detail regarding my dad's training techniques. I'd like to say I didn't wish for him to die so I could finally tell the world what a son of a bitch he was, how he had crippled me. I'd like you to think well of him. But there was a time I wanted the world to know that none of how I turned out was my fault. I wanted to blame him for all the bad, and give credit to myself and my mama for all the good. Years of therapy unraveled and sorted all that. But hang with me here while we head through the vinegar cellar.

Somewhere along the way, I grew up, wised up, or maybe it was having kids. I started looking and acting more like my dad, and I started understanding myself, and him, better. He was never diagnosed, but he was clearly borderline a whole lot of things, with touches of bipolar disorder, seasonal affective disorder, social anxiety disorder, and adult attention deficit disorder. He must have felt fear, powerlessness, inadequacy, and a whole heap of responsibility in a whole new world. Horses and horse-drawn wagon and machinery to maintain, crosscut saws to manage, log cabins to build, moose to shoot, fish to catch, wood and coal to keep up, a living to earn, kids to raise, a homestead to improve upon, land to clear and plant, and on and on. Not to mention his social and cultural responsibilities as senator. I can't imagine a reason he wouldn't have felt overwhelmed! All of this added to his already complex and highly driven personality. These and more pressures brought out his darker colors, and sadly, he didn't often show a brighter color on the homestead or to his kids. Likely, he couldn't often feel that way.

I was left alone on the homestead one winter when I was sixteen. My older sisters had moved on after high school. My dad was in Juneau playing senator, my mom and the youngest kids had gone to California for the winter. It was no big deal. I had a blast, learned a lot, and blossomed. I honed and practiced old skills and learned brand new ones, having no adult supervision all winter.

My responsibilities were no different than they'd always been. Only now there wasn't anyone there to check up on me. I had to keep alive thirty beef cattle, ten horses, and a bunch of chickens, ducks, and geese. All I had to do was give 'em food and water and gather eggs before they froze solid and burst. And I had to milk the cow. I had to keep the water pipes from freezing and bursting, as well. Keep myself clean, dressed, and fed. Oh, yes, I also went to school—well, when I wasn't skipping.

I got in touch with my inner alcoholic. I flunked the whole year. I partied and stayed lots of nights in town. I turned the calf loose with the cow so I wouldn't have to milk her. In town, I broke and entered, did some joyriding, and shoplifted.

Critters got skinny, and so did I. Drank more than I ate. Chicken eggs burst, hens quit laying, water pipes burst. I partied. The worst of it was one horse starved to death. I think next to finding your dog dead, finding one of your horses dead is a real sadness. Of course, if it died because of your own negligence, that's probably the worst.

I found Strawberry in the middle of a big open field, where she had been for weeks, pawing through the hard, deep snow, to get to the grass beneath. As I approached, I thought it was just an old stump or a pile of branches. Then I saw the birds. She was frozen solid, but they were still pecking away at her. Eye sockets empty, body cavity open, her half-eaten frozen innards on display. The wolves and coyotes apparently hadn't found her yet. Her hip bones looked like hat racks. Ribs stood out like bars on a xylophone. Her hooves were worn to the quick. They had served her until she had no more strength or energy to paw through the ice.

You can only stand there so long looking at that kind of thing, seeing the movie in your head. It brings up too many feelings. I went home and had a home brew.

The only time I saw the homestead in daylight was on weekends, since I was in school in the light of those short winter days, or supposed to be anyway. During the darkest part of winter it was light from ten in the morning till three in the afternoon or so. Even some weekends I stayed in town, just running home to throw the critters a little hay. It was a whole lot easier not thinking about what I was neglecting when I couldn't see it.

Out of laziness, I had not been opening the water hole for the cows. I reasoned it wasn't the worst thing, they can live on snow. Over the long haul though, melting cold snow burns up a lot of precious calories. And cows with all their stomachs need lots of water, more than horses.

One weekend when I get home during daylight, I break trail down to the spring to chop it open. The cows have long since given up on it, and the trail is snowed over. The water hole is about half a mile below the feedlot, a natural spring we'd dug out near the alders at the upper end so the water could pool.

In the summer, a cow or horse would bog down clear up to their belly around that whole area. Once the boggy ground froze though, critters could walk right up to the edge and drink. It took a long cold snap to freeze the spring itself, that's when you had to chop a hole with an ax. As a little kid, I thought it was the scariest looking thing, bubbly and foamy, brown and sulfur smelling. When it started getting cold, it would be steaming like a hot tub. A very scary place! We had no way of knowing how deep it was and never wanted to find out.

Cows fell in once in awhile but they'd drag themselves out. We'd have to help them out either by hand or a jeep winch. In the winter, if you didn't keep the hole chopped open, the cows might stand on it and sometimes break through.

Anyway, I finally get down to the local watering hole through all that snow and I take off my snowshoes, lean 'em up against the big old spruce tree that doubles as toolshed, grab the ax, and step up to chop the snow-covered spring. There's a lump under the snow and a branch sticking up. Just debris. Happens all the time. Even before scraping off, I take a mighty swing with my ax to sheer off the branch at ice level, but it's solid and sends shock waves through my spine. Chipped snow flies.

It's a cow's horn.

Another shock wave as it sinks in. I drop to my knees in the undisturbed snow. I take off my gloves and with bare hands I start digging. Which one is it? I can't tell by the horn. With stinging fingers, I carefully wipe the last of the snow off the white blaze face. It's Rene. Our first purebred Hereford.

I remember my dad's excited yodel that woke us all up the morning he and our hired hand Rene found her as a wet newborn. Kneeling there, I think of my dad and shiver.

I'd started reading signs long before I started talking, and I knew exactly what had happened. She'd broken through the ice. She wasn't able to turn around to climb out to solid ground, and she couldn't keep breaking the ice in front of her. It was too thick, and only her head was out to break it with. She'd struggled for some time. Chunks of frozen mud were slung here and there, and I imagined her churning legs. Her bloody chin, still frozen to the ice, had been the only tool she had for breaking ice, prying, and pulling.

She couldn't have lived more than a couple of hours. I didn't want to see how thick the ice was over her body. I was too ashamed of how long she'd been there. I began to wonder how many other cows were missing, and I was shivering. I don't know how much time passed, but my knees felt like part of the ice. The sweat from the effort of snowshoeing was freezing on me. My hands were still bare, fingers numb, and I started hurting bad, and not just in my body either.

But you push on. Life as lone ranch foreman continued. I paid more attention for awhile. Snow kept falling. Temperatures dropped. My conscience froze. My hoodlum friends came out to spend the night, and we drank my dad's good Swiss schnapps and all the home brew in the cellar. Good, stout, dark ale. Those city kids got drunk on one bottle! Nothing like partying in the safety of a remote cabin in the beauty of nature among dying animals.

Relatives of my inner liar started dropping in left and right, and we took to each other like long-lost friends. Soon the whole damn bunch moved in! The Rationalizers were among the first, the Deniers were close behind. The Procrastinators were a big tribe, they just kept on dribbling in. I got to meet 'em all. We were so much alike. We all played an important part and kept each other company. It took a lot of good hands to run that spread. I was a strong young man. I was a child, alone and lost. I knew how to do it all. I needed serious help. I was just a boy of sixteen.

I made it through the winter without going to jail. Most of the critters made it to see the spring. Mama and the kids came home. All was well ... until dad came home. My dad's radar was uncanny. He could sniff out a lie like a hungry wolf could find a half-starved moose, and he was just as relentless and ferocious once he found it. To outwit him, to throw him off the scent when he smelled blood, took skill. I did it time and time again. I had learned well. Survival of the fittest, kill or be killed, it was pure self-preservation. And I was almost ready to take over the pack.

Another thing I had going for me when my dad came home was his poor memory and the fact that he had pretty much turned the cow and horse operation over to me.

"What happened to that white face cow we called Rene?"

With just the right amount of confidence, and irritation at his poor memory, I interrupted with short, confusing, rapid-fire half-truths. "Remember those cows the Lewises wintered for us winter before last? That one we gave them in payment? And then that other one that died? So we actually gave them another one and traded for this one ... I'm gonna finish this fence before it gets dark."

"What the hell are those bones I found in the back pasture, there by the Indian thicket?"

I never missed a beat. It wasn't rehearsed; it was just there, as natural as anything, like it was part of who I was, and therefore true. "Don't you remember when the Willards drove their cows through here last fall and those two got caught on the wrong side of the fence and no one knew they were there?"

On and on it went, the interrogation of my winter sins. It was serious business. I could show no fear. He would have smelled it like a shark. Even when his eyes were rolled back, showing only white, I met him head on. Calm. Strong. With steel cold eyes, quietly challenging.

"I've looked all over hell for Strawberry, what the hell is going on around here?" She was the only draft horse we had left, the last of an era, all the others were saddle horses. It was his special horse.

This time his lip was curled in a snarl. Saliva. Fangs. Wise, knowing eyes that could almost see through me, hard and ready to strike. I had to up the ante.

"Goddammit, Dad!" I shouted. "I stayed here all damn winter, held down the fort, now every little thing wrong is my fault. I don't mind taking care of the cows and horses, but it was you who decided to leave Strawberry at the head of the bay to see if she could graze all winter. We agreed to leave her up there. The Lewises were gonna keep an eye on her. It was a worse winter than any of us expected. I'm getting tired of this shit!"

It was my best; it had to be. Chest to chest, wit to wit. Youth, cunning, and strength against age, wisdom, and treachery. For him, fear of losing control, losing his memory, fear of deception, fear of powerlessness. For me … fear of … no. There was no fear, only well-honed instincts and skills.

I had undergone years of being questioned, cross-examined, and quizzed. I had had countless traps set for me. He had sure ways of catching me. He booby-trapped, so when I lied he could prove I was lying by the thread I had broken, by the fine powder that had been disturbed. He was a pioneer, a hunter, a tracker. Only the wisest of wolves survives and learns to outsmart the trapper. There were plenty of times he accused me of things I didn't do, thoughts I never had. I think he also might have been just a tad bit paranoid.

I will never forget the time he lost his second bid for the senate. He felt rejection, hurt, deception, and anger beyond words. I was driving with him to town. Alone with him in a car. His favorite place for grilling, accusing, and lecturing. Granted, just having lost the election, he was a lit fuse. "I bet you're happy that I lost!" he screamed out of the blue, red in the face. Anyone who knew him knows he spit a lot when he got excited, bad or good. This was one of those bad spitting times. It lasted the whole way to town.

There is no way to talk reasonably to a psychotic, to someone in an altered state of consciousness. I was defenseless, cowered against the door. I could tell he was not going to let up. I had to choose between denying the accusation and letting him think I suspected he was temporarily wacky, or telling a lie and admitting that yes, maybe I was just a little happy. At least my false confession broke the stalemate, and things wound down. That was just one of the many times I lied, even though I was innocent, just to get it over with.

Never knowing what might set him off or give him some ammunition with which to accuse me, I learned to choose my words carefully, to always leave a way out, to have a quick mind. Many years later, in therapy with my second wife, my therapist said to me, "Atz, you have a rare gift of knowing what is best for your wife."

"Oh, yes," I answered, "I'm glad you recognize that."

Probably one of the most useful skills my father taught me was to read other people's minds, and to know what was best for them. This is a rare gift he passed on to me through years of patient role modeling.

It's hard to argue with someone who claims they know what you're thinking, or that they know what's best for you, that they know you better than you know yourself. Saying that he knew what I was thinking saved a lot of time and was a hell of a shortcut. It went right from the accusation, which to him was already a hard fact, straight to the sentencing phase.

Yes, to counteract his claim of being able to read my mind, I had to learn a different type of lying, and become a persuasive arguer using a new kind of warfare.

Oh yes, the tone. How could I forget? Even when your voice was perfect, the rage in his ringing ears distorted it to sound like whatever he feared: insolence, impatience, snottiness, smart-aleckiness. So I learned another valuable skill. Always keep a flat, monotone, unemotional yet respectful and noncondescending voice. At the same time, I was trying to determine which filter he was listening through so as to know how to counteract it, and give him the right antidote.

Similar, but with a little twist, was the face. Depending on his mood again, what he *thought* you were thinking or feeling or had done, he could *see* on your face. The best policy was a stone face, and even then, too stony could also get you into trouble. This might sound like something out of a movie, unless you know someone like this.

It was only after having been slapped very hard enough times for having the wrong voice or face—the head-twisting, spine-bending, chiropractic-nightmare kind of slap from a big, calloused hand—that the emotionless voice and face became embedded in my cells.

One of the proudest moments of my high school life was when I was a senior. On second thought, it wasn't *one* of many, it was *the* proudest moment of my life up till then: getting the most valuable, all-around outstanding athlete award. (I may have lengthened that title a bit over the years.)

Put in perspective, this was a small school of maybe a hundred and fifty, and thirty in my graduating class. All boys of any athletic aptitude at all went out for several sports. My senior year, I lettered in five sports.

Alaska tends to have a whole heap of record setters: first hockey-mom governor and vice presidential candidate, first woman to win the Iditarod Trail Sled Dog Race, first Swiss immigrant to be elected to the Constitutional Convention, and again and again and again. A friend of mine up the road set three records for the Iditarod in the same year. He also set the record for catching the most fish as a commercial fisherman. They call 'em highliners. Then there's that carpenter who became a famous author and is best known for leaving the light on for you at Motel 6. And of course, that blond singer-yodeler homestead hick chick.

I lettered in track, cross-country running, skiing, basketball, and wrestling. Skiing and basketball seasons overlapped, so I did both.

On the night the awards were given, the whole gym floor is full of tables all decorated with fancy tablecloths and candles. Students are sitting at separate tables, Mom and Dad with other parents. I'm with my best buds and I'm in heaven! I'm also in a rare mood. Even though I know my dad is watching me, I am trying to relax, put some life into my voice, some excitement. I'm trying to lose the stony face, so I'm cutting up, laughing, joking, and flirting. I'm eighteen and top dog of the athletic heap, having spent most of my high school career an unpopular hick who'd flunked a grade and was only recognized in sports.

I sneak a peek at my dad and catch him sneaking a peek at me. I wonder what he's thinking and feeling. Pride in his son? Happiness? Satisfaction?

We get home and something sets him off. One thing leads to another and he ends up with his face in mine. "I saw the way you were acting at that table," he rages with a red face, "laughing with that stupid laugh of yours, looking like a dumb clown. You looked just like your uncle Hugo."

Uncle Hugo, my mother's brother, who my dad openly did not like, had a lopsided kind of cocky smirk. Uncle Hugo's grin must have triggered some sick inner child in my dad, and he was forever running him down.

In his attempt to show me how I had looked at that table with my friends, he makes the most grotesque, twisted faces. What a convincing job of acting, flopping his head and rolling his eyes. It's not just the faces, though. That's the least of it. What really hurts is the feeling he's putting into them. Such hate, such malice, such venom to his disgust!

I go out into the subzero night to do chores. Those few face cells, not yet stiff and frozen, slowly join the rest. "You want stone you son of a bitch? You want ice? Well, you finally got it." Only the cows and horses hear me as they munch their hay.

In the '80s, while working as a social worker in Anchorage, I went to the Matanuska Valley where my mother and father first lived when I came to Alaska. They grew potatoes to make enough money to buy the tools and supplies needed to begin homesteading in Homer. While I was there, I met a man who knew my dad in those early days. He couldn't say enough good about my dad. He went on and on, I was sure he must be talking about somebody else. It took him a while to say it all, but he said my dad was the kindest, most generous, most helpful, friendliest, wittiest guy he'd ever met in his life. It had been forty years and he had never forgotten him. Talk about conflicting emotions! I was grateful, but my overriding thought was, *I sure wish that was the guy who raised me!*

At home, the clown and the wiseass and the hostile youth kept leaking out. Sideways. Indirect. Sarcastic. Angry. The clown learned better tricks, the wiseass got wiser. Something about the fear of using the wrong words, the wrong voice, the wrong face, makes it hard to express yourself real clearly.

Fortunately, I still remember the first time someone said I had a great smile and told me I expressed myself well. That came years later though, and was to begin the long, slow process of rebuilding and retraining cells. The stone face and flat voice still grab me at times. Mostly around family of origin. They crop up at the most inopportune times. When most normal folks would break into a big ear-to-ear grin and exclaim great excitement or joy, I go stone face and flat voice.

How in the hell I ended up on the stage, using my voice, face, and words, I will never know. Must have been my unconscious rehab program—plus, it got me lots of applause. Of course, most of the time alcohol helped me relax.

Maybe hiding how you feel is about as dishonest as it gets. Yes, I think it is the very worst kind of lying.

Why in the world would a kid keep doing "bad" or "wrong" things, even after being beaten, screamed at, or shamed? Why would a kid just keep adding more bad to their already bad, sad personality, keep right on getting better at being bad? How are psychopaths and mass murders slowly molded? Or are they born defective? How much credit or blame can parents take for how their kids turn out? Of course, to confuse things even more, there are all the examples of good kids from bad homes, and bad kids from good homes.

I'm not sure anyone has the answer. Even with all my schooling, my social work with some pretty messed-up institutionalized kids, having raised my own kids, and having taught others' children, it's still a mystery to me.

What I do know is this: I give thanks every day for all the *good* my parents and the wilderness gave me. For all the strengths, talents, and skills, all the tools and maps. Whether knowingly or not, with the disease, they also gave me the antidote I needed, the tools to turn the raw manure into rich, useful compost. It was their wisdom, determination, and work ethic I used to find the answers I needed through schooling and therapy.

I call that growing up—transforming the bad into something useful and finding a way to get all the good you never got.

It's a lifelong process, and I don't think I'm going to run out of work anytime soon. But like clearing a field, you can make it as smooth as you want. Just know, the more you look, the more roots, twigs, and rocks you'll see.

And how long it all takes just depends on how smooth you want your field.

# CHAPTER 3

## *Homer Hooligan*

As a teenager, I never spent much time contemplating why I was so dishonest. Why I stole and lied. Why I broke into Homer businesses or residences. Sometimes I just browsed, sometimes I stole a few items. I shoplifted for years. I did some "joyriding," a nice way of saying stealing cars and then returning them. Although I was picked on for being a homestead hick, I became a bully myself and beat up my share of innocent kids just because I could.

All I knew at the time was that it felt good. It was exhilarating. It filled some deep, dark need to be in charge, in control. It also gave me some friends of similar persuasions. But many of the things I did that were dishonest or illegal, I did alone.

Only years later, as a young adult with a master's degree in social work, when I found myself working with the same type of young hooligans who had become institutionalized, did I better understand all of this. The youth I worked with came from two systems: either from corrections, having broken the law, or through social services.

They all had severe social or emotional challenges. The difference was that some of them broke the law by acting out, while others had such extreme difficulties in the school system or at home that the state had to intervene. Believe me, working with these kids, I felt right at home. That is the reason I went into social work; it was a field I already had quite a bit of experience in. This field, of course, also required that I get involved with a lot of family therapy and marriage counseling—also a field I already had quite a bit of experience in.

It became apparent to me, as I was getting my degrees in psychology and social work and doing a lot of research on child development, that kids from certain dysfunctional homes were more prone to having certain issues. I believe all eight of us children ended up with some good solid issues to work through in our lives. I did not get a bigger helping of dysfunction than any of the others, but I certainly turned my share into more acting out—in my family, the school system, and society in general.

But here again, I also have to thank something in my upbringing for the fact that somehow, I had enough sense to turn that desire into useful college degrees, and into a career that I was pretty good at.

Of course, my early social work training wasn't just as a Homer hoodlum. While I was at the University of Utah, I was doing my master's fieldwork at a boys ranch. I had some reliable evidence that one of the boys had stolen a car while he was on a weekend home leave. This boy was already on thin ice, and if convicted of this car theft, it could send him to juvenile hall to be locked up.

My wife and I were co-ranch parents, and we tried to get the truth out of him. He had a beautiful story and beautiful alibis. He swore up and down that he was innocent, that he was being framed. He even cried. But the old Homer hoodlum knew he was lying. We put pressure on the kids. We put pressure on all twelve of the residents. They, in turn, put pressure on him. We were running our boys ranch under the peer pressure philosophy—a debatable method, but highly effective in young men with severe behavioral issues.

Day by day, he remained steadfast in his story. And I remained steadfast in my belief that he was lying through his teeth. I knew it in my own inner delinquent's lying gut.

My wife eventually got worn down and started buying his sob stories. And one night, it reduced her to tears.

"Atz, can't you see he's telling the truth? How can you be so cruel and without feeling? If anybody could get the truth out of him, those other eleven hooligans could."

"You just have to trust me on this one," I said. "He's close to cracking."

Just then, there was a knock on the door. All twelve young men came into our room in the big ranch building where we lived. They wanted a group meeting. It seemed the young man in question finally had something to confess.

There was another time I couldn't find any of the young men. They were not in the recreation area or in their bedrooms or anywhere in the yard. They had all vanished.

*Now where would I be and what would I be doing if I were in their shoes living here at this boys ranch?* I asked myself.

Immediately, I knew where they were. I set out sauntering across the field toward a deep gully with a lot of underbrush at the bottom. I was playing it up and whistling to myself, and when I got to the edge, I hollered out, "What a beautiful, steep gully! I think I'll start throwing some big boulders down into that brush."

I began doing just that. Boulder after boulder bounced and rolled down the steep hillside and crashed into the brush below. "Stop! Stop! We're coming out."

Maybe not the safest method, but it was effective.

Back in my hooligan days, if you were a boy in Homer wanting some extra excitement, I was the guy to hang out with. Guess you need to know how I define "excitement." Basically, delinquent activities of almost any kind. I was good at being sneaky and not getting caught—or lying my way out of it.

One windy, dark September evening, a few of us are riding around in my friend Steve's Impala. We're bored, waiting for a movie to start and we pass the old Svedlund place where there's a *huge* new political sign, the first such monstrous billboard in our little town. Senator Gruening's face is smiling at us in the headlights and he is clearly taunting us.

Something has to be done.

We tie a rope to one of the eight-foot-tall legs of the sign and take off, throwing gravel and dirt to get from the parking lot back onto the road. The eight-foot face comes tumbling down and is suddenly bouncing along behind us down the gravel road.

We are yelling and hollering like the wild, rowdy teenage boys we are. This is big small-town fun. We head out toward Miller's Landing. We have no plan of what to do with the sign, but before long, old Gruening is pretty much chopsticks. So we untie him right there in the middle of East End Road, for what good is a trophy if you don't leave the evidence for people to see?

Well, someone saw it, and they saw us. And wouldn't you know it just happened to be old Officer Jack, the only cop in town. He catches up with us somewhere close to the airport and he takes us in for questioning. Only the cop shop also doubles as his house—sort of a landmark, old and green, and one of the few with a traditional white picket fence. Or it was white at one time, anyway.

Jack had a real easygoing, friendly way about him, at least until he lost his temper. He normally cut us boys some slack, gave us some room to grow up. But that night, for some reason, he was pretty heated up about that Gruening sign. Perhaps since the man was running for US Senate, we'd broken some federal law. That seemed to be the kind of thing he might lose his temper over. We'd all heard stories of how he'd worked over some of the town's older and tougher hoodlums pretty good at times.

"Well boys," he begins real slow, "someone saw you pull over that sign. You wanna tell me about it?"

I'm ready. Way ahead of the pack. This is what I was trained for. This was gonna be easy. Poor old Jack didn't stand a chance. He was dealing with a PhD graduate of the Kilcher School of Lying, a decorated veteran and survivor of the POW Interrogation Academy. All I have to do is jump in before one of the other boys opens his mouth and blows it.

"You talking about that pile of splintered lumber by Mickey's Market?"

"You know what I'm talking about." Jack's eyebrows cast long shadows.

"We almost hit it coming in. Damn near went in the ditch swerving to miss it."

"Coming in from where?"

He faltered and I knew I had him. "Maybe someone saw us turning onto Kachemak drive."

"What were you doing out there?"

"Coming in from the homestead," I said. "Steve and the guys came out to pick me up. I went home on the bus and did chores. Hell, you can see the hay seeds and cow shit still on my boots." There was the evidence on my boots, like it usually was.

"Why did you go around Kachemak Drive instead of straight in on East End Road?"

"We were gonna pick up Billy, but you stopped us before we got there." I was cooking now. "Hell, Jack, you know that Senator Gruening and my old man are friends. He's been out to the place for dinner for God's sake! Why in the hell would I tear down a family friend? If I was gonna tear down a sign, it sure as hell wouldn't be Gruening's. More like Leo Rhodes."

I made sure to use his first name, and add in a little swearing to help to cement the male bond of equality.

You see, lying is all about control. Act in control and you'll win every time. And that day, I put on an Oscar Award–winning performance. I improvised to stay on my feet when cornered, I bought time with confusing counterquestions. But most importantly, it has to be ingrained in you, part of your basic molecular structure.

Long before we got to Officer Jack's house, I had a plan, a map, a foolproof script. I knew this called for playing a careful hand. I would play the responsibility card, the homestead, and chores. The political connections with my dad, the dinner. I knew the "good ol' boys" club would win. I even knew I had the "we're all men here" card.

Well, the questions go on for some time. Jack is slow and methodical. I give the other boys subtle cues as to who should talk and when. Once I see they know the script, I let them have a few minor lines they can't blow.

It was by no means an easy gig. But we finally got through it. We walked out through the spruce branches and the broken front gate to the safety of our waiting car.

Why do I remember that evening so well, right down to the slant of the crooked gate? Right down to the peeling paint and that branch that I had to duck under?

I guess there's just something about your "first" experiences, the major life-changing ones you never forget. That night was the first time I had experienced being totally taken over by an alien. That evening, I became an innocent person who did not have to lie, but only tell "the truth." Previously, with my dad, there was always the fear of being found out in the back of my mind. After all, he had known me all my life. Something about Jack and the threat of jail must have pushed me to the next level. The ultimate level. It was an exhilarating, heady, and addictive feeling.

Who wouldn't remember their first Oscar? And boy, did we ever celebrate that night!

Looking back, that was the moment I truly knew I was living a double life. Part of me was still good, wanted to do good, but part of me was clearly very bad. And that is pretty much the human condition, the angel and the devil that hang out on all our shoulders. The difference is only a matter of degree, just how big and how deep the disparity is between that good and evil inside us. Just how evil that evil side is, and whether or not that bad inner self is curbed with telling a little white lie now and then or is fed and encouraged until it becomes a mass murderer.

There was one side of me that was a friendly, helpful people-pleaser. I was fairly well liked by a small circle of friends and was becoming a fairly good and well-accepted athlete. The talented member of a well-known local homesteader family. My father was a politician, my mother, a writer. I was in the public eye and knew that level of scrutiny well.

But the other side of me that few knew about wanted to lash out, to cause problems, and it caused me plenty of problems, shame, and guilt. It was the side I had to keep hidden.

Maybe the biggest part of all of us wants to be loved and accepted by our peers, our parents, by our teachers and the community. And yet I still pursued doing many of the things that, if discovered, would bring exactly the opposite result: punishment, pain, and rejection. From a rational perspective, it makes no sense at all. But anyone familiar with these things will recognize that simple cry for help that knows no other way out.

The fear that people would discover the "real me," and that the real me would be the bad one, would last many years. Figuring out myself, who the real me was, would take many years. But even that fear wasn't enough to keep me from branching out to stealing from my friends and even those I deeply respected.

I'll never forget my stalemate with the guy we called "Big Red."

Clearly, I was a kid with some pretty serious habits to support in high school, and never enough money to support them. Actually, I had no money. My folks, being from the old country, didn't believe in that good, old-fashioned American value of allowance money.

The little bit of money I earned selling lettuce and radishes didn't go far enough to buy nicotine and alcohol. So those basic needs, which my parents chose not to provide for, I had to provide for myself, usually by stealing. What I couldn't steal, I had to buy or have someone else buy. That meant stealing money. Elementary economics.

My main source of revenue was the fertile, ever-renewing gold mine of the locker room. During PE class, after-school sports practice, or any kind of athletic event open to the public, there were countless "pokes" waiting to have a bit of "dust" pinched from them. Sounds simple, yet kids got busted all the time. Of course, many precautions were taken to prevent theft. Sometimes the locker room was ... what's that word? Oh yes! *Locked!* Some paranoid kids even had locks for their lockers.

But there were times when things were more lax. Like during PE class or if you were an athlete during an after-school function or had to use the bathroom. It also helped if the coach trusted you, if you were a top athlete, a trustworthy and hard-working homestead kid, or a senator's son, not to mention being a Kilcher. We were all damn good actors. To this day, when talking about certain, shall we say, darker aspects of our childhood, old locals will say, "We had no idea!"

It also helped that I was well trained. I didn't press my luck. I only stole once in a while, and from different groups of kids. Sometimes it was from basketball practice, other times track or wrestling or PE. And the all-important trick was taking just a little from a lot of pockets. It was all about percentages: one dollar bill out of ten, two dimes out of seven, one quarter out of three. You had to know the kids who wouldn't miss a little change, or a bill or two. Similar to farming, you didn't want to deplete the field. You had to let it renew and be careful not to overharvest.

Public events with concessions or a dance where athletes were more likely to have spending money with them were always good opportunities, and thefts could easily be blamed on anyone attending. The out-of-town team's locker room was always a good choice too, but it took a lot of skill and speed.

I had lots of accomplices in other stealing endeavors around town but always worked the school scene alone. I wanted the freedom to steal from anyone. Also, those caught stealing from their friends were scum.

I was desperate, and I was good. And no one could know.

Now, the year before high school, I cut the tendon of my right index finger, and it didn't heal properly. I had to go to Anchorage for surgery and numerous follow-up visits, but for some reason I can't recall now, I always went alone. Apparently, my folks totally trusted my adult skills and abilities to care for myself, and they let me hitchhike over two hundred miles to get there. The trip could take anywhere from five or six hours to a couple of days. Teachers and other parents either turned a blind eye, didn't know, or thought it was just a normal way of getting around back then. I don't remember. Funny, looking back now, no one even asked me about it. I could have died out there, or sure as hell gotten hurt.

It's Thursday afternoon and I'm going to leave for Anchorage right after school. I'm hoping to catch the Anchorage cold-storage truck heading that way because I know Henry will give me a ride. Of course, this was a trade-off, as most of life is. A sure, warm ride with meals thrown in for the pleasure of politely deflecting the unwanted advances.

Henry was a big, likable, Wyoming cowboy. He was friendly, chatty, and generous. We had a lot in common, though he was old enough to be a father figure, sort of. Our commonalities hit an abrupt fork in the road at our sexual preferences. Putting up a clear stop sign for Henry was easy for me. I was big for my age, and strong. By then, I'd gotten good at standing up for myself. He listened and respected me, but he kept trying. And he kept driving the only road he'd ever known.

I eventually gave up the comforts and security of the produce-truck ride. Sleeping in abandoned cold cabins and walking for miles to make it to the house of an old family friend ultimately became easier than holding up that stop sign for Henry. It started getting too heavy.

At any rate, with another trip to Anchorage approaching, I realize I need to do a moderate locker-room harvest to take care of my travel needs.

"Coach, I need to go to the bathroom!"

"Kilcher, you better make it damn fast or you're gonna owe me fifty laps!"

Coach Bill would yell while smacking his paddle against his hand threateningly. These were the days when a teacher could still fully express himself with words or a blistering paddle.

I run full speed. I know where the ripe fruit is and I do my usual "take a little from many" routine, maybe taking just a tad more from more pockets. I blaze around the locker room gauging how long it might take to do some legitimate bathroom business, if that's what I were really doing. I don't want any suspicion. I don't want someone coming in.

Then I hit the mother lode. The bulging pockets of Red's big khaki pants. He was the oldest of the Calhoun boys, one of Homer's rich fisherman kids. Not many guys in high school could have gotten away with wearing khaki pants. Somehow Red pulled it off.

Red held the shot put and discus records for our school. He was our heavyweight wrestler, and he was a strong fisherman. He could be really mean, but only when cornered or pushed. A new kid in school, Gary, a six-foot-two basketball player, found that out the hard way one day. He made the bad mistake in the locker room of flipping Red with a towel. We all heard the *pop* of wet towel on naked flesh. Everyone turned to see who got stung this time and our eyes stayed glued. This was going to be good! Poor Gary's size and basketball skills were of no help. He and Red ended up in the bathroom stall. Close quarters. A wrestler's dream.

Red was only five eleven, but he was all shoulders and head, no neck. He gave the term "swirly" a whole new definition that day. There wasn't much water left to swirl by the time he let Gary pull his head out of the pot. He left Gary gasping for air, slumped over the pot. Red had lots of red hair everywhere, hence the brilliant nickname, but his whole body was red that day. He looked like a ferocious animal. We all gave him plenty of room to cool off.

Big Red's pockets make me a tad greedy. I do a quick calculation of how much more I need and I lift a good fat third of the coins out of his bulging pocket. He must have broken his piggy bank. I also take a few bills out of his nearly-round billfold. I rehang my now heavy, happy Levi's, and sprint back out to do my fifty laps.

When showers are done and we're getting dressed, I go to put on my Levi's and my heavy, happy pocket flips upside down. It's a silver shower of hard cash! It's raining, it's pouring! Coins go rolling and bouncing merrily from wall to wall. I move like a cheetah crossed with an octopus, my arms are everywhere at once with lightning speed. And oh, yes, all the while I'm trying to act calm and keep the guilt from oozing out of my pores. I'm imagining something like being forever shunned and labeled a locker-room thief.

Now it just so happens that at the exact same time, Red is reaching into his big pocket, which is not so bulging anymore. As his fingers are sending his brain the message of missing coin, it all hits the fan.

"What the hell!" he bellows like a mad red bull.

I stand to feign surprise at his yell with all the others. In no time, this heavyweight with his big, red, all-shoulders-no-neck face is nose to nose with mine!

My memory of what exactly happened next is sketchy. Suppose fear will do that to you. I'd been through some strong fear up to that point in my life, but there in that locker room, I may have broken the world record.

I knew this was it: my entire identity was at stake. I had two lives, and the transition was where dirt road met gravel. I had worked hard to build my new, phony life. I had to overcome the hay seeds in my hair, the cow shit on my boots. It's a hard business to rise above the smell of hick, especially while battling demons you can hardly keep hidden. I was the son of a liberal, almost socialist immigrant from somewhere next to Germany! That was all some people needed to know. But worse, we sang and yodeled in public, and it was even rumored that we ran around naked out there in the woods, sweating together in saunas as a family!

Enough kids hated me just because their parents hated my loud, liberal, abrasive dad. "The senator's son" was used like a racial slur. It had been a long, obstacle-strewn slog up the mountain of acceptance and new identity, and I had finally found a comfortable niche to sink my roots into. I was doing well academically, I was a top athlete, I played lead in a couple of plays, and I had started playing guitar and had even played at a couple of school dances. I had pretty much pulled away from Homer's delinquent element and had some solid friends. Yes, I still stole from them, and perhaps some deep shame was right there with the intense fear I felt that day.

But there was a lot at stake. In some ways, there had never been more at stake. And it's at times like these you start making crazy promises to God.

I force numbness to erase my fear, transforming it into anger at being accused. All the while, my mind is racing. *He can't prove I did it. But neither can I prove I didn't. I'm on my way to Anchorage, which justifies me having money. No one else had noticed any money missing.* I imagine my dad's face on those massive shoulders and I stare unflinchingly into his eyes. I know how to do that.

I think of arm wrestling, the moment it becomes clear that neither can put the other down. We're still toe to toe, and we both know we're there. We let that decision wash over us. And we back down and apart, slowly and simultaneously.

It's another first in my life: a stalemate! Little does anyone know, but it's a giant step in helping me turn an important corner in my life, one of many more to come, but there will never be another one like facing Big Red. He's become part of the concrete foundation in the story of my recovery, bringing me the realization that it didn't feel good stealing from my friends. There, in the locker room, I had to face the fact that I didn't feel good about a lot of things I was doing, and I needed to change my life.

You can't properly thank those in your life who influence you so profoundly. You have no idea at the time. But I owe a debt to Red, and thinking about that, I realized I should call him. So I did. I told him this might be the strangest call he'd ever get. I started off by confessing and apologizing for stealing some money from him all those years ago. I told him I wrote about the incident and how it affected me, as well as some other locker-room shenanigans. He didn't explode or slam down the phone and come knocking on my door! Instead, we had some good laughs about it. He reminded me of the time he and I worked together on a geophysical survey ship just after high school. He was in the galley cooking, and I was on the recording crew. He remembered that at the end of a long, hard day, sometimes working up to twenty hours straight, we would collapse on our bunks and I used to crack him up late into the night with stories.

He said he'd been thinking about me lately too. He's a fan of Jewel and her husband Ty. We talked about what the chances were of a girl from a little town like Homer becoming as well-known as she has. I told him that as proud of everything else as I was, I was the proudest of how she has handled her fame, what she has done with her life, how she is living it in a balanced and healthy way. How amazing it is to see your kids go out and do more than you ever could.

After I hung up, I just sat for a while, thinking. Talk about full circle. Here I am writing a story about him, and he tells me he remembers me telling him stories way back then. I had forgotten about that. I'm glad I called. I'm glad Red's part of my history. He's a great guy, and he's not even mad at me.

It feels so good to get some distance on that young man of long ago and better understand him. What would make him steal from his friends? As always, I try to see the lessons. I try to forgive that self of long ago, and yes, even be grateful. Grateful for the fact that I did nothing worse. And mostly grateful that somewhere out of that wilderness family, first in the forest and later at the end of a dirt road, surrounded by nature and an imperfect family, some good sense and wisdom came too, somehow knowing when to quit and how to grab that deeply ingrained moral compass.

# CHAPTER 4

## *Farewell*

Losing animals on the homestead was part of life. You did everything to avoid it, but it often happened anyway, for a variety of reasons.

Horses were always the toughest to lose. Some of them were pets, but even if they weren't, you had a personal relationship with each one. You trained them and learned how to communicate with them. They were an important part of farming and ranch life. They were used for cattle drives and roundups, and they provided transportation to places otherwise impossible to get to. A horse and rider were a team, each relying on the other. Many times, your safety and life depended on them.

There was colic, poisonous weeds, bad hay, difficulty birthing, strangulation, harsh terrain, cliffs, high tides, bottomless bogs, and fast-moving rivers to contend with. They all were ever-present dangers. Show me anyone who owns and uses horses, and I will show you someone who has lost some, no matter how careful.

It's always cruel and shocking to find a dead horse. Only thing worse is being there while they are dying, or having caused it and having to say farewell as a shot from your rifle sends them to those green valleys beyond.

Dawn was the first horse I owned. That by itself would have been reason enough to make losing her so painful. But there was a whole herd of reasons. If I had to pinpoint why her death has stuck with me all these years, I'd say because of what she represented. And the fact that she died as a direct result of my laziness and dishonesty.

Dawn was a palomino in a class all her own. She was the perfect golden color of a prizewinning marshmallow, the one everyone around the campfire "oohs" and "aahs" about. A perfectly white blaze down the middle of her face, with matching white mane, tail, and stocking feet. Oh, she was a beauty.

We were raised with Percheron work horses—big, slow, plain bays, which were brown with a black mane and tail. They were built for strength, not for show or speed. They were broke to ride, but we didn't ride them much. We had to do the splits just to sit on them, and they were never in a hurry.

But the summer I turned twelve, my life changed. Finally, we got a stallion and two mares, the horses of my dreams. Small, quick, and compact, real cow ponies like in the movies and Western novels I lived in. They weren't registered anything, but I didn't care. The stallion was black, out of Canada, and we named him Dusk. He might have been part Arabian. The mares were mustangs off the Navajo reservation in New Mexico. The blue roan we called Blue of course, and the palomino was Goldie.

They were much more than horses to me. No longer locked between the covers of Zane Grey and Louis L'Amour Western novels, they opened the door to a new life for me, a new world of real cowboys, rodeos, the Navajos, and horse training. They could go fast and they had endurance. On their backs I found my first sense of independence and privacy, and my earliest concepts of the identity I longed for. They led me into deep wilderness, and through them I was introduced to a large extended Mormon family who helped me learn to train them.

There was speculation that there was some Appaloosa and Arabian in Blue. She came to us pregnant and threw a leopard Appaloosa. Just so happened my idea of perfection was Appaloosa and palomino. Her Appi filly died as a yearling, but Blue faithfully gave us a new foal every year for a long time, though never another Appi, and I was disappointed.

The amazing thing is that some twenty-five years later, I was to get another Appaloosa filly and we traced her color back to the original Appi filly Blue first had when we bought her. The Appi genes had been dormant all that time. Offspring of those original three horses are still on the Kilcher homestead today.

Goldie and Dusk produced two palominos, both fillies. The first broke her leg in the dead of winter and I had to bid her farewell. That's a whole other story. But the second one we named Dawn, and she became mine.

As Dawn grew and I started working with her, I fell deeply in love. Since I trained the horses and did most of the riding in those early days, I considered them all mine in a way. But Dawn actually *was* mine! I was finally living the fantasy life I had only been reading about. A herd of horses to train and play with, one of my very own, a herd of cattle to care for, and wide open spaces. This homestead boy had achieved a dream; I wanted nothing else.

Dawn was as intelligent as she was beautiful. Her strong athletic body had horsemen thinking there must be some quarter horse as well as Arabian in her. She could have been that model horse on the cover of a horse book. She made me think I was a natural horse whisperer. I was learning about horse training from our Mormon neighbors at the time, and she made me look like I knew what I was doing.

Without knowing how I did it, I trained her to throw her head up and back and smack me right in my nose, a most annoying trick. I rode up to the Tietjens' to ask Tom for advice. "Tie her head down by her reins to a stake in the ground in the corral. She'll get tired of fighting it, and learn to give in to the pressure," he advised calmly. We visited a while, and I had supper with them as I often did. After supper I went out to ride her home but she was gone! I walked home in the dark, worried sick. She wasn't in the barnyard, so nothing I could do till morning. There were hundreds of acres and miles of fence line for her to get caught in while dragging her reins. I tossed and turned all night.

Come morning, I saddled up another horse to go find her. I

figured she would try to get to the other horses, so the first place I looked was the pasture fence. Sure enough, I found her there with her reins caught on a root. Looked like she had been there all night, next to the fence with her head held tight to that root. I was glad she hadn't gotten tangled up in the barbed wire, or gotten her legs caught in the reins. I got her untangled and leapt on her and led the other horse alongside. The first time I tried to stop I was pleasantly surprised when she tucked her head down instead of flicking it up. She'd been cured overnight, as if she'd been doing it all her life, as if she'd been trained! And by God, she was. She'd tied herself to that root and been broken of her bad habit in one night. I think I might have started believing in the Mormon God that day.

More important than everything else was the fact that to me, owning Dawn was a right of passage. My dad gave her to me as payment for some work I did for him—the very first time he ever paid me, despite a promise he had once made me previously.[1] When I lived at home, I did my part as we all did, and payment for work was never even considered. But when I was seventeen, he'd promised to pay me whatever he received for wintering the Cattlemen's Association bull, a bribe to keep me at home after I threatened to run away. I stayed, but I never saw any payment.

In this case, I'd built a fence for him on the Clark Place, at the head of Kachemak Bay. It was an old homestead my uncle Edwin owned, but was always considered ours. He promised to give me what the Farm Bureau would pay him, about a thousand dollars after materials. Seemed a good deal for doing something I had done for free all my life. I was a year older than the last time he hadn't kept his word, a legal adult, and I never questioned our deal. I have often been accused of being a slow learner.

1. Even back then it was dawning on me more and more that my dad had a real giving issue, a selfish streak. Perhaps it was a deep inner fear of not having enough, being frugal and making do with what you had, especially with a family in the wilderness. That made sense. But I see now it ran way deeper than that. It wasn't that he was a dishonest man or took keeping his word lightly. And it also had absolutely nothing to do with anything I had done. But he broke his word to me so many times, I eventually lost count.

The job done, I asked him about the money. He said it had long since come and gone to pay taxes or buy groceries—who knew? I was angry, but I considered my options, feeling like a man now and getting ready to go to Vietnam. I know he still needs me for the fall harvest, the roundup, and butchering. It's August, and I don't leave till January, so I know I have some bargaining power.

"Then you can give me that two-year-old palomino," I say, with utter confidence that he will.

He does, and Dawn is finally mine. A thousand dollars would have meant far less to me then that three-hundred-dollar golden palomino.

Shortly after my dad gives me Dawn, I make my second adult deal. My uncle Edwin agrees to sell me the Clark Place land for fifty dollars an acre. I agree to buy the old one-hundred-and-sixty-acre homestead and start paying on it once I move there.

Four years later, I am twenty-two and back from Vietnam and married. My wife and I decide to live at the head of the bay in an old cabin ten miles past the homestead where I was raised, at the new end of the gravel road. From there, we take a three-mile trail, the last part of which is a series of steep switchbacks down a three-hundred-foot bluff to the beach, twenty miles from Homer.

I know nothing about moving up in the world. I just moved farther out.

When I get back from Nam, life is good. I'm a married man with big plans and dreams. My life is ahead of me. It feels good to be out from under my dad's rules and roof. I had been a cook in the army. I plan to cook for construction camps in bush Alaska part of the winter, and raise cows at home, the two things I now know. I have one cow and two horses and one hundred and sixty acres on the shore of Kachemak Bay—a damn fine start.

One spring day in late April, I can't find the horses. Dawn is six years old and ten months pregnant. Near the end of May, I am going to have my first foal out of my very first mare! And who knows, it might be another palomino. Seems to be a pretty strong gene.

I track them and find that for some reason, they've gone exploring up to Windy Point. Why would they leave the sea-level pasture where there was green grass to go up to the snowy high country? Cabin fever, I suppose. They've been cooped up too long. But they have never gone up the steep hogback trail before. I can see where they nibbled some grass shoots on the south side of the steep ridge as they zigzagged their way up.

After climbing the near-vertical hogback, my heart is pumping, but I find them standing in three feet of snow in the sunshine.

I will never figure horses out.

I turn and look back down at the cabin, smoke curling lazily up to meet the scattered morning clouds. It's breathtaking.

Greening meadows roll toward the beach, bordering the dark-blue bay. Across the water on the shadowed side, north-facing mountains are still cloaked in snow almost to the sea. It's the perfect little nest I've created for our first home. I'm eager to get back down to green, to spring, to my bride and my breakfast. But how, and what's the best way to get the horses down? That's when reality sets in.

Decision-making hasn't been one of my strong suits up to this point in my life. I have been too busy ducking and dodging, making excuses and lying, doing what I am told, or sneaking around and doing what I damn well please. My dad told me what to do till age nineteen, and then Uncle Sam took over. And I've been married less than a year at this point, so the tiny little unimportant life skill of decision-making, well, it's shriveled, or never took root in the first place.

I have always envied people who can make wise decisions quickly and easily. Some pray and hear an answer, others hear their conscience[2]. But between the id, the ego, and the superego, the inner child, the lost child, the many sides or many selves, how the hell does one know who to listen to?

---

2. And then there are the lucky ones who don't even need to think about it, they just choose the best thing every time. Of course, there are also those New Agers who piss me off, saying, "There are no mistakes, everything happens for a reason, everything holds a valuable lesson we need to learn."

So here I am, trying to figure out how to get my runaway horses back home. "Back down the same way they came up," I say to myself. Quick as a flash myself answers back and says, "Like hell you are. We're taking the long and sure three-mile way around the top of the canyon through the deep snow and down the switchback trail."

I was by no means an expert in these matters, but it was obvious to me that a couple of leaders had emerged in this important decision-making drama. Don't know who they were, but they both had some excellent points. Could have been my dad arguing with Uncle Sam. Could have been me and my dad. It came down to, "You are a lazy risk-taker!" and, "You are an anal, overly cautious, border-line paranoid personality!"

Lazy risk-taker wins out. He argues brilliantly that he will stay on the thawed-out south side of the ridge, and stay off the trail where it winds to the frozen icy side. The north side is a lot steeper, with a twenty-foot cliff at the bottom, where it drops off to the creek. Actually, it's pretty much "straight-uppendicular," as my old home-steader friend Bruce Willard used to say. If it were a freckle steeper, grass wouldn't be growing there. So, I put a rope around Dawn's neck, and start leading her down the trail.

The other two horses quickly run ahead, eager to lead the way. As soon as they get to the first place where the trail switches to the north side of the ridge, they take it. The footing seems good as I don't see them slipping, so I follow with Dawn in tow.

In a blink, all three horses slip off the trail. The two out front quickly turn their heads downhill when they realize what's happening. They know it's useless to try to scramble back up to the trail on that icy section. They also know enough not to be caught sideways on a steep hill! Like two big sawhorse sleds with locked wooded legs, down the slope they slide! Their balance amazes me. They are almost sitting down, their front legs way in front of them.

When they get to the bottom, the ground gets rougher and less steep. If they keep sliding they'll hit the first hump and go flying head over heels, they are sliding that fast. I watch them start running at top speed, trying their best to keep up with their bodies, and slow down enough to curve away from the cliff at the bottom.

I will never forget that sight. One was a Shetland pony I was wintering for a friend. His short, chubby little legs were a churning blur of gray. I couldn't believe how fast they were moving, trying to slow him down. Their intuition and sense of timing was unbelievable, as only animal instinct could be. The whole thing couldn't have taken more than seconds. I let out my breath, my heart pounding in my chest.

Dawn is standing just below the trail and I am still on it. I have one foot up against a little birch tree. Dawn is facing downhill with very little footing, but she's not sliding. I can't let her do what I just saw the other two pull off. She would never make it with her huge belly. So I make a split-second decision and pull her gently to try and get her back up to the trail. This turns her sideways to the hill. But her feet go out from under her and she is on her side, sliding.

I'll never know, but had I let go of the rope right then, she might have been able to get her head in front of her and maybe regain her feet as she was sliding. I take a quick dally around the birch tree, but all this does is keep her head stationary while her hind end keeps sliding. And now she is basically hanging. If I don't let go she will choke. Up till this point I had many choices, and each one led me to where I had but one left, or none really.

I let go of the rope.

It took her a couple of seconds to start sliding, like time was suspended. She hung there in time, just long enough to burn herself into my memory. Her big, helpless, pleading eyes locked with mine. Then she was gone.

It's still unbelievable to me how fast she slid, not changing position till she hit the rough ground. And then she was airborne, bouncing and flopping like a giant rag doll, over and over and over. My heart was in my throat and I don't know if I let out a yell, but I probably did. She disappeared over the cliff into a patch of alders.

I slide down the steep slope almost as fast as that Shetland. I hit the rough hummocks at the bottom and keep right on running. I don't see where I am putting my feet; my eyes are locked on the alders where she went over that cliff.

When I reach her, miracle of miracles, she's standing! I can't believe the luck. Then I look more closely. Her right leg is shattered just below her hip, protruding bone, and bleeding. Then she turns her head, as if to show me the side I haven't seen yet.

I suck in air. I don't know how she can be conscious, much less standing. Adrenaline, I suppose. Her skull is broken, bashed in. She is groaning like a human, as horses only do when they are in extreme pain. That picture of her is branded in my brain as a symbol of courage, strength, and hope.

I run for the cabin and bust inside. Nedra looks at me as I reach for the rifle. She asks what's wrong. Till then, somehow I am strong, showing no emotion. As soon as I try to talk, only sobs come out. Deep, hard ones, age-old and brand new. I can't talk. I can only choke out the words, some of the hardest I've ever had to say, "Dawn is hurt bad. I have to put her out of her misery."

I run back up toward the spot she is waiting. I am no longer crying, now I am angry. I need to blame someone. "Someone" assured me, no, someone *promised* me it would work. That someone lied. I should never have listened. I am so furious, I am numb. Maybe I am preparing myself. I say farewell to her in my heart as I stumble back up the canyon.

Forgiving myself will come much later and take a long time. Right now, I am trying to make peace with what is. It is my job to take the life of this horse. In a situation like this, you have to. I know there is no way I can be sentimental once I get there and still do what needs doing.

I've been here before. I know where my head needs to be. No veterinarian, no painless needle, no putting to sleep. Just me alone with my first rifle. Just me alone with my first beautiful horse, Dawn.

The rifle shot echoes up the canyon walls. Sometimes I hear it still.

Farewell, Dawn. You won't soon be forgotten. Run free.

Today, a fifty-six-year-old man takes a walk up that canyon.

He finds the jawbone of a horse. It is mostly decayed, but some of the teeth are still in place.

Slowly he carries it back down to that old cabin. He hangs it tenderly above the door.

It's still there today. To him it will always be a gentle reminder that forgiveness is possible, that we can indeed accept the darker deeds of our past and finally make peace.

# CHAPTER 5

# Moose Hunt

Some years after the hard-learned lesson with Dawn, I was headed back to the homestead, and I was more excited than I had ever been in my life. Who wouldn't be excited, coming back to their village as a hero? My expectations were so high I was about to burst. Of course, I did not recognize them as expectations. I thought I was full of joy. And satisfaction. And a deep sense of self-worth and accomplishment. Pride.

You see, I had left my small hometown of Homer feeling like a failure. I had failed one year of high school. I managed to barely graduate in four years with an extremely low GPA. I had a reputation for being a juvenile delinquent. I was not popular nor well liked. I felt that I was viewed by most peers, as well as adults, as one of those marginal kids headed for trouble. But now, I felt a glimmer that possibly there was more to me than bad grades and bad behavior. True, I had gotten fairly good grades as a senior and was a top, well-respected athlete, but I still had no solid proof yet. I had also recently joined the Mormon church and cleaned up my act after honorably serving my country for two years in the army, spending a year in Vietnam. Yes, I had even recently married a wonderful local Mormon girl with good standing in the community.

But old stories recorded over a lifetime are slow to be unlearned. Perhaps they can only be replaced with new, stronger stories. It can be hard to get others to read and believe them. Hardest of all, of course, is believing them yourself.

But I was coming home a hero. I had graduated second highest in a college of five thousand, summa cum something, 3.9 GPA. I had worked my way through college with part-time jobs and a GI Bill. My wife Nedra and I had three children and had worked through the grief of losing one to SIDS. I had a BS degree in psychology and was excited to return to my community as a recognized hero. But most of all, I was convinced that my father and siblings would welcome me with open arms. I was convinced they would see me as that highly qualified person who could now understand and even help them, motivate them to change, and thereby lead the entire Kilcher family and homestead into positive harmonious nirvana.

Of course, you already know where this is headed. Oh, the naïveté of youth. However, mine was a special kind of naïveté, that of a dysfunctional, out-of-touch youth, armed with a little hope and a little education. I was smart enough to know I needed further educa-tion, smart enough to design and enroll myself in the very class my deeper self knew I needed: *Reality 101.* But I had no idea how difficult that reality would be.

I was twenty-seven. My brother, Otto, was twenty-two. My father was sixty-two. Finally, we were all adults, and we all held in common a love of the hunt and the great outdoors. Just to demonstrate my cluelessness, I planned the perfect bonding experience. I planned a moose hunt. Finally, we would bond as family, as men, as humans. No doubts, no fears. I had visualized the entire trip and seen only success and happiness. Such was the strength of my hopefulness. Such was the strength of my dysfunction.

I have no clue why I chose a moose hunt, and an extreme one at that. At the simplest end of the moose-hunting spectrum, you can jump in a pickup, hit a back road, shoot one close to the road, and your hardest job is packing the meat to the truck. Or, you can be dropped into remote desolation by bush plane, track for days, and then pack what you shoot on your back for many miles to a pickup point. And at the farthest other end of the spectrum of difficulty, you have horses, which require a whole other set of responsibilities and potential difficulties.

And yet, you could also be one of the crazy homestead hunters who forgo the bush plane and horses and opt for skiff.

I had yet to learn there is a much more realistic and reliable way to gauge the difficulty of a hunt. It has to do with how many working parts and pieces there are—how many things could and will go wrong. The more people you add to the mix, the more firearms and knives, the more machines and horses and saddles and pack saddles, boats and airplanes, propellers and engines, high tides and sandbars, and, of course, bad weather, the more things there are that can go wrong.

Assuming things will go wrong at some point, you may even need to allow for extra days, which means extra supplies. And along with all of this realism should come an evaluation of your physical, emotional, and mental strength.

In the end, you may just want to ask yourself how badly you want this free meat.

My plan to go by skiff may have been off the highest end of the spectrum. We would launch from Kilcher beach at high tide and head toward the head of Kachemak Bay about fifteen miles away to find the mouth of Fox River. Our destination was a small trapper's cabin about ten miles up the river. In the best-case scenario, we would find a bull moose along the riverbank. Otherwise, we would hunt close to the cabin so we wouldn't have to haul our meat very far on our backs.

In my easy, safe, and perfectly manageable family scenario, we first evaluated any potential dangers. We tried to imagine what could go wrong and plan for it. We'd be dealing with ten miles of rough seas, ten more miles of swift-flowing glacier river, tides, sandbars, fallen trees in the river above or below the waterline blocking our way, the outboard motor quitting, and, of course, falling into the glacier-cold water and dying within moments.

Homesteaders come prepared. We had spares and extras including food and clothing. We'd camp out if we couldn't reach the cabin. We'd bring a good set of oars. We thought it all through, except for one major piece. I don't know about Otto, but I was not at all prepared for the fact that my father had not changed, and that he would react the way he always had in a crisis, real or imagined.

I thought I'd prepared for everything, but I wonder now if I've ever been so unprepared in my life.

\* \* \*

The warning signs started before the journey even began. Otto had towed the skiff on a trailer to the end of the Homer spit by the harbor. From there it was pretty much a straight shot to the Kilcher beach about ten miles up the bay. Here, he was going to pick up me, my father, and our gear.

The first leg of my plan, just me and my father hauling all our gear to the beach in our tractor and trailer, went without a hitch. In the distance, we could make out the tiny dot on the water as Otto and his skiff got closer. It was close to high tide, but we timed it so the tide would still be coming in to prevent the skiff from going dry as we loaded it.

Otto came in as far as he could, picked up his motor when it became shallow, and stepped out in his rubber boots to pull it up to the dry beach. Because the tide was coming in, it would be no trouble getting the skiff back out to deeper water.

And here is where the mood slowly began to shift, like the sands on the beach. The ever so gradual dawning! The glacially slow creeping awareness that possibly nothing had changed in my father's personality, in our dynamics, in my reactions. Denial was putting up a valiant struggle, but was rapidly sinking beneath the cold salty waves of reality. Numbness, with her familiar seductive smile, was returning to my soul. Yet the hero, the returning warrior wielding shining sword, was undaunted. He was still fresh; the journey had just begun.

My dear old father reacted in a very predictable way to the stress at hand, to that which he perceived as potentially dangerous. And of course, I fell right into doing my carefully choreographed and well-rehearsed steps to the age-old dance. I perceived my father's screaming, hand gesturing, cursing and belittling, oar waving, spittle-flying wrath and red-squinted angry eyes, as a threat. He was afraid of the situation, and I was afraid of him. But neither of us understood our triggers back then. He was just a hard-seasoned pioneer, using the same few coping tools he had always used. And I was just a young son of a homesteader, dreaming of a hero's welcome. Dreaming of miracles. And magic. And happily-ever-afters.

"Real or perceived dangers and threats" was a phrase I had learned somewhere during the past four years of my college journey. I didn't really understand it. Even though, due to my childhood PTSD and what I piled on top of that in Vietnam, I was still a helpless victim, reacting to situations that were not real, that were long since dead in the past.

PTSD: Post-Traumatic Stress Disorder. According to the letters, it's a disorder that occurs after the traumatic stress. Did that help? Okay let me give you a simple homestead, country-boy, cowboy definition. First you go through some kind of traumatic stress, could be one big event or a whole string of little ones. At the time of the original stress or stresses, your body reacts exactly the way it should, the way it was designed to. That's what the body does to protect itself from extreme physical, psychological, or emotional pain. Your defense could be anger, a readiness to fight, or it could be fear, a desire to run away. You might go numb and freeze up inside.

With common or short traumas, the body and mind recover, you realize your reaction was not helpful, and you learn how to change and deal with that type of situation should something like that happen again.

But that is not what happens with good ol' PTSD. Your body, mostly meaning your complex network of interactions between thoughts and feelings and emotions, becomes almost permanently damaged, like a scar you carry. Every time a situation reminds you of that original trauma, you react the way you did the first time. It is the definition of irrational, of overreaction. It is unwarranted and it is hurtful to you and those around you.

Of course, everybody reacts differently to trauma. There are many variables. We all are wired differently, genetically speaking; we all have different thresholds. Whether the PTSD is mild, moderate, or severe, it gets in our way. On the mild end of the scale we may just come across as jumpy and be difficult to be around. On the more extreme end of the scale, we may be extremely moody and angry or antisocial and withdrawn. We may have extreme difficulty with relationships or tend to abuse drugs or alcohol to find relief. And, of course, the most extreme ways of dealing with one's PTSD is by committing suicide. A sadly far-too-common occurrence.

So, let us not compare scars. Let us not say that the soldier who returns from war is more entitled to his crazy than the Alaska native who has lost his culture and identity. Let us not assume that any child once brutally abused is more or less seriously affected than another child. Let us not say that hitting a child leaves more serious scars than causing a child to watch his mother beaten. It's all bad. It all leaves a scar. It all has to be dealt with and healed to live a healthy and productive life, and to ensure those cycles aren't repeated.

A screaming parent, a belittling elder, can do damage a person carries all their life.

The origin of my PTSD in a verse of the song I recorded on my most recent album called *PTSD* may say it best:

> *Could have been the mom and dad I had,*
> *those times when their very best still was*
> > *pretty bad,*
> *could have been that year in Vietnam,*
> *my soul was rearranged,*
> *came back, was called a killer,*
> *they said I was a deranged,*
> *I went looking for that young cowboy,*
> *I left riding out on the range.*

Given what they had, my parents always did their very best. They also did a whole lot of good to make up for the rest. I have long ago forgiven them and am truly fine with it all. At some point, as you're growing up, you realize it's pointless and nonproductive to decide what gave you the worst scars and who to blame and be angry at. You have to get to a point where you accept who you are and what made you that way, forgive, and begin the long, hard healing journey.

Triggers and reactions. Reactions to reactions. Like a Ping-Pong game that snowballs into war. With every volley you get in deeper and the ball gets bigger till you can't remember what the score is or who started the game. But whether you walk away or pick up the table and hurl it at your opponent, you always come out a loser.

Anyone raised outdoors who spends time there learns to read the weather. The more your life or your livelihood depends on it the better you get at reading it. Watching for the subtle mood changes in my father was no different. Just a slight shift in the wind, slight drop in temperature, and clouds move in, dark, rain-filled thunderclouds could be headed in my direction.

Life becomes an emergency, a matter of survival. Children are not prepared to be experts in reading accurately and responding appropriately.

For my mom and us kids, our weather station was always the front window where we'd watch how he would walk into view as he came home.

What caused my father to start shouting that day is a mystery and probably doesn't matter a bit. The anger and blame was piled onto me and my brother. I'd let myself believe I could stop watching the subtle nuances of body language, facial expressions, and tones of voice. But the old storm had caught me off guard yet again, and my father's tide turned.

Whatever set him off, he calmed down again. As we got into deeper water, the outboard started humming as we headed toward the head of the bay and the mouth of Fox River. Fear ebbed and my spirits lifted.

But it's always tricky to locate the precise mouth of a river. We could still run aground on the shallow mud flats. If the tide is too low and not yet in the river, it is too shallow to navigate. If it's too high, it covers the bank on either side and you don't know if you're in the river or at a bank in shallow water. So, timing is everything. You need the tide to be high enough to carry you up the river to where the water is deep, but not so high that you can't tell where the mouth is. Too low, and you'll run aground.

As fate would have it, we hit the mouth of the river a hair too late. We were going to have to use our oars to check the depth of water to make sure we were in the proper channel. Not a big deal. People do it all the time. But we were late, and late is what my dad hates. Late in any form would bring out his worst, his certain knowledge of our inevitable destruction. Had I been smart, we'd have called off the trip right there. My dad was ready to turn it into a national disaster.

My brother, Otto, was running the motor, so that left me and my dad on each side of the bow sticking our oars into the water. My dad was running his own oar and telling me how to run mine. A familiar scenario. At the same time, he was screaming at my brother, telling him to turn left or turn right. I was not speaking fast enough! Otto was not turning fast enough! We bounced from bank to bank, our propeller churning in sandbars and our motor clogging with glacier silt. We stopped to unclog it and started drifting. Then the screaming started, a rage of hateful words blaming us for everything. Blindly, he unleashed his inner pain on those closest to him, as he always did. Once again, he'd taken my hopes and dreams and smashed them into dust.

I didn't want to fall into old patterns of fear and numbness, but instead, by choice now, I decided to be more understanding and forgiving, so I tried to keep my mouth shut.

You have to understand of course, that it took me twenty-four years to get to the point where I thought going on a wilderness moose hunt with my dad and my brother was a good idea. It also took me that long to get to the emotional point where I could actually make a choice about how to act or react to my dad. Growing up, I had always been the one to stand up to my dad or challenge him, to just spit right back at him in the same tone and language, including swearing.

For the first time, I recognized my old ruts and wanted desperately to stay out of them. I had my Mormon God riding on one shoulder, and the great spirit of the Eagle of the Fox River Valley on the other. There was a whole lot riding on the success of this trip!

My own inner struggle was far more intense than our struggle to find that deep river channel. This was now episode number two since our journey began an hour ago. The coward versus the hero. Old, familiar, well-worn ruts versus the new and untried higher ground. Doom and gloom seeing more disasters ahead, and Mr. Hopeful believing redemption is just around the next bend.

Finally! We are in the channel. My father is no longer screaming. The motor is no longer screaming. But my nerves are still screaming. I've been working hard to dodge the old triggers.

There are stretches of the river where we can sit down and relax. These are the places where there's a well-defined channel and it's easy for Otto to see where to go. Anytime the river broadens out, meaning shallower water, it requires that my dad and I go back to sounding with our oars on each side of the bow and directing Otto. Both my dad and I are sitting up front, keeping a vigilant eye for submerged logs, as well.

We finally get to that place in our journey where the slow-moving Clearwater Slough enters the Fox River. At this point, we only have a couple of miles to go up the Slough to reach our cabin.

And then miracle of miracles! Just up ahead we see a bull moose grazing at the edge of the river. He seems totally unaware of the skiff approaching. Either he is not hearing us or he is used to skiffs in the river and sees them as harmless.

We had not planned how we were going to hunt. We certainly did not have a plan for what to do in case we encountered this kind of situation. But being homesteaders and sons of homesteaders we figured it out in a hurry.

"Otto," my dad harshly whispers at the decibel level of a small windstorm which could probably be heard by the bull moose above the outboard motor, "keep the motor going slowly so he doesn't notice the change and slowly take us over to the bank." In some circles, they call that a stage whisper. My dad had that one down cold.

We both grabbed our rifles. My brother stayed on the tiller, slowly putting toward the bank. When we nudged the bank my dad again whispered instructions. "Atz, we are going to jump out of the skiff as it is moving. Otto, keep the skiff slowly moving upriver. The moose might not notice that you let us off."

We both jump and land safely. Behind us we hear Otto putting on up the river. My heart is pounding. This is it. The dream! The great payoff! How lucky could we be? There is a legal bull moose right beside the river; he won't stand a chance against this awesome team.

As soon as we got our footing and looked up, we could see the moose looking back at us. When he saw two hunters with rifles on the bank and the skiff motoring toward him up the river, he began to run around the left of a spruce thicket. At this point he was about a hundred yards away. Again, there had been no plan. My dad brings a rifle to his shoulder, hesitates a moment, and takes a shot. The moose doesn't miss a beat and disappears around the far side of the thicket.

"I'll follow him and go around the left of the thicket," my dad now says in a screaming stage whisper, "you run around to the right."

So, I run toward the right of the thicket for about fifty yards. Indeed, the moose is circling in that direction away from the noise of the river. I bring up my rifle. I shoot. He drops. The returning hero rejoices. He has returned to the village. He has planned a successful hunt. He has shot a bull moose. There will be meat for the village. There will be feasting and storytelling around the fire tonight. He has brought the bull.

Oh, shit. The very moose the Great Man had failed to bring down.

As he watched his father approaching the dead moose, his nerves were alive reading the signs. It was easy to read his father as he walked through the deep grass. Enough similar scenarios replayed themselves in the young hero's mind that it was as simple as reading a well-worn memorized manual. There was no guesswork involved. There was only waiting.

Yet he felt hopeful, that young returning hero. Perhaps his years spent in more gentle climates and his degree in psychology could help him rewrite a new ending. After all, these were old scripts he was remembering. Yet the launching of the skiff on Kilcher beach and the battle into the mouth of Fox River cast a shadow over his optimism. The dialogue for which he thirsted, he knew was not to be:

"Unbelievable, my young son! What a shot! I can't believe you dropped him; he was at a full run! I'm sure glad you dropped him before he hit that timber. I can't believe I missed him. Man, I had him broadside!"

"Thanks, Dad. I can't believe I dropped him with one shot either. Bummer that you missed your shot. But I was quite a bit closer than you were. But hey, we're a team! Here comes Otto!"

Otto would shout excitedly, "What a well-tuned machine we are! I distracted the moose with the skiff. Dad, you guided him over towards Atz, and he nailed him! Yahoo!"

"I am mighty proud of both of you boys! Come over here. High-fives!"

With excitement in the air, and that feeling of satisfaction that only a job well done can bring, father and sons would stand admiring the downed bull. They all know this is a big moment for many reasons; nothing needs to be said.

The vision slowly fades. The father is almost to the son who is standing by the moose, which he, the father, has missed.

"Hold steady," says a new voice, my inner warrior. "This is going to be tough. But you'll be okay. I'm right here with you."

The atmosphere is turning. Tension is thick in the air. A feeling of a powder keg and a fuse and the match. The ingredients are in place. Only the timing remains a mystery.

Because I never had a casual, cheerful, let's call it a "normal" conversation with my dad at a time like this, I had no clue what it would sound like or how to begin such a conversation. If I had had a clue at that time, I hoped it would go something like this:

"You know, Dad, I think it's been six or seven years since I shot a moose. Of course, I butchered cows every fall but cleaning a critter lying down on the ground like this is sure harder than butchering a hanging cow. There are so many details I don't remember. How about you? How long has it been since you've field dressed a moose?"

"You know, Son, I'm not sure. It has been a few years. But like you said, butchering cows and moose are pretty much the same thing, except one's hanging and one's laying down. Whatever we don't remember we can figure out together and we'll do just fine."

Attempting this never-before-attempted casual conversation at a tense moment like this was obviously the wrong place to start. But, then again, chances are that any time I chose would've spelled disaster.

We had the moose turned up on his back with his neck and nose stretched out, and his mighty rack somewhat keeping him balanced on his back. His four legs were pointing skyward. My dad, with his razor-sharp hunting knife, was slitting the hide from tail to nose. I slit the hide of each leg from the hoof down to the center cut my dad had made. Otto was holding legs and helping the moose stay upright. We were humming along at good speed, no chitchat, only terse instructions from my dad. Finally, after laying the animal first on his left side, then on his right, we got the hide completely off. Now it was time for gutting, or cleaning, him. The moment has arrived!

This is probably the trickiest part of the whole cleaning process. You are now opening the body cavity. You follow the path that you used when you slit the hide. Only now, as you are slitting that layer of muscle and tissue that holds in all the intestines, you have to avoid puncturing the intestines or that huge stomach or paunch. There is a way to put your hand under the knife pushing the intestines and stomach out of the way of the tip of your knife. There are knives with special points that help avoid a puncturing issue.

So, my dad had one hand inside the body cavity pushing the

intestines down while his other hand was holding the knife doing the slitting. It had been a little while since the moose had passed, and during this time, all the partially digested willow leaves he'd been munching had been expanding the huge stomach with gases. It was tight as a drum. Puncturing a paunch is not a pleasant picture. It is not a pleasant smell.

Now, anybody familiar with moose droppings knows that they're fairly dry, compact little packages of digested leaves and stems. Harmless. Not in the paunch. Before exiting, it is a pea-green soup of green prepoop. Not the strong poopy smell, but an overpoweringly foul, sharp willow-poop-soup smell.

My dad had successfully slit the body cavity from the pelvic bone forward and was now skimming his knife mere millimeters over that taught paunch ready to explode. And for some reason, that seemed like the perfect time to ask the question that would open that golden door into a brand new conversational territory:

"So how long has it been since you butchered a moose, Dad?"

My dad interpreted my innocent question as a competitor's challenge to his wilderness prowess. I barely got the question out before the screaming exploded from his mouth, angry words and spittle flying, along with a green willow-poop-soup and the thunderous noise of the gases escaping through the tiny cut the knife had made, all of which hit me full force.

I'll never forget the anger and pain and fear in his eyes. As he screamed, his trembling hand accidentally stabbed the knife into the waiting time bomb of the willow-poop gas-filled paunch. The sound almost drowned out my father shouting. Flying willow-poop-soup covered my face that my father had just covered in spittle. The green geyser fell from the sky and covered the entire scene—son, screaming dad, and moose.

"MOOSE! COWS! BUTCHERING! IT'S! ALL! THE! SAME!"

The thunderous roar of escaping gas and green willow-poop sounded like a giant fart! The long, gigantic fart of a giant! Like an enormous whoopee cushion. *FLAAAAAARRRRRPPPP!!!!* But my father continued screaming, unabated.

The geyser hit us on its way up and again on its way down. My brother had the good sense to duck and run, a script he had learned well in the past: run while older brother takes the shit.

I have no memory of what happened next. It could be my memory recorder got turned off there for a while, like when you're going into hypothermia and your less-vital systems shut down. I was in survival mode.

Somehow, we got the meat over to the river and washed off, loaded up the skiff, and continued upriver toward the cabin. I was already returning to the safety of old retreats.

Several miles up the river, just short of the cabin, we suddenly came to an abrupt stop. We were all surprised because the Slough was fairly deep there. I jumped off the bow like I had many times before. Expecting to land on a sandbar, I hit the surface and just kept going down. I never did hit bottom. It was glacier cold. Now I was numb outside as well as inside. In the twilight, I hadn't noticed we'd hit a submerged log.

Mercifully, the cabin was just around the corner. We left the meat in the skiff to cool overnight and took our gear into the cabin, an old trapper's cabin with part of the roof missing, but it served our purposes. I put on dry clothes, and someone started a fire while the other prepared our simple food. We ate, then crawled into our sleeping bags, but I couldn't sleep. I was still shivering, thinking, feeling, and processing. And still trying to figure out how it is that I had stepped so blindly into that deep, dark water. So trusting, not a thought.

Of course, what counts is that I fought my way to the surface again. What counts is that I'd brought dry clothes with me and I knew how to get warm. What counts is that I'd learned I had choices, and that while glacier water will always be cold, I can either be prepared to take it, or learn to avoid it.

There were no village celebrations to mark my rite of passage that night, no welcome home for the hero. No elders' voices saying, "You have passed the test, Son. Now you have become a man." There was only that inner warrior's voice whispering to me in the darkness, in the slowly dawning warmth of that old trapper's cabin.

"You done good, boy. You done real good. And you'll be fine."

* * *

Postscript: We hung that moose rack on the gate to the homestead. Two years later, when I returned the next time to the homestead with my master's degree, there was a WELCOME HOME sign spray-painted on a rough-cut board nailed to that gate, right beside those moose horns.

My dad and siblings were there to welcome me. Somebody took a photo of my dad and me there next to those moose horns and that sign.

Years later, the biggest newspaper in the state did a series of stories about children raised on homesteads. I was one of the people featured. The interviewer asked me what difference it made in my life being raised on a homestead. I said I thought it gave me more tools for survival. That photo was on the front page: a picture of me and my dad, a WELCOME HOME sign, and an aging pair of antlers.

# FINDING MYSELF

# CHAPTER 6

# *Shootout on the Flats*

Every summer, people come from the Kenai Peninsula or Anchorage and head to "the end of the road"—the Homer Spit—to camp out or go fishing. The Spit is four and a half miles long, the second-longest in the world. At high tide, it isn't much wider than the road, maybe a hundred yards wide at the end, where the businesses, canneries, harbors, and condos sit. Every year, the Homeroids will say, "Yeah, got us a real bad case of dry mouth—ain't no Spit left!" What part of the Spit isn't covered with water is covered by people and people stuff.

On the poor side of the tracks, it is pretty much wall-to-wall tents, from the high-tide line to the road.[1] Back in the day, there were loads of hippies. Locals joked that we always knew when spring was here because the birds and the hippies returned to Homer.[2]

1. It's usually the typical mix of tenters you would see in most campgrounds. This sea of tents, however, is probably inhabited by more young folks, many of whom are looking for summer employment. By the look of the tents, as well as some of the more temporary Visqueen shelters draped over driftwood, this tenting crowd may be from the lower end of the socioeconomic scale. It is probably also a more diverse crowd, making it all the more interesting to go "tourist watching." Well-dressed and clean-cut may be walking side by side with barely dressed grunge-cut, headed for the Salty Dawg. Nobody comes to Homer, especially the Spit, regardless of where they're from on the ladder of life or how they dress, without visiting the world-famous Salty Dawg.

2. Anyone camping out on the Spit was a "hippie" to us; it was simpler than trying

On the other side of the road, it's wall-to-wall everything else. Car campers, cars pulling campers, cars pulling boats, and motor homes of all sizes. I've always loved seeing those "big dog" motor schooners, the ones with the tip outs, the carpet, the TV, the barbecues with two propane tanks—really roughing it! Every once in a while, you'll even see a campfire going strong close by.

The harbor is buzzing. Every square inch of boardwalk, tourist shop, pavement, and gravel is hopping. People walking to or from somewhere carrying fish, fishing poles, gifts, and lattes. Here is where the tent dwellers earn the big bucks, either to send themselves back to college or to buy up the new businesses and condos for which there is no more room. They are hauling fish, filleting fish, cleaning fish, and smellin' like fish! I love the smell of fresh halibut. Smells like the sea on a breeze.

But now it's Fourth of July weekend, 2006, and I'm down on the Spit itching to get out of all this busy holiday traffic. So, I decide I'm going to saddle up my sorrel mare, Sundown, and head for the head-waters of Kachemak Bay, what locals call "head of the bay." Boats are leaving or returning to the harbor in a steady stream, a memorized pattern, like bees bringing home the pollen. And though their honey keeps Homer sweet and keeps Homer the halibut capital of the world, I long to leave behind all the noise. The hustle and the bustle of the locals and the tourists has the end of the Spit looking and sounding like a beehive. Soon the fireworks will be starting.

I make it back to the homestead, saddle up Sundown, and

---

to distinguish between folks. At the bottom end of the spectrum were the "Spit rats," though by the end of the summer they were all Spit rats because by then, they were really hard to tell apart. The great majority went home in the fall, chuckling all the way to the bank. The fishing docks and the canneries welcomed their hard work and motivation. Sad to say, back in those days, I was a narrow-minded hick who hated them all equally because they were not part of our town, they looked and dressed differently, and they made pretty good money, while I was working my ass off for free on the homestead. The hippies are all grown up now and running Homer. Many of them own businesses on the Spit, doing their best to fleece the tourists to make up for those years they were discriminated against for being lowly "Spit rats."

fortunately, by the time I get down to our magical, clear-flowing spring that comes straight out of the canyon close to the beach, I'm beginning to relax. I've been riding for less than a mile, but it's my first and favorite stop. I love the coolness of the leafy alders, the smell of the rich dirt, and the sound of the surf. What a combination! I get off, breathe deep, and take a long, cold drink, and Sundown drinks too.

It always takes me getting at least down to the beach to unwind, to get over the "departure anxiety" I inherited from my dear old papa. Horses make it a little worse because of the added responsibility and preparations they require. The heavier I pack, the heavier my anxiety. Today I am packed pretty light, one horse and minimal gear, so I'm feelin' good.

As a young adult, I once told my dad about my anxiety when leaving, and asked about his. I didn't know it was anxiety. All I knew is that I got uptight and usually argued with whoever was close at hand whenever I was leaving. I was horrified that I was turning out just like my dad, but I thought maybe sharing this condition could be a bonding moment and shed some light for us both.

In the early days, whenever he got ready to leave the homestead, especially if it was for a long period of time, you could count on a spectacular departure scene. It was like a blast-off countdown: 10, 9, 8 ... The air became charged with electricity. Then there were sparks. Then thunder and lightning. Then shit hit the fan. Then all hell broke loose and it was every man for himself. *Fire in the hole! Run for cover!* At an early age, us kids got really good at learning how to quietly slide right through the cracks of the log house, blend in with the farm animals, and fade into the forest.

My dad's response blew me away. Either he didn't hear me or decided to sidestep it, or was in denial. "I don't know what it was about your mother, but whenever I got ready to leave she would make a scene, like she just couldn't let me go. She would start a fight with me every time."

All I could think was, *Wow!* Since I had been on my own for a while, and I thought our little chat was going good, I took a little risk.

"Well, Father, according to my memory, and that of the rest of the family, we saw it totally different." And I told him how those times appeared to me.

His response blew me away again. "I'll be damned," he said, contemplating. I decided not to take that bonding experience any further.

After relaxing a bit at the spring and breathing deeply, I head down the rest of the canyon trail to the beach. A cool breeze is blowing, and I can see the surf rolling in.

When I reach the beach, I am in another world. Silence, except for waves and sea birds. Privacy, three-hundred-foot cliffs on my left, beach and water to my right. I can see all the way to where I'm going. The cabin where I'm headed is at the brush line, where grassy tidal flats meet the low willows, alders, and spruce trees of the valley. The fifteen-mile distance will take me three hours of leisurely riding.

I always divide the ride into three sections. First there are ten miles of beach which gets you past Fox Creek. Then, the mud flats, which can be three or four inches of squishy, squirting, blue-gray, silty mud. And I don't know how it happens, but even riding alone, your horse always somehow manages to send a splat of mud straight to your eye. By the way, the cows also take this trail, so it's not just mud. When riding with others, you learn to stay apart to minimize the mud bath, unless you have it in for someone. Then it can turn into a game of tit for tat. When you're chasing cows across this stretch, you can count on coming out the other end a blue-gray blob. We'd generally wear slickers.

Just across the first of the three branches of the Fox River, you hit grassy tidal flats. Mud gives way to various velvety, colorful grasses. There are no motorized vehicles of any kind, since thankfully they can't get across the rivers, which keeps it nice and quiet in the valley.

This is the home stretch. This is where the Fox River Cattlemen's Association keeps their cows from May through October. Unless they are up the valley, you can see hundreds of cows grazing in any direction you look. This is also brown-bear country, and big-packs-of-wolves country. Not many folks come here for pleasure, usually hunters or cattlemen. Most who do come up know each other, so they keep an eye on the cows while they're here and watch for predators or poachers.

There are no cabins allowed on the association lease, except for three small "line shacks" placed so cowboys can stay and check on their cows. In the old days, cowboys used line shacks when they rode for days checking the miles of fence line on the open prairie. They were generally placed a day's ride apart.

Since I'm a part-time range rider for the cattlemen, when I come up here, I'm on brown bear, wolf, and poacher patrol, always looking for cows in trouble.

Just before I cross the first branch of the Fox, I see two four-wheelers coming down the trail out of the brush. It's the one place where wheeler trail and horse trail meet. They catch my attention right away. They're not your usual four-wheeler riders. The wheelers are humongous and brand new, with all kinds of racks, mostly for rifles. They have lots of gear tied on, and it appears they are looking for a place to camp. Apparently, I'm not the only one trying to get out of town.

Closer, I see there's a man and woman riding double on each wheeler. Each is heavily armed—sidearms, and both women are carrying shiny shotguns. The men driving have theirs in an easy-to-reach scabbard alongside. The guns all look brand new, shiny and gleaming in the sun. I can't tell by looking at them if they're just prepared for bears or plan to shoot in the Fourth of July.

But it's not just the metal on the wheelers or the rifles that catches my eye, it's the metal in their faces. They have studs and rings, posts and pins in places I didn't think you could put things. Ears, eyebrows, lips, noses like bull rings. I'm glad my hat is pulled down low so they can't see me staring. I gotta say, they looked scary! The tattoos on their sleeveless arms completed my picture. The guys might have also had some tattoos on their faces but it was hard to tell beneath the splotches of mud.

I nod at them, and our trails that converged, ever so briefly, separate. I cross the river, and they go on up the valley looking for …

whatever. I have nothing against guns. I have nothing against bear protection. I have nothing against shooting or target practicing. I have nothing against body piercing or tattoos or even someone wanting to put all of these together on a couple of four-wheelers. But I know danger and I was uneasy. Maybe it was the unfriendly look, like they were on something besides Fox River grass. They were the kind of guys you'd definitely want on your side if the chips were down. I'm glad to be riding my horse in the opposite direction, farther away from civilization.

I settle in at one of the shacks for the night. The next day dawns on the Fourth of July and I make the rounds of the cow herds. All is quiet and peaceful. No bears, wolves, or humans. Toward evening, I build a campfire by the river, grill me up a couple of juicy, fat-splattering-in-the-flames, organic beefsteaks, and bake a couple of taters in the coals. I wash it all down with some cold, fresh-from-the-glacier, silty river water. Later that night I hear some shots in the distance, but things here are nice and quiet. I get what I came for.

The next day as I'm riding home, something catches my eye in the distance. Something is chasing two calves, dark gray and long tail, could be a wolf. I pull out my binoculars to get a better look. It's a big dog, looks like a German-shepherd-husky-type mix. And he isn't just having fun, he is hunting, chasing fast.

I don't know how long he has been after them, but the calves are getting tired and finally bunch up together, unable to run anymore. In a herd, the big cattle would normally form a protective circle, but these two little ones are alone. The dog is striking at their legs, circling, and keeping them in tight together.

I can't believe it. I'm angrier than anything. That damn dog belongs to someone and he's about to kill one of those calves.

Not on my watch.

I am about a half mile away and still have one branch of the Fox to get across. I put Sundown into the fastest gear she's got, four-hoof drive, mud flying. She knows something is up. She always knows when she sees me pull my long-barreled .44 magnum.

We splash across the last branch, water flying. Now I'm within range. The dog, either oblivious to me, or, more likely, unafraid of humans, keeps right on trying to grab a calf leg.

He's clearly not just playing. I've seen what the breed can do to chickens, livestock, or moose calves. One look at this dog's face, teeth bared and snarling, tells me this ain't no pet dog just out here playing a game of tag.

I jump off my horse on the run, hook the reins over my left elbow to keep her from jumping away, and fire at the dog.

*KERBLAAAM!*

Damn, it's loud! The mare jumps sideways and drags me with her! I make a quick circle, and come back around to take another shot. The dog starts running for the brush. The mare jumps again and pulls me, but I circle around her and shoot again. The dog disappears into the willows.

I don't think I hit him. Maybe.

I am steaming! I settle down my mare and get back on. I check the calves, they're fine. Their mothers have finally caught up with them. Bad mothers! Up here, calves don't last long without overly protective mothers. Could be they weren't worried about the harmless-looking dog. I've seen wolves bring down calves right in the middle of a herd and next to the mother. They seem to have learned not to worry from being around barnyard dogs.

About that time, I hear a wheeler start up. Sounds like a big one coming from the Wallace place. It's an old homestead in the mouth of a canyon about half a mile away, where folks like to camp. It's where I saw those heavily armed and studded wheelers come from two days before.

I'm beginning to build a picture in my mind. When I saw them, they had just left their camp to go exploring and they'd left their dog tied up in camp. Today, their dog was loose and out chasing cows for a little vicious fun while they were in camp shooting, piercing their bodies, drinking, and searching for psychedelic mushrooms in the manure-laden valley. They hear four shots, and soon their dog comes limping back to camp, wounded and bleeding. It's their favorite attack dog trained to kill policemen who come snooping around their meth lab. Now they are agitated. The two guys grab their big guns and head down to deal with the dog shooter. They leave the women to guard the drugs. Or maybe they send the women down to do the dealing, because they're too out of it. All of this flashes through my mind as I calmly pull the leather thong off the hammer of my long-barreled *bad .44*.

I turn my horse toward the wheeler trail. Whoever is coming will, any minute now, pop into view. I am very calm. I have no doubt if it is one of those scary dudes, and they are mad or berserk and pull a gun on me, I will shoot first. If they merely have a gun, I will wait. If they start to raise or point it, I will shoot them.

Having made that resolve, I am stone calm. No different than when a brown bear is attacking the herd and I have to shoot it. No different than when I was in Vietnam. Though I fortunately did not have to kill anyone, I was trained to. It is a mind-set you put on, like a uniform. You have to be calm. You can't afford to be otherwise.

A motorcycle with a lone rider comes into view. As soon as he sees me, he stops and keeps his hands in plain sight on the handlebars. So far, so good.

"Did you shoot that dog?" He was careful to send me the message with his excited encouraging voice that he was rooting for me, like a hunting buddy.

"No, I missed. He was trying to kill a calf, I watched him long enough to know he was serious, so I treated him like I would any predator." I still hadn't figured out the connection between this guy on a motorcycle and the dog.

"Me and my boys are up here camping and that dog has been following and bothering us for a couple of days. We tried to tie him up, but he kept getting loose."

He talked some more, trying to convince me way too hard that it was a bad loose dog and he was trying to help. Something smelled fishy. I told him I would shoot the dog if I saw it again, and rode off.

I didn't know the real story, but I did know his was phony.

When I get across Fox Creek, I see my sister Mossy and her husband, Konni, at their cabin on the beach. She was up on the flats the day before, checking on her cows. I told her about my run-in with the dog, and the guy on the motorbike. Then she told me the rest of the story, or the *real* story.

She and Konni had just crossed Fox Creek, when they saw a commotion up ahead on the flats. They saw a man on a motorcycle, and two kids on four wheelers having a grand old time—you guessed it—chasing helpless baby calves, little ones. They were running them ragged.

Then they hear a ruckus over on the hillside, and guess what? You guessed it again. There is a big husky-looking dog doing the same thing he sees his master doing, chasing calves.

So, Mossy tears over to the hillside on her horse to chase off the dog, while Konni hightails it out to where the wheelers are having their fun.

When the man sees Mossy closing in on the dog, the one he claimed he did not know, the one he claimed he was trying to get rid of, he whistled for it, and it ran straight out to where he was.

Mossy rides out to where Konni is now talking to the man, who has the two kids on wheelers and his dog gathered around him. By now there are no calves or cows grazing on their range, having all run for cover, exhausted. Not a great Fourth of July for the cattle.

Well, they chewed him out, and he was nice enough and apologized. They went their separate ways.

A few days later, I was back up there and found a dead dog. He looked to be the same one. Things have a way of working themselves out. Though, like always, you can never blame the animal; it's the human's fault for not training them. Too bad the animals are the ones who suffer.

Other than when I was in Vietnam, this was the first time I was prepared to kill someone. Of course, I am glad it didn't happen. But sometimes it's good to have a test like that thrown at you. You learn things about yourself. I learned a little bit about how it might have been in the old West. How those cowboys lived and died for the brand they rode for. These were my friends' cows, my brother's, my sister's. I was protecting my family. Mean, untrained dogs, brown bear with a taste for cattle, or scary-looking guys with big guns. It was all the same.

We all draw the line somewhere when it comes to protecting our lives or what is ours. We need to know where that line is for us and what we'll do when it's crossed. We need to be mentally well rehearsed; sometimes even a moment's hesitation can cost a life.

I only came to get away from the noise and frenetic energy in town. But there was no escaping. The crazies followed me. Just another reason I'm thankful for my homestead upbringing that taught me to always be prepared for the unexpected.

# CHAPTER 7

## *Yodeling*

Yodeling is a rare and dying art. Well, I don't know about dying, and it isn't all that rare. My oldest son, Shane, did a college paper on the fascinating origins of yodeling. He compiled a CD of over a hundred different styles of yodeling from Pygmies in Africa and Indians in India to American Indians, Hispanics, and, of course, the Swiss. I come from the Swiss branch of yodelers, but I've thrown in a fair bit of cowboy yodeling and added some of my own style too.

From Shane's research, it seems that yodeling goes way back. I imagine as long as humans have been using their vocal chords, the yodel technique of jumping from the lower chest voice to the higher head voice has always been around in some form or another. Once you know what to listen for, you hear it in the music or chanting of most cultures. Mostly, though, especially here in America, we think of yodeling as what the Swiss or Austrians do, or the old Jimmy Rogers cowboy-type yodel.

At the first concert my wife, Nedra, and I did for the Homer Arts Council, I called someone out of the audience to teach him to yodel on the spot. It was longtime Homer resident and friend Bruce Willard. After some coaching and having to yodel to the audience, he was thoroughly humiliated and embarrassed (but all in fun). I commented that at least he had someone to teach him, and I explained how I had taught myself many years ago.

As a kid back on the homestead, I found a three- or four-foot-long piece of old flexible exhaust pipe from our gas-run washing machine. It was about one inch in diameter. Being an inquisitive and creative kid, I put it to my mouth and yelled through it. It sounded kind of cool, had a reverb echo sound to it. I played with it for hours. I made all sorts of sounds, but the ones I liked the best were when I went from a low "ay" sound to a high "ee." Or a low "oh" to a high "oo." Before I knew it, I had me a "yodel-ay-e, yodel-o-oo, yodel-ay-e-ti" going. I loved it! I was hooked. I relayed the story to the audience, lamenting on how I had no one to teach me, and how fortunate Bruce was to have me as a tutor, and if they thought he sounded bad, they should have heard me going around the homestead, scaring the animals and my family half to death.

Well, wouldn't you know, my dad later informed me it hurt his feelings that I gave him no credit for teaching me to yodel. Truth is back in those days, the more credit I could give myself for anything, the happier I was. I didn't understand what my dad meant till years later when I had kids of my own and I began wanting a little credit for what they learned, for who they turned out to be. No, he never sat me down and gave me yodeling lessons. Yes, he taught me how to yodel, just as he and my mom taught me how to sing. I was exposed to it all from an early age. Nowadays, I give my mom and dad the credit for everything, just to cover my bases and be on the safe side. And realistically, regardless of how you look at it, they may not have taught us every little thing we know, but our parents certainly set the stage.

I'll never forget the first time I yodeled for someone else. Singing in public or to a non–family member for the first time can be scary, but nothing compared to yodeling. A mistake in yodeling can sound like a dying pig. And even yodeling well can make people laugh. I swear it happens every time in my experience, although I imagine all cultures react differently, depending how commonplace it is.

Velva Hatfield was my first audience, a safe one-person audience. She lived just up the hill from Kilcher Road, on—you guessed it—Hatfield Hill. That's what you get for being the first ones to settle a place; they name it after you.[1]

The Hatfields weren't just neighbors, they were friends. They had five kids roughly our age and we went to school together. We walked out Kilcher Road; they walked down from Hatfield Hill. Their oldest daughter Dianna ended up being my sister-in-law, she married my wife's brother. As a teenager, it was one of my favorite places to go and hang out. Could've had something to do with their three daughters. Floyd, the dad, knew a lot about horses, so we also had that in common.

There was something very motherly and inviting about Velva. When she was excited, her eyes lit up and she giggled like a girl. Sometimes to further express her excitement, she rubbed her hands together. She was a happy, exuberant person. To me, it was the uninhibited happiness and excitement which was lacking in my home, and yet another draw to the Hatfields.

So, I chose Velva to be my first yodeling audience because she herself was a yodeler, and I decided that she would be forgiving and understanding. I was a young teenager at the time and had been a barnyard yodeler for a few years already. I had been singing at home and performing with my family for years, so singing in public was no big deal. With my yodeling though, I felt I needed some private practice.

I've never forgotten that first public yodel to Velva. My throat went so dry I could hardly swallow, much less yodel. I was sweating before I even started. The song was "Chime Bells." It's an old, standard yodeling song. Everyone over a certain age recognizes it and smiles in recognition after you barely get started.

1. I'll never forget some friends from Switzerland who visited Homer. They went to our museum and they came out laughing in disbelief.

"What was so damn funny in there?" I asked them.

"In Switzerland, things in the museums are actually old. Here, you Kilchers are historic!"

"Well," I said, "here in Homer, we Kilchers are really old, we've been here longer than most other folks."

*Up on a mountain, so gay and so free*
*There lives a maiden she's waiting for me.*
*Out on the lake, we'll drift with the tide*
*And hear those chime bells ring.*

That part was a breeze, it was just singing. Then came the dry-throat part, my first public yodel ever.

*Chime bells a ringin', yodle-e-ti*
*mockin' birds a singin', yodle-e, yodle-e-ti*
*hush little lover, yodle-e-ti*
*up on a summer's eve.*

Oh my God, I did it. Now for the second verse.

*Moon beams were shining as I kissed her*
*there*
*night birds were singing, perfume filled the*
*air.*
*Each little star twinkled above,*
*and heaven smiled on our love.*

Then I did the chorus again, more relaxed than the first time. But then came the really scary part—no more words just straight, good old yodeling. The grand finale. Okay! Deep breath! You can do it! Too late to back out now!

*Yodel-i-e-i-ti yodel-i-e-i-ti*
*Yodel-i-ti yodel-i-ti*
*Yodel-i-e-i-ti yodel-i-e-i-ti*
*up on a summer's eve!*

Whew! I did it.
Velva jumped up! Her eyes, dancing and sparkling with glee, she

was alternately rubbing and clapping her hands in excitement.

"Yes, yes, you got it! That's it! You sounded like a real professional!"

I think someone must have set her up to say all the things this teenage boy needed. I smiled and breathed deep. All first experiences should be as well received, celebrated, and applauded as that first yodel. I loved her even more after that. To her death, I considered her a dear friend.

That experience was another of those building blocks. Another brick in my entertainer home. Another rung in my ladder of self-confidence. I walked home thinking, *I'm not just a singer-songwriter, I'm a yodeler too.*

"Chime Bells" is the first yodeling song Jewel learned. I think I taught it to her, but she might remember differently. Every time I hear her perform her version of "Chime Bells" now, with her jazzy scat-singing-yodeling, I think of me yodeling to Velva back in 1962.

Yodeling is unique, no way around it. People love it and I could fill a lot of pages with just yodeling experiences. I'll have to limit myself to a few highlights.

Possibly one of the earliest, if not *the* first, real yodeling heard in Alaska is a story about one of my dad's earliest explorations of the area.

When I got out of the army in 1968, I worked as a longshoreman loading logs onto a Japanese boat. I was out on a raft of logs jumping from bundle to bundle, hooking up cables. Once they were hooked up, the winch operators picked the bundles of logs out of the freezing icy water, and stacked them on deck. It took about two weeks to load a ship, both the holds and the deck. Good money for a young guy just back from Vietnam. The winch operators were from the longshoremen's union out of Seward. Seward is on the other side of the Kenai Mountains from Homer, a three-hour drive by road, a six- to ten-hour ride by water depending on the speed of your boat.

One of those Seward longshoremen heard someone say my name, so he came up and asked if I was related to Yule Kilcher. I said, "Yes, he's my dad." He said, "My name is Val Anderson. I gotta tell you about the first time I met your dad." The Andersons from Cooper

Landing had been longtime family friends of the Kilchers, and I was about to find out how and when they had met. So, he starts his story, which I have never forgotten, and I know you won't either. It's that kind of story.

"Way back in '36 we were living on our very remote homestead on Caribou Island, in the middle of Skilak Lake. Rarely did we get off the island to see other people. Visitors to our homestead were rare. There weren't many people around this part of the world back then! Early one morning, we woke up to one hell of a racket. We couldn't figure out what it was. We got up and went out to the water to see what we could see. The fog was thicker'n pea soup, couldn't see more than maybe twenty, thirty feet in front of you. We listened and heard it again. The noise was coming from out on the lake. At first, we thought it was a wounded or dying loon or some sea birds excited about something. It sounded like a wild animal screaming, except it had a bit of a musical ring to it. Then we recognized it as yodeling. Now we were really curious. We just kept waiting … watching … listening. The noise kept getting closer. Then something began to emerge out of the fog heading straight for us.

"Here comes this crude hand-built raft with a man standing on it. The sail he'd fashioned out of his yellow rain coat. And that wasn't all. As it got closer we could see the man was naked! Floating through the fog on his raft in the middle of nowhere, but on his way to some-where, keeping himself company yodeling at the top of his lungs. His clothes were stashed to keep them dry. He was fearless, Yule Farenorth Kilcher. Yep, that was the first time I met your dad, my introduction to a fine man who became a lifelong friend!"

I loved that story then, and I love it now. Back in 1936 my dad had just arrived in this country when he was all of twenty-three. He arrived in Seward by steamer, and had tried walking to Homer. If you look on a map, which I am sure you have in front of you, keeping me honest about where Skilak Lake and Caribou Island are, you will see that the shortest line from Seward to Homer is across the Harding Icefield, down to the head of the Fox River Valley, and then take the beach into Homer. That's the way my dad intended on getting to Homer. But it didn't work out. The icefield proved too vast and dangerous, and, being a Swiss, he probably thought there would be a little *Gasthaus* every few kilometers. So, he turned back. It could have had something to do with almost falling into a crevasse, but that, as they say, is a whole other story.

So, he decided to walk through Moose Pass and follow the river to Kenai, and then down the coast to Homer. No roads in those early days, just trails and rivers. When he got to Skilak Lake, you will see on your map that it's a pretty big lake. Instead of bushwhacking around the perimeter, he used his Swiss ingenuity to build a crude raft. Smart guy, this dad of mine. Everyone I've met who knew him in those carefree, exploring days of no responsibilities say he was the funniest, most brilliant, kind, and charming man they ever met. That's my papa![2]

Nedra and I were performing at a church social back in our college days in the seventies. After our performance, which included yodeling, a woman approached us to ask a special favor. With her was an elderly woman who was originally from Norway but had been in this country for some time. She had lost her sight and hearing as a young girl, so I guessed that she'd been blind and deaf for close to seventy years. The woman asked if I would yodel for her elderly friend. She had never heard yodeling and wanted to take this opportunity.

You can imagine what I was thinking right then. How was she going to hear me? The woman answered my unasked question. "She will put one hand on your guitar and the other on your throat." I can't say I was nervous, but it sort of felt that way. It was more like I knew I was about to have a rare, first-time experience, the kind I wouldn't forget. She walked up to me and I loved her instantly. White hair, petite, probably eightysomething, with the most delightful smile. She

2. An interesting side trail, or dogsled trail, happened years later when another Swiss man named Martin Buser won the one-thousand-forty-nine-mile-long Iditarod Trail Sled Dog Race from Anchorage to Nome. With what the newspapers called "Swiss ingenuity," he fashioned a sail out of his wind parka and used the wind to scarcely beat out his closest competitor. There was a hearing, but Martin's victory was upheld. After all, ingenuity and courage is what settled Alaska.

placed one hand on my Giannini classical guitar that I played in those days and her other hand on my throat. This was going to be harder than I imagined, I was half choked-up already.

And no, you can't yodel half choked-up. I've tried it. It doesn't work.

Well, I got into it, at first with my eyes closed so I could concentrate and block out that tender image. Then I opened them. She was smiling such a radiant joyful smile, swaying from side to side in perfect rhythm to the rhythm of my yodeling, totally getting it!

I couldn't stop. She responded to all my dynamics: faster, slower, louder, softer, she was *hearing* it all. We were a duo performing together. I finally stopped, tears running down my face. The mingling, dispersing audience had all regathered around us, having recognized this was the *real* performance.

I'll never forget it as long as I live. Those kinds of experiences stay with you forever in some special safe inside.

I went home and wrote a song about it that had to do with being thankful for our senses. What a gift my dad passed on to me. What a gift my new elderly friend got that night, and what a gift I got in return. The vibration of vocal chords and strings, felt through fingertips—an unbelievably simple yet profound gift.

And now, I've got to tell you about Yo.

Yo started out as a curse to me, but he became an unbelievable blessing. It all started one night at the Putter Inn. I'm driving out East End Road and I see a whole pile of cars at the Putter Inn, so I stop. I walk in and find out an old friend of mine's daughter got married and this is the wedding reception. There is great food, a great band down from Anchorage is playing, and I get a chance to catch up with a lot of old friends all in one place. Before long, there is a tap on my shoulder and I turn around. I see a gray-haired man, about my age. He smells and looks drunk. Even before he talks, I can tell.

"Areyougunna (hiccup) yooodle t'night?" he slurs, weaving from side to side.

I don't know where I first heard it, but the term "sailing three sheets to the wind" comes to mind.

"Nope I'm off duty tonight. Just here to enjoy myself." I quickly lose myself in the crowd, which isn't hard to do.

A little later, I am dancing out on the crowded dance floor, and I feel a tap on my shoulder. It's the same guy. Oh no, not again. And he hasn't changed his line, he's stickin' with it. Head bobbing, eyes blurred, "Are ya gunna y-yodel fer ush ternight?" I say no again. I'm not even going to dignify this guy with a full sentence. I waltz away from him as he stands in the dancing sea of people, swaying. I have a few drinks, dance some more, nibble from the buffet line, and go to the bathroom. As I'm standing at the urinal—*yes*—I feel a tap on my shoulder. *It can't be*, I think. But it is. He asks again, and I say no again, this time more emphatically. I have learned from years of performing in bars not to engage with a drunk, or to take them too seriously.

Now, it's getting late and the crowd is just beginning to thin out. At this point, I'm sitting at a table chatting with some friends. Guess who pulls up a chair and sits down? I guess he's decided on a new approach. I have to admit, at this point, I'm beginning to be impressed with this guy's tenacity. He seems to love yodeling, and my yodeling in particular. Can't blame him for that!

He holds out his hand. I ask, "What's your name?" He says, "Yo." I'm thinking this guy is drunker than I think he is, so I ask again. His head sways, his eyes blink, he swallows, burps, and says the same thing, "Yo."

"Your name is Yo?" I ask.

"Yea m' name's Yo. Ah-heaard-ya yodlin' down at Hobo Jim's a—while back. A-I jus' love yo' yo-dlin. Yer the besht, man. Love that—yodlin'."

Okay, so I've had a few drinks, but *his name is Yo, for God's sake!* No wonder he loves yodeling. But I just don't feel like getting into the performing mode, not even for my newfound fan, Yo. So, I lie to him and tell him I have to go home. With that, I say goodnight to the table, and head out to my car.

Here's where the liar in me gets me into trouble. I plan on sitting there a while, hoping Yo will get discouraged and leave, and then I'll sneak back in. I sit there quite a while just waiting, then I open the door ever so slowly and quietly, and start to head back to the Inn in a half crouch.

There is Yo, behind the next car, patiently waiting.

"Okay, Yo," I say, "let's go do some yooodeling!"

I know Rod, the leader of the band. I tell him my dilemma and he is more than delighted to let me steal the spotlight for a yodeling tune. The band heads for the bar for a break.

Yo comes staggering right up to the stage, with an angelic smile on his face. He looks like he's died and floated up to heaven. I suddenly realize I've never had a fan like Yo in my life. He stands there mesmerized on the floor. He starts clapping and stomping when he hears my yodeling cry.

I do my old standby yodeling song, "Chime Bells." When it's finished, he has a big grin on his face and his eyes are closed—could be he's sleeping standing up, smiling and drunk. Quick as a cat he opens his eyes and slurs, "I wanna hear shu more." I think, *Oh, what the hell*, and yodel another song. The crowd loves it too, so we're all happy now.

When I get home later that night, something in me says I just have to write about being bugged all night to yodel by a guy named Yo. I mean, how many times in your life is that going to happen?

Some years later, I'm performing at the Kenai Peninsula fair in Ninilchik. A television crew approaches and asks if they can film a segment of my show for a commercial for the State Fair Association to use next year. I'm honored. Yes, sure. By now I've had great feedback on my song "Yo," so I decide it's the perfect song for the commercial.

The film crew is standing out front, the cameras are rolling, and I'm yodeling my heart out. It's one of those good days when everything's clicking and I'm hot, what can I say? My eyes scan the crowd as I usually do, left to right, front to back, when who do I see way back by the admittance gate?

Yes! It's Yo! Like a moth drawn to a flame, he hears yodeling and he's weaving toward the sound. I need to catch you up just a bit here.

Since that night I yodeled for him at the Putter Inn, I have not seen or heard from him. He has disappeared from my life. He doesn't know it's me up there yodeling. He doesn't know the song he's hearing is about him. And I can hardly concentrate on my song for watching the expression on his face.

He's delighted, moving ever closer to the source. At some point, he sees and recognizes me, and that brings an even bigger smile. He's quite close now and stops. I see it's dawning! The light is slowly dawning! It's like I can see his thoughts slowly forming, as though his entire body is mouthing the words, *OH MY GOD!*

*My yodeling hero is singing a yodeling song and he's yodeling about ME!*

Now it's just me and him as he inches closer to his music, his song, our song. Then, from in front of the stage, he turns slowly to survey our audience and notices the cameras rolling. And Yo must be part entertainer himself, because he sits himself down on one side of the stage on a bale of hay, crosses his legs, and smiles for our cameras, his new fans.

And this would be a great story if it ended right there, but there's more!

Later, Yo and I get to talking. He would just *die* for a recording of that song and he asks if I would consider coming by his place just outside Anchor Point to record it on his cassette boom box. What can you say to a fan like Yo? Surely only yes. We set a date and a time and I went to his place and did my first recording of the song "Yo." I find out he's a commercial charter-boat operator who takes tourists halibut fishing during the summer. He entertains them with tall tales all the way out to the fishing grounds, and then back to the dock. Sometimes that can be a two- or three-hour run each way. He wants to play "his" song to them as part of the package. His lucky clients should have the song memorized at the end of the day or be sick of it!

A month or so later, I'm talking to someone at the post office when Yo walks up, gives me a big smile, and sticks out his hand to the guy I'm with. "I'm Yo," he says, fully confident my friend has not only heard of him, but is dying to meet him. While we're standing there a few more friends stop to chat with me, and with great pride, Yo introduces himself to them too. He's a true celebrity making a rare appearance for his public. And the fact of the matter is that at least half of them *have* heard the song and *are* indeed excited to meet him. I walk out of there thinking, *This story just keeps getting better.*

A couple years go by, and I am in New York City. Jewel is performing at the Sony Studios, filming a Live at the Hard Rock series. She calls me up onstage to yodel with her. And yep, we do "Yo." A few days later, someone tells me it's on the internet. I google it, and sure enough! Yo's song has not only made it to the Big Apple, he is now on whatever it's called … "My Tube" … "Your Space."

Now, I'm standing in Dulles International at baggage claim. The guy next to me is staring. At me. I move away. I realize I'm not in LA, so nothing to really worry about. But he keeps staring. Finally, the line I've used myself a few times comes out: "Don't I know you from somewhere?"

"I doubt it," I say, "I'm from Alaska, just passing through."

But I'm not off the hook that easy. "No, I never forget a face. What do you do?"

"Well, I'm a schoolteacher, used to be a social worker, been a part-time musician most of—"

"… THAT'S IT!" he shouts. "You're the Yo dude I saw yodeling on the Live at the Hard Rock series!"

Some years later, a rare opportunity comes along for me as a songwriter. I'm asked to perform at an all-Alaskan songwriters showcase featuring a songwriter from the lower forty-eight. His name is Steve Young, and he has written songs for Hank Williams Jr., Waylon Jennings, and Joan Baez. He wrote the hit song "Seven Bridges Road" for the Eagles. I am officially blown away! One of my very favorite songs! Now I'm going to be famous because he is going to fall in love with my original songs.

I agree to perform, of course, and when I go on, I perform my very best, most melodic, meaningful, and thought-provoking songs, showing off the depth and breadth of my songwriting. I also open for him in Homer and he stays at our house. I am in heaven! No, I don't become famous. The concerts are soon forgotten, except in my memory, of course. But a year or so later someone recognizes me as having been one of the performers at the songwriters' showcase. *At last,* I think to myself, *someone remembers my unforgettable songs.* With such enthusiasm they say, "I've never forgotten that song you sang ... about that guy named Yo."

And that, my friends, is the curse of yodeling, that's what people remember. All my other songs fade away with time, but the yodeling remains. So now most often when I'm recognized or remembered, it's, "aren't you the guy that yodels?" Once, I even received a letter addressed to "The Yodeler, Homer, AK."

Thirty-seven years have yodeled by way too fast since I taught my six-year-old daughter how to yodel. I am visiting her in Telluride, Colorado, and she has some friends over for dinner. They're an unbelievable family—close-knit, talented, athletic, spiritual, successful, and a joy to be around. Their sixteen-year-old daughter Sarah, who plays guitar and is a budding singer-songwriter with a gorgeous voice, asks me to teach her how to yodel. Not sure why she didn't ask Jewel; maybe she was too bashful. Since Sarah's father, Greg Steil, has a company that manufactures bows, I tell her I'll make a trade, a yodeling lesson for a bow. It's a deal. I teach her the same yodeling song I first taught Jewel, "Chime Bells," and Sarah actually performs it the next evening. Yes, she's a gutsy young lady and has a great future ahead of her.

I was feeling a little guilty, afraid I'd taken advantage of them, comparing a simple yodeling lesson to a world-class bow worth $1500. I was sure I got the best end of the deal.

But Sarah still stays in touch. She sends me videos of her performances, which always include a yodel. At one performance, she did a Pink Floyd song followed by yodeling and she brought down the house! Now, I'm not sure who got the best end of that deal. I know I'll be using that Elite bow until my arms and shoulders are too weak to hold it up, and I know that Sarah will be blessing many audiences far into the future with her beautiful voice and her unique yodeling, to which she has added her own personal touch.

* * *

As I said, yodeling is often the thing people remember most about a performance. I recall this was one of the reasons Jewel hesitated to yodel much at first. Even though she was new on the world stage, she knew enough from her early yodeling experiences that she could easily become stereotyped as the blond yodeling chick from Alaska.

In case I haven't been very clear so far, parenting was a struggle for me. One of the biggest aspects of parenting is teaching. I look at my kids now and see the qualities or talents they have, and can't help but wonder how much of it is genetic, how much did I actively teach them, and what did they learn just by watching and listening to me, both the good and the bad. Pathetic is the word that jumps into my mind when it comes to the role I did as active teacher to my children.[3] I can guarantee you that if they picked up anything from me, it was mostly accidental.

Oh, I started to teach them things like riding a bike, running, skiing, working with horses, singing, playing guitar, washing dishes, on and on, but I never got past the starting phase. Thankfully, their mother would come to the rescue and take over. Of course, it was doubly hard for her then to not only teach a new skill, but to first soothe their hurt feelings, dry their tears, and rebuild their confidence.

My daughter, Jewel, was a bit of an oddball. I have thought about her a lot, and still don't know for sure what all the differences were. Could have been the daddy-daughter thing. Could be she had

---

3. Here is a good definition of pathetic. We would be sitting on the living room carpet learning a new family game involving cards, dice, and boards with little squares on it. Within minutes I start getting frustrated and impatient, rolling my eyes and huffing, maybe even sputtering. My wife would send me out of the room, and then teach the kids how to play. Once they learned, I could only play along if I was on good behavior, and if I reached the red line, I would get put on time out.

more of an appetite for music and horses. She definitely had a higher tolerance for my bullshit. Regardless, horses and music are two things I set out to teach her and she got both. She took to horses like a duck to water, both the riding and the training. She spent countless hours on horses as a young teen. They were an important part of her life, as they were mine. This, no doubt, contributed to the reason she ended up marrying Ty Murray, the only seven-time World Champion All-Around Cowboy.

Jewel spoiled me when it comes to teaching anything to do with music. There are many ways to describe it, but the image that fits best for my visual brain is of molding or shaping modeling clay. Jewel's voice was like a piece of modeling clay, and she could do anything I wanted her to.

As a young girl, her appetite for learning certain things was as great as my passion for teaching them. I found out when she was still very young, five or six or maybe even four, that she could do amazing things with her voice. I would say "try this," and she would just do it. Even if I didn't know the term, like "put a little more vibrato into your voice," or, "transition into your head voice," I would do what I wanted her to do, and she could do it, just one octave above me. My challenge was figuring out how to say what I wanted her to do. I would make up my own vocabulary or use hand signs. I'd point to a note somewhere above the one she just sang, and she would know which note it was. She could imitate any style of singing, which we later incorporated into her yodeling routine.

Of course, she'd heard yodeling since she was born, which I am sure was a helpful factor. She was a proficient yodeler at age six, but once she'd mastered that flip of her voice, she had to learn the nonsense syllables and repeated vowels. The first song I taught her was, of course, "Chime Bells." And the most important part of this whole story is that Jewel practiced day and night until she had it down perfectly. I got a call from her elementary teacher one day: "We have to do something about your daughter's yodeling. She yodels in the hallway, on the playground, in the bathroom, even in the classroom!"

I can hear that same teacher now, telling her friends with great pride, "I used to be Jewel's teacher, and she yodeled all over school like a little von Trapp girl in the Alps!"

A few years later, when I moved back to Homer with them as a single dad, her fourth-grade teacher actually did approach me with a glowing report. She said that usually new girls at school are quite shy at first—not my Jewel. The first day in class she taught the whole class how to yodel. That's my girl!

It was the same with teaching her to play the homestead flute, which was made of anything hollow—a piece of garden hose or copper pipe or a dried stem of something. You'd blow across the opening much like you do a bottle top to make a whistling sound. The only thing is, it's a lot harder. It was the same with teaching her to put a warble into her whistle. She practiced relentlessly until she got it. That was just her nature. Sometimes I drove her, yes, but most of the time I'd say she pushed herself and got real joy from learning something new.

When she was only eight years old, she had already been onstage with us for at least two years. We put a small band together with Jim on bass, and Shonti on fiddle. Through the Alaska Council on the Arts, we did a tour of bush Alaska—the small rural communities, Alaska Native towns and villages surrounded by wilderness.

Our tour included one larger bush town, Bethel, and three smaller bush villages, St. Mary's, Aniak, and Akiak. Imagine a school gym out in remote Alaska, packed with natives who seldom get entertainment, much less a little white girl yodeling. People in these villages tend to be quite uninhibited. They were as free and expressive with their laughter as they were with applause, and there was as much whistling and stomping after a song as you could imagine. Let me tell you, it is a rare treat for any musician to play for such an appreciative audience.

Unfortunately, when Jewel got done yodeling, the roaring response was mostly laughter—loud, raucous laughter. It was the wildest response I had ever heard to anyone's yodeling, let alone to a little girl's. Well, she was quite used to taking care of herself while not on stage, and we never worried about her, but I finally found her out in the hallway flattened up against the wall like a fly, a large group of adults and children crowded around her. Some were stroking her hair and others farther away were reaching for her. She wasn't crying or hiding her face, her stage presence was intact, but it was easy to see she was terrified.

We took her back to the classroom serving as our dressing room and she burst into tears. "What were they doing?" she sobbed, "why were they all trying to touch and grab me?" We explained they didn't get to see little white girls with long golden hair very often and they were curious. They liked her. We tried to give her examples, like the time we got a new red horse and hadn't been able to keep from stroking its long red mane. I'm not sure she was even listening through her sobs.

"And they all laughed at me when I yodeled!" That's when her sobbing began in earnest. It broke my heart. In my experience, there is no pain like watching your child suffer. I could feel her humiliation and sense of rejection. Having had a good dose of that in my past, I had some trouble not joining her in her sobbing.

Instead of doing what good functional parents should do in cases like this, which is help her get in touch with her pain, let her know that what she was feeling was real, get her to tell us more, pour it all out of her small heart—in short, validate her—we tried our best to plug the bursting dam with all of our adult explanations.

I was afraid this might be one of those pivotal moments in her life. It might change her forever. If I gave the wrong answers, didn't do a good job, she would never set foot onstage again. It was hard to talk in a calm, reassuring voice when I felt such a sense of urgency, as well as pain from my own childhood. "Oh, but they loved you! They weren't laughing ... well ... but not at you ... it's like ... they were happy! They were laughing instead of clapping, and it just seemed like they were making fun of you." We kept trying to console her, and eventually her sobbing subsided. Maybe she bought our line of goods, or maybe she realized she survived and was not going to give up. At any rate, she has thrived. And yes, she still yodels.

Jewel started performing with us full time, as did her two brothers, Atz Lee, six years old at the time, and her older brother Shane, who was eleven. Atz Lee played his little fiddle, and after I paid him his quarter, he would take a flying leap off the stage and run to the candy store in the lobby of the hotel. Shane ran the film and slide projectors as well as the spotlight and sound system. If I remember correctly, Jewel did only her yodeling act. Like a puppy, we'd call her out, she'd do her trick, and then go back offstage. Only later did she play her banjo and sing. And only much later did she take over the whole damn stage, pack it up, and take it to California with her to become world famous without me.

We had worked up a little routine. Since discovering that her voice was like modeling clay, we used it in her yodeling act. I would say, "Lay-dies and gen-tle-men! Now for the act you have all been waiting for—the youngest yodeler in the world! She has more yodels up her sleeve than Alaska has mountains! First she will do her underwater yodel!" Then she would puff out her lips and strum her fingers over them up and down while she was yodeling, to make it sound like she was bubbling under water.

"Amazing!" I would shout in disbelief. Then she would do her Indian yodel. While yodeling, she would slap her mouth with her open hand like an Indian whoop. Now she would be whooping and yodeling at the same time. Then came the opera yodel. As you might guess she would yodel in a very high soprano vibrato opera voice. People went wild over that one. As if they weren't going wild already, she did a more Swiss-style yodel, which doesn't have as much flipping back and forth, but is more melodic in the higher register. She would end with her lightning version of the standard cowboy homestead yodel I had taught her. Let me tell you, lay-dies and gen-tle-men, it was a showstopper.

We used the same routine to advertise the dinner show we were doing in major hotels in Anchorage. We had Jewel yodel in the lobby. We tried a lot of other things, like me dressing up in a brown bear skin and singing with Nedra. We tried me yodeling. But believe me, nothing brought 'em out of the woodwork, the elevators, the cafés, the hotel rooms like little Jewel's yodeling routine. No wonder she left Alaska and became famous at such an early age—to get away from that childhood slave labor!

It is always an unbelievable thrill when Jewel calls me onstage to sing one of my original songs. If she wants to do one with me, I choose "Fox River Grass" which is one we did back when we sang together. All the rush of the big stage, screaming fans, lights, state-of-the-art sound system is a drop in the bucket compared to yodeling with her. Now *that* is an indescribable experience. Father and daughter. History. Memories of a six-year-old looking up to me and watching my face and throat intently for any cues of changes in rhythm or melody or patterns. It still boggles my mind when I think about it. All those years she watched and listened and learned, not just *singing* harmony, but *yodeling* harmony.

I have to mention one of my very favorite Jewel yodeling stories here before getting back onstage with her to end this show. We were doing our hotel dinner show and Jewel did her usual brilliant yodeling routine. Even though I was always thrilled, it had all become familiar to me by now and I had started taking it for granted. After the show, a well-dressed, sophisticated-looking elderly woman came up to the stage before we headed to our table to sell and sign albums of our original Alaskan songs. She had the most serious, dubious, quizzical look on her face. I sensed something big was coming. You could see a question or statement slowly forming in her mind on her face.

She wisely began by giving her credentials. She was a retired music professor from a big-name college, and she had spent her life conducting choirs, being a vocal coach, and basically knowing all there was to know about vocal chords and what they could or could not do at various ages or stages of development. Then she said, in the most carefully measured words of disbelief that I will never forget, "A child that young with undeveloped vocal chords is just not supposed to be *able* to do those kinds of things with the voice." There was a moment of silence. She hadn't said it in an accusatory way, that we had done something wrong. It was more that she was saying it to herself, that she could not believe what she'd just heard.

"Well, it's a good thing no one told me sooner or I never would have taught her," I said.

Yes, Jewel may have been an exception. And yes, there are other exceptions out there, call them gifted, call them talented. The key is discovering those talents and developing them carefully and leaving it up to the individual to take each step with joy and enthusiasm, with a sense of discovery. That's the way it was with my little Jewel. This taught me an invaluable lesson I was later to use over and over again when I became an elementary music teacher. Even if there was only one five-year-old in my kindergarten class who had the talent or gift, to sing on pitch or play the recorder or, yes, even yodel, I gave 'em all a chance to try.

Yeah, sometimes I pushed 'em too hard, and sometimes other music teachers cringed and advised me to wait till third grade before teaching certain things. I would always smile and say thank you, and go on doing my homestead intuitive thing. It thrills me to think of all those precious young minds and hearts I had the privilege of touching and teaching.

So, when Jewel asked me up onstage with her, it happened to be Father's Day back a few years ago in the Twin Cities of Minneapolis–Saint Paul. Of all the yodeling-with-Jewel-on-her-big-stage experiences, this was the crème de la crème. I forget now what theater it was, but the place was packed. When she called me onstage, the crowd went wild. I stood there beside her, looked out at the sea of faces, and as always, I felt such pride in what she had done with her career, what she had done with her humble beginnings.

I recall the seating came up close to the stage, or else they brought in extra chairs. I remember looking down, and people were bending their necks to look up at us. We started our daddy-daughter yodeling, and well, little buckaroos, we were hot! I did my usual, average, meat-and-taters yodel, but Jewel was the dessert plate, the frosting, and the flowers in the vase. It was one of those nights where no matter what I threw at her, she was there.

I can't say for sure (because I don't think you could write it down), but yodeling has lots of 32nd notes and probably some 64ths as well, like trills in trumpeting. Regardless, some of it is damn fast. Sometimes she was with me note for note, doing harmony, other times her rhythm was a little faster or slower, but it didn't matter, because no one, not even us, knew. We were improvising as we usually do. Seldom did she look at the audience, she was watching me for cues. When I glanced at her, again I saw the four- or five- or six-year-old girl watching her daddy, and I was struggling hard to yodel all choked-up! An unforgettable experience!

At one point I remember looking down, and the exquisite joy on people's faces ... it was incredible! I am not sure if there are different degrees of standing ovations. You know, there are those where a few stand and finally the rest of the audience stands just so they can go home. Then there are those where you can tell it's spontaneous, and the audience all stands at the same time. Well, this here standing ovation we got in those Twin Cities gave the term standing ovation a whole new meaning. All at once, at exactly the same instant, the crowd leaped to their feet. I swear, they jumped up so fast they got air under their boots, and they landed back on the floor with a thud.

But that's yodeling for ya! Everyone loves it!

Fast forward ten or fifteen years from that jumping standing ovation in the Twin Cities. I get a call from Jewel and she asks me to join her for a Christmas special to be aired on CBS. She also invites some other members of her Alaska family. And then real casually she asks, "I'd love it if you could write a homestead yodeling Christmas song."

Without even thinking, I say, "I'd love to!" And I go out to the shop and start a fire in the old woodstove, pull up a chair, and take out my guitar to set the stage.

And then it hit me! This was the big time! This was CBS television—national television! A yodeling homestead Christmas song, there wasn't a doubt in my mind that this would be the first yodeling homestead Christmas song performed on national television. Well, I wrote it, and I have to go to my favorite line from that song, the one that sums it all up: "My mom and dad were cooking up a secret recipe, a homestead yodeling Christmas harmony."

My mom and dad *did* have a recipe for raising creative children in the middle of the wilderness. It was a good one! It landed their granddaughter Jewel on a national stage, and it landed her dad there beside her for a nationally televised Christmas special. And doing what? Yodeling! The audience went wild, the producers loved it, but who doesn't love a dad and daughter yodeling a homestead Christmas harmony?

# CHAPTER 8

# Horses in the Oats

Horses. You gotta love 'em. Or hate 'em. Depends on which day and what kind of mood you and them horses are in. I always tell folks I have a genuine love-hate relationship with horses. They bring out the best and the beast in me.

I think it started when I was a boy and used to listen to my dad screaming obscenities at his team of workhorses as he logged and cleared the land on our homestead. I also have memories of many tense moments as he trimmed their huge feet. In the early days, he used a razor-sharp ax; he later switched to the more conventional method of hoof clippers. I dreaded helping him with that chore more than anything.

The dread was due to a combination of factors. First of all, I was little, so the horses were huge, with feet like dinner plates. When they stepped on my usually bare feet, it hurt for days. I'd have bruises. You learned quick, so that didn't happen very often, but the sheer size of them terrified me. Remember, ours were draft horses. Sometimes I had to hold them, other times I had to hold the tools. Regardless of which job I had, I could guarantee I'd get hollered at and cussed at about as much as the horses did, which was basically every time they moved or set down the hoof my dad was trying to trim.

I much preferred holding the horses—they were more predictable. The thing I really hated, and was actually terrified of, was holding the tools. Later he switched to using hoof clippers, rasp, and hoof knife, all of these were very sharp. When he was done with one, he would slam it behind him into my waiting open hand, and I would give him a new tool. The madder and more frustrated he got, depending on how well or how badly the horses were cooperating, the harder he slammed those tools. I got cut and scraped on many occasions.

When I was living on the homestead again as a single father, I had the rare privilege of reliving that horse-hoof trimming experience. I came home to see a horse tied in the yard, and as I got closer, I could see my dad bent over on the far side of the horse. He was trimming its hooves. I heard him yelling, so nothing new there, but when I got closer, I saw my little Jewel was his assistant.

Immediately, I went on red alert. He swore at her for not giving him the tool quick enough, and then he angrily reached behind his back with the tool he was done with, and tried to slam it into her hand exactly as he'd done to me. Only this time, it wasn't there. I had pulled her away. He kept taking swipes at the air where he thought her hand was. And that's when he dropped the horse's hoof and turned and saw me. I sent Jewel into the house, and he and I had us a good old-fashioned heart-to-heart, father and son. Sort of a horse-whispering session. And I forbade him to ever trim hooves with her again.

I have trimmed countless horse's hooves in my life. Your legs and back ache and cramp, and when you're done with one hoof, you can barely stand straight. After a while, you're all nerves. I've done my share of yelling and yanking horses around or smacking them with the flat side of the rasp. I trim hooves alone. Wouldn't want to put my kids through it!

Growing up, more times than not, horses were the source of much frustration. Of course, it is all in how you deal with it, like anything else, and my dear daddy just seemed to have a low threshold for what some might call the many unpleasant and unplanned problematic details of life. Horses definitely presented many of those challenges.

Having horses means putting up hay in summer and feeding

them in the winter. It means making sure they have water, which, in the old days, included chopping ice at the water hole. It means building and repairing fences. It means trimming hooves, saddling, harnessing, keeping tack repaired, staking out or tethering, grooming, and on and on. It means death by natural causes or choking at the end of a rope. It means doctoring as best you can in those early days or watching helplessly as your horses suffer. If you are not a person who likes a lot of drama, excitement, and many unplanned problems, don't get involved with horses.

The most traumatic of all aspects of being raised with horses was when they broke out. This meant they could get on the main road where they might get killed or cause a serious accident. This meant getting into neighbor's hayfields or gardens. Still today, but even more so in the old days, you did not mess with someone's garden or hay fields. Gardens meant food for staying alive. Hayfields meant food for your animals to stay alive. Mess with someone's garden or hayfields and you were messing with someone's life. It's right up there with messing with someone's wife.

Of course, the more often your horses got out and wreaked havoc around the neighborhood, the angrier your neighbors got, and the more afraid you were to go get 'em. Usually it was us kids who had to go and get 'em—and take the heat as well.

So, to make a long story short, when the horses got out, things got just a little tense around the old homestead cabin. No matter whether they got into the neighbor's stuff or into ours, things got real hot.

One incident that stands out far above all others was the time our horses got out and into our newly planted oat field shortly after a visit from my uncle Edwin. I could take you back to countless horses-getting-out episodes. But I'm gonna tell you about the most stand-out-in-my-mind horse-got-loose story that involved both me and my daddy. I believe it was the summer I was sixteen.

Now, first, I gotta backtrack just a little here and tell you what got me to thinking about this experience of forty-four years ago. Oh, I think about it quite often, but a while back something happened that caused me to remember it more clearly—seven of our horses got loose.

Atz Lee had come out to the homestead to go sledding with *his* six-year-old son, Etienne. Between my brother, Otto, and I, we have ten horses total. Four are already being fed hay up at his feedlot, but the other six are still grazing in the pastures below the homestead. It snowed quite a bit, about a foot and a half, so they're getting short on grass and I need to move the pasturing horses up to the feedlot.

Now, I've moved a lot of horses in a lot of different ways, so taking six of them the half mile to the feedlot was not gonna be that big of a deal. Of course, you can't lead horses through the snowy forest in the dark, with one of the horses being blind, without running into a problem or two.

I catch two of 'em and tie a rope around their necks—same rope, different ends.[1] I tie those two up and catch two more with the same one-rope method. While I'm letting 'em through the pasture gate, one of the ropes holding two horses slips out of my hand and away they go, up through the snow-covered hayfields. At least they're headed in the right direction, I think. They take turns leading each other. Sometimes the rope is under their legs but most of the time they figure out how to avoid that. They disappear into the white snowy darkness. They were both well trained and used to ropes so I'm not worried I'm gonna end up with a broken leg or a choked horse. Well, not too worried.

I take the other two and head up to Otto's place. The two loose horses took a more circular route, but we all got there at about the same time. I put those four in with the four that have already been there a few weeks, and they commence getting reacquainted. My son Atz takes time out from sledding to help me open gates and keep the "in" horses in, while I put the "out" bunch in with 'em. Atz gives 'em some hay to help settle 'em down while I go back for the blind one

---

1. That way you don't have to deal with two ropes. But you have to be careful not to get your hand caught in the bite of the rope, and if you lose one, you lose 'em both. It's a method I don't recommend.

called Sweetie Pie and the old mare I named Damn You.[2]

I halter both of them and tie the lead rope of the blind one around the neck of the old mare, kinda loose-like, with a big loop. This way Damn You is pulling Sweetie Pie, pretty much like the collar of a harness is designed to pull a wagon, so her sounds and scent can lead him instead of having him step on my heels the whole way. This works perfectly and I put them in with the cows so Sweetie Pie won't be bullied by the other horses, but can still have some horse companionship, so come spring he doesn't think he's a cow.

Mission accomplished, Atz Lee, Etienne, and I head into town for a little family dinner of Christmas leftovers. Little do I know that just as we're startin' to get supper together, the phone will ring with the loose-horse alert.

My sister Catkin's place borders Otto's, and her daughter Catty says she counted seven horses that look like ours running by their place. Yep, we had a holiday jailbreak going on. Otto isn't home, so it's up to me to go after 'em. Atz Lee says it's no job for a lone cowboy in the dark and cold and insists on coming along. I say I'm sure I can get 'em all back in, but he'd certainly make the job easier and faster.

It was a low-key crisis—how hard is it to follow tracks in the snow and lure them back with grain or hay? Easy enough to follow their trail and see where they broke through the fence. The biggest risk was if our horses visited the neighbor's horses across the fence and broke another fence in their excitement.

I couldn't remember if Atz had ever chased horses with me when he was younger, or if he'd just forgotten how much fun it hadn't been. Maybe he'd forgotten any nightmarish memories. Or maybe he was looking to heal some old wounds of his own.

We hand our supper-fixin' off to Jane and Nikos, and tell them we won't be long, though I know it isn't likely, and out we go on our first

2. By the way, since Sweetie Pie is owned by my sister, she was the one who named him that. Just so we're clear. Damn You, on the other hand, was all me. I was training her with my dad and she just wouldn't cooperate. I kept shouting, "Damn, you! Damn, you!" and, though my pops protested, it stuck.

big adventure together in a long while through the dark and the cold.

My son suggests we go via the upper road to see if they went to the neighbors and eliminate that option first. We do, and seeing no tracks, we know they're still up on the homestead. At Catkin's driveway, new tracks tell us that, indeed, they were headed down Kilcher road to the very place they escaped from. Of course. Otto's haystack was there.

We get to Otto's and they're not at his haystack. Atz thinks he hears them over at the other haystack. He suggests we use Otto's snow machine. It has no headlight, but we have headlamps on, so off we go with him driving, heading toward the haystack. No sign there either, but Atz sees them up in the hay meadows. I'm already glad he's along, hearing and seeing things I don't, due to my *more seasoned* senses.

They hear us coming, and head for the forest, so I get off and Atz goes up around them on the snow machine while I go the other way on foot. I'll head off any escape while Atz herds them back down to Otto's. We get them, settle them back in and then backtrack to find where they went over the fence. There's a tree fallen on it, probably from the last wind storm. And since we can't find a chainsaw at Otto's, we take a big ax to go chop the tree in half and get it off the fence so we can temporarily prop it back up.

But as you might have guessed, the ax is so dull it barely cuts, so we have to go borrow one from Catkin's place. Meanwhile, I lose the rope I was going to use to tie the cable fence to my temporary fence posts. And I haven't been able to reach Otto on his cell, which is probably a good thing, actually, considering how angry I was in the moment. I'm sure I would've said some things I'd later regret.

We start hacking away, and by this point, my inner cauldron of frustration over past horse breakouts has gone from a low simmer to boiling point. I am mad, but at this juncture in life, I'm not fully cognizant of the latent source of my misplaced anger. All I know is I'm mad Otto has no ready chainsaw available, and I'm mad his ax was dull—*Who in the hell even has an ax that dull, let alone doesn't sharpen it? Surely not any son of Great Axman Yule Kilcher!* I'm mad the wind blew down a tree. I'm mad Otto has not checked his fence after the storm. I'm mad at the dark and the cold. And, of course, I'm mad at the horses just a teensy bit too.

I am *not* mad at my son, who by the way, is being perfect. He's saying and doing all the right things. We *must* have done this together before, 'cause he's sure good at it. Also, he must have had an inkling I might be challenged by my inherited predisposition. At one point, he stops hacking to say, "You know, I'm actually enjoying this, getting my blood pumping. I don't get many opportunities to do something other than play and sing. This is a great father-son experience!" That's damn near exactly what he says to me right then. Gotta love that boy of mine!

Finally, Otto shows up with his chainsaw, right after we've managed to chop our way through the eight-inch tree trunk with Catty's little ax, which is also dull. A couple of beavers could have done a cleaner job.

My old self wants to fill Otto in on all I'm mad at him about. But my newly enlightened inner cowboy holds a tight rein on that malignant, mutated, calcified part of my heart. Though my silence fools nobody.

"Say, bro," Otto says, "I'm sure sorry you couldn't find the chainsaw and that the ax was so dull. Sorry you had to deal with all of this. It couldn't have happened to a more understanding person, though."

I keep my mouth shut tight. Whether he really thinks that and isn't picking up my angry vibe, or he's salving old wounds, it feels good.

As we we're leaving, Catkin and her family return from town. Someone comments about loose horses and fence repairs in the dark as one of the downsides of living in Alaska, to which my son replies, "Actually, we had a lot of fun, and it was a very healing experience for all of us. I got to spend some quality time with my dad and my uncle."

On the way home, cell messages told the story of dinner long since over, dishes done, and now all gone home. But no one was disappointed, no one's feelings were hurt, and all had been taken in stride. I should also mention that my son only gets his boy once a week, so he'd given up some of that precious time to travel quite a different father-son trail than he'd planned.

I think he knew something I didn't.

And now for that old horses-getting-out story that I'll never forget. The one with *my* daddy.

When I was sixteen, my millionaire uncle from Switzerland came for a visit. And much as I took comfort in knowing my uncle was a millionaire, the long and the short of it was that much of the time Uncle Edwin treated my dad the same way my dad treated us most of the time. But he treated us kids real good, which was just one more factor that pissed my dad off.

Uncle Edwin screamed at my dad, ran him down, and often belittled him in front of us kids. How awful that must have been for my dad (though personally, I loved it). Uncle Edwin wondered why Dad hadn't gotten more done since he'd been there last. Later, I'd learn that he'd loaned my dad much money over the years and the land was collateral, so in effect, it was as much my uncle's farm as my dad's. At least, that's how Uncle Edwin saw it.

What matters most about this is that it was the only time I ever saw anyone intimidate my dad. The only time I saw anyone able to put my dad in his place, call his bluff, even tell him to shut up. Once, I even saw Uncle Edwin raise his open hand in a threatening, abusive gesture to my dad, and to my wonder and amazement, my dad cowered. As I watched this, I felt myself split right down the middle. Part of me cheered for Uncle Edwin finally getting even for me. The other part felt as horrified and frozen in fear as when my dad would do that to us.

Seeing this may have helped me to realize my dad was battling something bigger than himself. He was not always abusive, and he did a lot of wonderful things for us kids. He had many good reasons for his moods, frustrations, depressions, rage, blaming, suspicions, and for feeling unloved and disrespected. And he suffered from many disorders for which he never sought help. He generously passed them onto us and divided them among us fairly evenly. I have been guilty of doing the same for my children. Happily, those qualities are becoming more and more diluted as the Kilcher gene pool mingles with calmer waters. Bottom line is, my dad did the best he could. Sometimes that was a shitty job. But I've learned to accept it, to take the good and leave the rest. I've learned from it all, and I've forgiven and moved on, but that doesn't mean I don't meander back down old trails now and again.

You can bet every time my Uncle Edwin left after one of those visits, my dad had some serious unwinding to do! I chuckle lookin' back on it now. This guy had no other way to express all his frustrations and inadequacy and who knows what else, having to keep his mouth shut and be on his good behavior and take the very shit he wanted to dish out. That had to be a mighty bitter pill to swallow. So, we used to get pretty good at making ourselves scarce after Uncle left.

At sixteen, I was full grown—five-foot-ten, and one-sixty or so. Still an awkward hick, but to my dad I looked like a man. Uncle Edwin's recent two-week visit had made Dad's cork ready to blow, especially after trying to take horses and a pack mule to go hunt some sheep at the head of the bay and never getting where we were going. I remember many tense and frustrating horse and mule moments, and my uncle riding my dad even harder than usual. I realized the frustration with horses ran deep in both my father and my uncle.

So, the great white whale was ready to spout! Like a cauldron, my dad started hissing, steaming, and bubbling. His eyes began smoldering behind narrow slits. His mouth started twitching and his nostrils flared for the blow! Looking back, I can't remember what in the world had kept me from long-since heading for higher ground. Maybe my age and size made me unafraid. Maybe I was also being a bit naive, optimistic, or just plain stupid.

"Go get a bucket of coal!" he roared. I got the bucket and headed for the door. I don't recall if I said something, mumbled something, or just moved too slow. Maybe I swung the bucket just a bit too vigorously, but whatever it was translated disrespect to him, so he hollered something else, and again I reacted wrong but tried not to speak, realizing the danger.

He ran outside to head me off and screamed in my face, "Come out and take your coat off and fight like a man!"

Wow! So, there it was! My first official challenge by my dad. Man to man, mano a mano! I recall this so vividly because of that challenge. My own father wanted to fight me, man to man. What the hell was that supposed to mean? I cowered and mumbled some appropriate apology while I went to get the coal. All the while, he berated and goaded me. Where the hell was my uncle when I needed him?

But no sooner did I get the bucket of coal inside than someone came up from the beach and informed my dad that the horses were loose and had gotten into the newly planted oat field. You didn't think this little story was going to end in the coal pile, did you?

Such a serious incident as horses trampling newly seeded oats would have been worthy of a major family crisis and blow up all on its own. But add it to the pressure cooker my uncle just left us with, and this was now at the level of national disaster. My poor daddy screamed so loud his vocal chords almost snapped! He sounded like a horse. He conveyed to me quite clearly that I was to waste no time in getting down to the bottom flat meadow to get the horses out and back into their pasture. Having never been big on spending the time or money on good fences, kids were his preferred method for corralling horses and were a lot cheaper. Plus, kids could be used for a lot of other things; fences were only good for keeping in horses.

Well, I didn't bust out of the starting blocks quite fast enough, so he screamed for me to halt, come back, and try again.[3] I can't recall now how many times he had me start over. I was not fast enough, my shoulders were too slumped, or I was not quite enthusiastic enough and had a bad attitude—who wouldn't by this point?

Believe it or not, I can't remember what straw broke the old whale's back, but the Great Blow of the Century was finally delivered. I must

3. This became one of my favorite training tools that I used years later on my own kids, much to their dismay.

have mumbled something and he called me to where he was standing. I knew right away this would be a biggie. It had that extra-heavy feel to it, sorta how I imagine it must feel walking to the gallows. I stopped in front of him and his fist came out of nowhere, caught me totally off guard. He'd never hit me with his fist before, though the open-handed slaps hurt plenty and I'd been sent ass over teakettle many a time. But this hurt bad.[4]

His punch hurt, but it didn't knock me down. I kept my balance and stayed on my feet. And before I knew what I was doing, my own fist was clenched, and I dropped my shoulder and came up with all the power a frustrated sixteen-year-old boy can muster.

It came from somewhere I seemed to have no control over. I hit him square on his chin and he went down like a tree. The next few moments I remember as though they just happened. It's an amazing thing how the mind can store some moments forever like they're trapped in amber. I stood there paralyzed by what I'd just done. I watched the dazed look on his face turn to hate. In his eyes, I saw what I'd only seen in wild animals or an angry dog. It was the look of wanting to kill!

So, I did the most sensible thing I could think of—I ran! He was up in a flash, but I ran around the pond we called the swimming pool, and he circled the other way to head me off. I went the other way and so did he. If I could get to the gate that led to the road, I'd be free, but he kept blocking me. Finally, I faked one way and went the other way, got a slight lead on him and sprinted for the barbed-wire gate.

*Shit!* It was closed! No time to stop and open it—I was a high-jumper in school and I told myself it was time to use the old barbed-wire western farm-roll. I jumped, but I caught the leg of my Levi's on the top wire and fell in the mud on the other side. That was all the time my dad needed. I looked up as he opened the gate and I thought, "Well, Lord, this is it."

4. My neck would be a chiropractor's delight for many years to come. The first bone cracker I went to asked me, "What did you do to your neck?" I told him it was just farmwork.

He reached for me and I started scrambling and slinging mud like a pig, gaining my feet and slipping out of his grasp to run up the slippery road I'd run enough times in my life to know I'd make it. I was one of the fastest milers in my school, but I set some new records that day! I hit the main road after a mile and a half and kept on running.

At Fritz Creek a couple miles down, I heard his car coming so I hid in the woods. After he went by, I hitchhiked into Homer, borrowed money from a friend, and then hitchhiked to Anchorage, some two hundred miles away.

My plan was to go to British Columbia where we had friends who owned a ranch. After that, I had no plan. The one thing I was very sure of was that I was never going back.

I stayed the night at my dad's duplex in Anchorage, which was my big mistake. I was roughly awakened the next morning by my dad's hand shaking me by the shoulder. I evidently lacked some basic long-range planning skills—kinda like robbing a house, then sleeping on the couch till the cops come.

He drove me back to Homer, lecturing me about respect and obedience and threatening to send me to the army. He told me he talked with the school principal and they'd arranged counseling for me. I was his captive audience for four hours and he took full advantage of it.[5]

*   *   *

This particular trail of the past has plumb tuckered me out. Some things are forgotten forever, other things fester in us and we never quite work through them. Maybe you make peace with some, but they still leave scars. Most of the time, they lie dormant inside and only come up every once in awhile. I still get edgy around horses sometimes, but I've learned to deal with it. However, I still feel old stuff when horses get loose and start causing trouble.

It took me all morning to realize why I felt so down and had

5. Another tactic I proudly used on my kids during many a long drive in years to come.

gotten so angry out there fixin' fence and catchin' those loose horses, especially since it had all gone so well. Then I remembered those loose horses of long ago. They'd come back to me in disguise to pay a little visit, and I needed to chew this memory over one more time.

And to my son Atz, I'm mighty thankful. Even though he knew all this about me, he still wanted to come along. Reckon his clearer vision was on another kind of round-up he might help me do, catchin' some loose ghosts of the past, and helping fix another fence from long ago, an old wound I couldn't see my way over between a father and son.

# CHAPTER 9

## *First Car*

For me, my first car was a big deal.

Okay, so, big deal—isn't it a big deal for everyone? It *is, and* it's also a bigger deal for some than others. It represents freedom, autonomy, adulthood, privacy, separateness, individuality. It was an important rite of passage for me where I had few such rights.

If a teenager has already experienced those things, say, a teenager who has a job, a bicycle, any freedom or respect as an individual and was encouraged to make their own decisions, a first car may not be as big a deal. For such a teen, a car is merely the next logical step in their growth toward adulthood. But I lived far at the other end of the spectrum of teenhood. My *hood* was in the forests of dysfunction junction. So, my first car was my first escape, my first taste of controlling my own fate for the first time.

Horses played a similar role, but my first car had doors and locks, a portable world I could take with me, a safe bubble that could take me where I wanted to go, where I was in control and could make all the decisions.

Strange how all of this flashes back to me now. I was a mere seventeen or eighteen then. I've forgotten much of those foggy years of survival, insecurity, self-doubt, shame, and pain. But today some of the exhilarating, deeply imprinted feelings surface to be felt again, to be shared with my kids and grandkids.

So many thoughts and feelings converge on me at once, it's hard to process them all, much less make sense of them in an intelligible form. Writing helps me organize my thoughts and feelings. Right away, my mind went to my kids, and I just knew I had to share this treasure with them. You find something special and you want to share it with the most special people in your life. Before I know it, I'm writing a letter:

Kids,

I write partly for myself, for my own joy of discovery, disclosing, reminiscing, and sharing. I also write in part because I wish my father had shared more of who he was. My knowledge of him was so one-sided, though my mother wrote us kids more and more as she got older. Just as my parents did not do for me, I did not give near enough information or road maps for your futures, nor did I show you my many other sides.

I am so glad I have more and more opportunities to interact with you now in different ways and settings. To get to know each other again as adults. It is always a joy to see qualities you have, how we are similar or how you have improved on what I did. It especially feels good when we can get past old stuff, old blocks or patterns of reaction, when we take time to do the hard work it takes to listen and understand each other and come away with a greater love and appreciation for what we've been through.

I plan on writing you all more often. If I do not even hear back from you that you received it, I am prepared to accept that and try not to attach judgments to it. If, in the process, we both gain from it and grow in love and understanding and all that is groovy, then cool. I am trying to become more involved in your lives by staying more in touch with what you are doing and telling you what I am up to. I encourage all of us to try harder to stay in touch more through phone and emails. If I am the only one who wants this, then that is okay. I have to say though, nothing feels better than having someone call, especially my kids, and say they just called to say hi and that they were thinking of me. On the hierarchy of calls it goes at the top. At the bottom is when someone calls because they want something and never calls to thank you. Next is when someone calls for something and calls again later to say thank you. Then there is a call just to make contact, to chat or catch up, for no reason. I am sure we have done all of those at times. I am not sure why it is such a challenge to do a better job of staying in touch. I think of you guys all the time, a part of you is always with me, beside me. It's even hard for me to stay in touch with those of you who live here in Homer.

I believe any of us who have kids have had similar goals of being the perfect parent that we did not have. We want to be loved and respected, asked for advice, listened to, have our kids hold us in a high place of esteem, be their idol, their rock, the one safe place to go in rough times. I certainly wanted that. Since I cannot go back, all I can do is be the best I can be now, to improve what we have, or create something new.

Of course, both people have to want something equally to make it work. But regardless, one person can still do a lot. If I want you to think or know I am a fast ski racer, I have to win some races. If I want you to think I am generous, I have to do stuff for you, give you things. If I want you to know sides of me I have not shown, I have to take opportunities to show them.

One of you calls more than the others just to say hi, that you're thinking about me. One of you remembers special days, like Veterans Day. Another of you once said, in the most nonjudgmental way, that you would like more contact with me. Some of you call once in a while for help, some don't; some of you remember to thank me, some (more like me) forget to say thanks. One of you once said something in a letter about my "pitiful occasional attempts at closeness." As I write this, I have to still that inner voice that tells me this letter is just such another attempt. Could be it is. Could be this is my best. Just could be this is who I am. What counts is that first I accept who and what I am, then for you all to try to accept that also. It is all good. You are all different. We each have a different relationship. I was a different father to each of you. One of you was the oldest, one was a daughter, one was the youngest—I bottle-fed you, whereas the other two got the warm breast. One has a different mother, was adopted out, and I only got to know you later. One followed the death of a son, one witnessed the death. You each had a very different childhood, and we each have a different relationship now. When I have a glitch, a run-in, hard feelings, or a stuck place with each of you, it goes differently with each of you because we are different with each other depending on our past relationship.

If I were able to give each of you a litmus test, you would all come out different in love for me, fear of me, wanting a closer relationship, your ability to deal with discomfort or tension. One of you, if I am uptight around you, will automatically start whistling or getting punny. It drives me crazy. Another of you used to say, "Easy, Dad," till I told you I was not a damn horse. One of you kids, when I fell out of a tree moose hunting, took off running, and when Mark came to see if I was hurt, thought to himself, *No! RUN!* And he was right. I screamed at him, "Why the hell didn't you hold me better?" I had to blame someone. Especially since my chickenshit oldest son wasn't there for me to scream at. Oops, suppose the cat is out of the bag. Sorry, Shane.

But believe you me, you ran for good reason. There were way too many times when you tried to inquire into my pain, and you got yelled at. So, all I can say is, if it looks like a tense moment and you think you might get the brunt of it like you used to, by all means, "Run, Forrest, run!"

Regardless of where each of you stands, in terms of wanting a better or closer relationship with me or wanting more contact, I want more. Not that I'm unsatisfied. It might simply be partly my work ethic. Might be wishing my dad had wanted more of a relationship with me. I'm not sure.

It's all good. It's all okay. We can all change to the degree we want to. We can all decide on the amount of time and energy we want to put into it. Just as I and my siblings all have different relationships ranging from "can't stand to be around them" to actually enjoying hanging out with them, so do each of you have different relationships with each other. Hopefully none of those qualify as "can't stand to be around you." My sibs and I inherited challenges from our parents, as did you.

How do we express feelings, especially those we call negative or hurtful, in a kind way? How to listen and not bring up our stored shit at the same time, but listen deeply and bring up ours later? That's one challenge I see both generations having. Yet those of you in long-term, successful relationships will agree that conflict resolution makes or breaks the deal. And while there may be many theories on how to do that, there are some constants. Both have to feel heard and listened to. Better if one talks at a time. Better when there is not a strong reaction causing a counterattack. Better when they're planned and well thought-out. Better when they're done often and not stored up.

I remember in college learning the term *gunnysacked* for stored-up negative feelings. I proudly told Nedra what

I'd learned, and she quickly pointed out to me that I was definitely the gunnysacker. Of course, she was right. I hope you're all aware that I did that to all of you repeatedly. I ranted, raved, and gunnysacked, gathering up a shitload of frustrations and then dumping it on you all at once. Oh, yes, and then I told you to have no reaction whatsoever to that load I just dumped. If you don't recall or you believe it didn't affect you or that you deserved it, that's not true. I'm thinking of organizing a support group for people called, "Adult Children of Homesteaders," ACOH. You can all come to our first meeting.

I have tried hard not to do that anymore, and when you have had things to say to me, I have tried to listen and not take it as an opportunity to tell you things I've been saving up.

If this has been merely for my own therapeutic growth, that's all right. My love for each of you is increasing, my desire to be a good human and dad is also increasing, as is my desire for us all as a family unit to grow closer. To see the good we have, what we have in common, what we can share, how we can support each other and care for and about each other as ideally as a family can. If I did hurt you, I want to know about it and have the opportunity to express my apology and ask for forgiveness.

I once said something well meaning which hurt one of you, and I heard about it later from another of you. I then tried to make it right. Since then, this same kid has told me several times when things I've said hurt, and it's such a wonderful gift. To be able to say, "Before I react, let me try to understand what you meant and maybe I can help you get it out and sort out your real intentions." That gives people the opportunity to say, either, "Yes, that's what I meant. And thank you for not reacting. Let me try again," or, "Oh, I'm so sorry. That was not my intention. Let me try to say it differently." Our feelings or reactions to intended or unintended messages are very valid, but that comes later, separately. Believe me, my kiddos, it is all fear which keeps us from asking someone what they meant by what they said. It is all fear which causes us to react without first checking what someone meant. It is fear and self-preservation, sometimes on a subconscious, primitive, reactive level. I know very well that of which I speak. It is exactly what I didn't model for you. Indeed, I modeled the opposite.

It's always hard to tell someone they hurt or angered you, always easier to gunnysack or simply tell someone else. Some of you may have gotten my Christmas letter. I mass-emailed it and said I would no longer talk to any of my siblings *about* other siblings, *and* when they talked or tried to talk to me about my siblings, I would only listen if they were willing to make a plan to talk *to* that sibling or look at their part in the conflict and what they could do to change *themselves.* I invite each of you, if and when you talk to each other *about* each other, to look at why you do that, why you don't talk directly, what your fear is, what's holding you back, and what it would take to change. Lots of good stuff to think about. Since I've stuck to that, my relationships with all my siblings have improved, but it wasn't easy to change old patterns.

With much love and hopefully a little wisdom,
Dad

Well now, we are a-ways from my first-car story. But driving has always given me many opportunities for reflecting on the past. Much of this thinking still happens today, at fifty-nine years old, driving from Bend up to Mt. Bachelor in my little green Subaru every day as I practice for the National Master Ski Races, just me and my skis in a brand-new place. I first found that freedom and privacy in my first car, my Renault, when I used to drive to Anchorage for ski races there.

I recall sitting in parking lots, not knowing a soul, just me and my skis and some food and a change of clothes, and one hell of a desire to win, to excel, to be someone, to do something I was good at, and yes, to make my papa proud. Physical accomplishments were something he could relate to. Athletics were the very first taste I got of being praised by others, and then developing a new sense of self-worth and identity, something I could genuinely be proud of. I could easily escape into athletics, and skiing especially played one of the more significant roles.

The summer of '65, I helped Dad guide a Swiss hunter, Dr. Grassli, whose name I remember after all these years for the simple reason that he tipped me three hundred dollars! I don't know what that would be in today's economy, but what was also amazing was that my dad let me keep it!

I remember it so clearly. We were partway up the road to Pferdewiese, and the good doctor thanked me and shook my hand.[1] I felt something between our hands and I could not believe my seventeen-year-old eyes. I'd never seen that much money in my life, selling radishes for pennies. Other money I earned was appropriated, usually by my dear mother, for school clothing or other needs, so I have to give my papa credit for allowing me to keep that windfall.

I've forgotten how or where, but that money bought me a tiny Renault. My first car! And like a first love, you never forget it, no matter its limitations or flaws. She was a beauty!

Up till this point I had to bum rides or stay the night with friends in town, which was always a source of embarrassment. There were many mornings I would get up at 4:00 a.m., do chores, and walk the mile and a half to the end of Kilcher Road and then another mile

---

1. "Pferdewiese" translates from German as "horse meadow." Any early settlers, out of necessity, had to name the places they frequented so they could know where to meet each other. Most often, for the sake of simplicity and clarity, they called a place by its most basic description, and sometimes those names stuck through the years—as it did for this particular meadow.

down East End Road to catch a ride at 5:30 with the only car going to Homer for basketball practice. After school in winter was skiing, after which I would hitchhike home, sometimes walking half the twelve miles back, do my chores and homework, then fall into bed after the usual dysfunctional family "acrobatic practice" and entertainment.

My first car changed all that, except for the highly emotional family workouts.

Before my first car, I barely knew what privacy was. Sleeping double in the early years, and later, several kids in the same room, I'd never known it. At one point, six kids were in three bunks in a room that measured about six-by-eight feet.[2] The lack of physical privacy was less damaging than the total lack of emotional, psychological, and personal privacy we endured, unable to ever escape. Being grilled in a frenzied rage of adult paranoia and insecurity as to where you were going, what you were doing, and why was one type of invasion. I learned quickly to lie well, be extremely defensive, have answers well thought-out in advance, and never be caught flat-footed. But the invasion of psyche and soul was much harder to protect against or be ready for. It required hardening, shutting down, building up calluses inside where there should be only softness.

The berating, accusations, cross-examinations, prosecutions, and harsh final judgments left their mark on me. Those were much harder to escape, and were what formed habits that were so hard to break. Boundaries were nonexistent. Log walls and spruce forests were no boundaries. The land had eyes and ears. I go back there now as a fifty-nine-year-old, fairly well-adjusted adult, and I still have to fight the urge to allow the memories to swallow me, to allow the past to invade the boundaries I've put in place.

My first car changed all that. Not sure how, but it sure as hell did. Yes, it sure as *hell* did! There were additional factors, like turning eighteen that fall, and my dad sensing my impending independence and eventual departure. But I give all credit to my first car.

2. When we turn that cabin into a museum, I hope to put two child-dummies in each bunk, and a full pee can under the first.

It was my own private world, and I had earned it. I had bought it. I was safe in it. What I did and thought in my car stayed in my car. I was an individual in my car. I had boundaries the exact shape of my car. I recall sitting, sometimes for hours, in my car at the end of the road, hanging out in my little world, soaking up the strength to enter my *other* world again. Sometimes I slept in it all night, ran home to do chores and change clothes, only to turn around and head back for school, or rather, to my *real* life—sports.

That summer, I earned some money and opened an account, only withdrawing from it for gas. For it was that gas that fueled my private world, my first taste of *separateness*. I stretched out that money like no resource I've ever had since.

Had it not been for that car, I wouldn't have been able to enter all the ski races I did that year and qualify for the junior nationals or eventually be ranked the number-two skier in Alaska, an accomplishment I'm still most personally proud of. Many a wintry, blizzardy, cold day, I would drive all alone to Anchorage. I would find the race, change, race, change again, perhaps stay the night, and then head back to the reality of homestead life.

So now, at fifty-nine years old, my little green Subaru Forrester takes me to the mountain every morning, closer to my goal of competing in my first National Master Ski Races. Something I've wanted to do for years. I am back to my high school weight and old muscles are reemerging. The top coach in the area, one of two or three World Cup coaches, has agreed to prepare me for the World Master's next year.

I'm still the new guy in a strange town, like I was in Anchorage years ago. But I'm getting to know folks, and skiers are a great bunch. I'm always running into someone who knows someone I know, or who I knew years ago. The other day, the wife of a top skier who I finally beat said, "So you are the new threat on the mountain." That tickled me to no end, of course.

As my little green Subaru took me off the mountain the other day, I contemplated how many things had not changed much from when I was eighteen. I felt that same thrill of being in shape, of doing well, of pushing myself and gaining recognition in a strange place for something I was doing on my own. I felt that same "peaceful easy feelin'" I first felt in my little Renault. Only now, that feelin' doesn't stop when I open the car door.

I felt so full driving off the mountain in the warm sun. I thought of the fact that I now have kids and grandkids, and how much I love them and am learning from them all.

So, I came home to write to them.

How many gifts they have all given me! And how sweet it is that my first car in the lower forty-eight, which takes me wherever I want to go—to races, mountains, and snow—also took me back to long ago, to my first car and the freedom I first found in a three-hundred-dollar Renault.

# CHAPTER 10

## *The Bar Five*

It takes getting older to fully realize the main influences that shaped you, those that were stronger and bigger than the others.

Things like going to war or to college or getting married are obvious. But sometimes it's the friends we grow up with or folks we spent a lot of time with. Somebody we looked up to saying just the right thing at the right time, or reading that book we happened to be ready for. Some of the most life-changing influences can also be small things that happen along the way, people we meet briefly that gently nudged our personalities to take shape.

When the Bar Five crew, so named for their brand, moved into my neck of the Alaskan woods, I had no idea the far-reaching effect they'd have on my life between ages ten and eighteen.[1] They had a profound effect on me during that period of my life.

I was lonely and not well socialized. Up to that point, I'd been homeschooled and attended two years of elementary school in my home country of Switzerland where we had been getting to know our relatives while my dad lectured and showed his Alaska documentary.

1. People who own animals pick a brand so that everyone knows who the animals belong to. It can be anything they want—a design and then a name to go with it. The symbols and letters used mean different things and all the cowboys know how to read them. The Bar Five brand was simple: a bar followed by the number 5, representing the five families and their siblings.

Before my two-year Swiss experience of total culture shock, I had been living remotely and quite secluded on a homestead thirteen miles east of Homer. We had only recently gotten a road, electricity, and running cold water.

I had a somewhat "split" personality. One of my selves was the homeschooled homestead hick. The other was a bilingual kid who'd attended two years of private school in Europe and was a son of a multilingual lecturer and filmmaker, quite well known in his home country of Switzerland. I got by over there but never really fit in or felt at home.

I'd run semiwild in the forests and meadows of the wilderness homestead, and then lived in a crowded Swiss town with trams, buses, shops, and people everywhere. I went to the zoo a lot and started stealing and lying a lot more than I already did, started smoking and running with older teenagers.

When I returned to my homestead hick self, I took right up where I left off: hanging out in the woods with the cows and horses and reading my Zane Grey and Louis L'Amour Western novels. I lived largely in my head, pretending I was a cowboy and telling myself I was important, that I mattered, that I was the emerging young man my father was proud of and loved. I was a sponge waiting for water, a duck searching for my pond.

The Bar Five were *real* cowboys made up of five families, hence their brand, Bar Five. They were adult siblings, four girls and one boy, all married, and most had kids. When they first arrived, they ranged in age from twenty to fifty. Gary Presley, the youngest of the bunch, was the only boy, and the sisters were Virginia Wilson, Edna Anderson, Lorene Lewis, and Marguerite Jacobs.

All of them were good-looking, and what added to the allure was something about those Presley genes. Yes, they were distant relatives of the King.

I had more to do with those who lived nearby, and the ones with children closer to my age. The years blur some things, colors have faded and run together, but when I think back on them and those years now, I think of the Bar Five collectively as an *era*. They were a "community" into which I adopted myself.

They had cows and horses they had brought up from New Mexico and they wore the Levi's with big belt buckles, turquoise and silver, and their authentic cowboy hats were something out of one of my novels. I was in heaven. They took top money at local rodeos, and if there were no rodeos, they started them. They held cattle drives and roundups where they branded, dehorned, castrated, and ear-marked their herd.

They also roped. And boy, could they rope! You name it, they could do it. As I learned to rope, I felt lucky to catch any part of the animal I was throwing my loop at, but they could catch their critter 'round the neck, horns, back feet, front feet, or any single foot in between. They'd "team tie"—one cowboy would "head 'em" while the other cowboy would "heel 'em," and their horses would stretch the critter out between them so it could be "worked," which meant it needed to be castrated—to control breeding—and ear-tagged and ear-notched, so the cowboys know whose cow is whose. To me, it was pure magic.

They were, in many ways, the antithesis of my main role model up to that point—my dad. They were slow in movement and speech. They laughed and joked. There was always time for everything, no rush, everything got done eventually. They were patient as they taught this tag-along kid the ropes of being a real cowboy. But it was much more than that. They showed me how to be a real man, a friend, and a person with self-worth and self-respect. They took me under their wing, valued me even as a kid, and they became my water, my pond. I soaked it up and paddled and quacked to my heart's delight.

I first got to know the Lewises. Lorene was married to Elvin, and they had one son named Milton, who was married to Dorothy. I was close to twelve when I met them. Their son, Milton, and Dorothy were seventeen and married, about the same age as my oldest sister. Milton was one of my earliest heroes, role models, friends, and a sort of older brother. He was bigger than life. Of course, I also loved and felt close to his parents and wife, but my main relationship was with Milton. I don't know how they viewed me, but I felt like I was a part of their family.

Before they arrived, there was only the head of the bay populated by a couple of homestead families. Now within a couple short hours' ride, I was in a Western novel. But instead of just reading it, I was one of the characters.

I loved to ride my horse the ten miles up the beach to go and visit them at their ranch. They lived in a very small cabin with no indoor plumbing or running water. It was cramped but cozy. Sometimes I went there to check our cows, which were summer ranging in that area, or to catch our loose horses. Other times I went to get away from home. As long as all my work was done and my dad thought I was tending our stock or helping and learning from the Lewises, he had no problem. I think he knew they could, perhaps, fill in some gaps in my upbringing.

I helped out with haying one summer, mostly just tagging along and doing whatever Milton did. I remember a lot of playing. As I got older, there was some singing and playing the guitar. We rode horses and hunted in the high wild mountains together.[2]

We shot a huge brown bear and roped a black bear. I say "we" rather loosely. We chased it up a huge rock in the mountains together. While I took a photo, Milton threw the loop over the black bear. Before he could get a good dally around his saddle horn, however, the bear bailed off the fifteen-foot boulder, causing the rope to sizzle its wraps off the horn, and the bear, with a loop still around its head, streaked across the mountain tundra. The rope luckily came off after a few hundred yards.

At cattle drives and roundups, all the cattlemen of the area got together. Cattle were separated into respective herds and then worked. I was fascinated as I watched seasoned cowboys do their thing. When you separated out a herd, it meant mothering up the calves with their branded mothers, so that you knew who belonged to who. That

2. See photo in insert.

always took some time and patience. I used to love to watch the older cowboys do that slow, careful job.

And all of this was done slowly, calmly, and methodically. Once a herd was in the corral, they were either run through a chute or roped off horseback and worked in the corral.

There was hard work and lots of good food. There was the smell of burning hair from branding, and the smell of blood from castrating and dehorning. Cows and calves were bawling and mooing. Everyone had a job. We young boys held down the calves as they lost testicles and parts of their ears for identification and got branded. We pushed the steers down the chute, got kicked, slobbered on, shit on, run over, and run into. By the end of the day, I was covered in cow shit and blood and slobber. I was sore and bruised, but my heart was soaring. The big smile on my face said I fit in. I belonged. I finally found my tribe, or they found me.

One year we finally got smart. Instead of gathering all the herds and driving them to the Lewises' corral, we built a corral up in the Fox River Valley. We used some barbed wire for a long channel to help funnel them in. Our building material was cottonwood logs fastened to upright trees with wire. It was high and strong, and again, I was amazed at these cowboys. They had the pioneering, homesteading spirit, and they figured out a way to do what needed done.

My prior cattle experience was very different. My dad had no corral or cow horses. We didn't brand or earmark or castrate. When we butchered, we lured our victims to the butchering tree with sweet hay or grain. If we wanted to get a rope on one of our cows, we set a snare in the trees on a cow trail. And it was all done to lots of screaming and yelling. The bumps and bruises at the end of the day were of a different type. No smile, no soaring heart.

The Wilsons and Presleys lived about fifty miles up the highway from our homestead at a place called Happy Valley. Their kids were quite a bit younger than I was, so I didn't spend much time with them. Most of my interactions with them were during rodeos or when the Bar Five had get-togethers.

Virginia Wilson was in her thirties and I had a crush on her. She was gorgeous: black hair, Levi's boots, turquoise jewelry and belt buckle, and Presley lips. She always looked neat and made up. Their two kids, Tony and Shirley, were too young to notice.

Gary Presley and his wife, Naomi, were probably ten years older than I when they first came to Alaska, early twenties. They were young and beautiful. He was your stereotypical cowboy in his well-worn Stetson and soft, deep, and easy voice. He had a way of making me feel seen, important. I also had a crush on his wife. I can still see her in her rodeo outfit and turquoise jewelry. They eventually had three kids, and I had more to do with the oldest, Danny—later on, he tagged along with us older teenagers.

In my midteens, when I became a minor outlaw, one of the local juvenile delinquents, it was Gary who played a significant role in helping me shape up. Though I never got caught (by some miracle), I had enough brains or fear to mend my ways before I got locked up like some of my friends did.

At the time, Gary and his wife and their two young kids lived about three miles down the road. I'd noticed Gary had really cool Western shirts and turquoise jewelry and a really cool pistol. And I wanted some of that in the worst way.

Any criminal, even a juvie, learns how to separate business from pleasure, how to keep their two very different lifestyles and set of standards in different parts of themselves. So, without any qualms or feelings of guilt, a friend and I set out through the woods. Far from guilt or feelings of betrayal, I was feeling giddy, quite resourceful, and crafty.

From our very back pasture, we sneaked through the woods, careful not to go near any houses. This wasn't hard as there were no houses between our homestead and the small cabin at the bottom of Fritz Creek, where we were headed. The cabin was right beside the only road into Homer, so we had to break and enter from the back.

I tried not to be too greedy, I did have some feelings, and took only a few things—a beautiful turquoise-blue Western shirt with black diamond buttons, a Levi's jacket, and a pistol. Back to the homestead, through the woods we went, feeling quite satisfied and successful.

For the life of me I can't figure out why I thought it was a good idea—obviously I wasn't thinking—but there was a rodeo coming up, and what better place to show off my new wardrobe? I did have enough good sense not to wear my new pistol.

How in the hell did this homestead hick never get caught, being the brainiac he was?

I got there early in the day, riding up to the arena on my little stallion we called Dusk. The first person I saw riding toward me through the crowd of mostly rodeo participants on horseback was, yep, my hero, my idol, and the man I'd have done anything to please, Gary. And right there is where my split personalities collided. I wheeled Dusk around behind one of the sheds and all I could think to do was either strip off my jacket and shirt and go as an Indian instead of a cowboy, or button up the Levi's jacket and hide that shirt I so desperately wanted to show off. Since most Levi's jackets looked alike, I chose the latter option.

It was a long, hot day but I kept my jacket buttoned up tight. I sweated to the point of choking all day. I was so miserable! Inside and out, body and soul. The hardened thief and the attention-starved teenager wanting to please fought all day while riding one horse and wearing one set of clothes and skin. It was a long but unforgettable day!

The best part was that that day was the highlight of my brief rodeo career, the day I won All-Around Cowboy in the Alaska Jr. Championship rodeo. My dream come true and more—it was like finally earning my PhD in cowboyology. I'm quite sure no one else saw it as I did, but for me it was a huge transition, a graduation from homesteader, sod buster, stump farmer, and goat roper to full-fledged COWBOY!

I had a wad of green in my pocket that could have choked a horse—over five-hundred smackeroos. I could barely fit it in my wallet. It was too big for my tight-fitting Levi's, so I stuffed it in the pocket of my coat. The next day I hitchhiked the two hundred miles to Anchorage to see our chiropractor. Many rides and hours later, in the chiropractor's office, I noticed the big bulge was no longer in my coat pocket.

For a moment, I was heartbroken, but I soon got distracted talking to a fellow cowboy there to see the bone-cracker too. He'd just won All-Around Cowboy at the Matanuska Valley Rodeo. We compared stories, bumps, and bruises, and the lost money was no big deal compared to sitting next to that cowboy as an equal, a man, a cowboy!

I've kept that trophy all these forty-six years through many moves, jobs, wives, boxes, and storage sheds. It's in many pieces now and the plate with my name, title, and date is long lost, but it matters not. I'm gonna get a new one made and put that puppy back together. I'm on my last wife and my last house; time to put 'er on a shelf.[3]

The day of that rodeo, most of the events I'd won were due to my fast horse. The only event I won on my own was steer-riding. All the other events relied on my horse. There were the typical gymkhana events such as pole bending, the keyhole race, and barrel racing, but there were a few others thrown in, like the cowhide race, where a person on a horse dragged a second person down to the end of the arena and back hanging onto a cowhide attached to a rope dallied to the saddle horn. The hide did have a rope loop in it to hang onto. The straight down and back wasn't that hard, but that turn at the end is what dumped most cowboys and cowgirls. I told my horse man to do a long sweeping turn and that proved to be the winning ticket.

Then there was the boot race. Everyone took off their boots at the far end of the arena and rode back in their stocking feet. At the signal, everyone raced to the end of the arena, jumped off their horse, put on a pair of boots, jumped back on and had to cross the finish line with the boots hanging on their feet in any fashion. I ended up with two odd small boots, but my horse was short, so I vaulted on without the stirrups.

3. See photo in insert.

The race that caused me the most pride was the all-out horse race, which was, again, down to the end of the arena and back. It gave me a chance to show off that little stud I had trained myself, under the tutelage of the Bar Five cowboys. I had raced him against other horses in our area before, at roundups and such, and he'd never lost. He had an extremely fast start, but due to his short legs he was better at races under a hundred yards. I was anxious to see how he'd do against the fastest horses on the Kenai.

One of those fast horses was a long-legged quarter horse named Chevrolac, owned by the Tietjen brothers. The second horse I was worried about was a quarter horse mare named Lil owned by Gary himself.

The flag goes down and we're off! Dusk gets the jump and I am hanging onto the saddle horn for dear life. He'd jumped out from under me several times racing him bareback so I learned to hang on. Even with a saddle on, I could end up behind the saddle if I wasn't firmly attached. We get to the end of the arena and did a quick turn around and just barely cross the finish line ahead of Chevrolac, ridden by my best buddy, Andy Anderson, son of Edna and Elton Anderson, also of the Bar Five, and Lil, ridden by Gary and Naomi's son Danny, I believe.

It was the last event of the day and I was feeling high knowing I had a good chance at All-Around Cowboy. I hoped winning that last race would put me ahead of Andy, which it did. He won second-highest money. The interesting sideline was that Andy and I also doubled as clowns—maybe I thought a clown outfit was better than hiding in that Levi's jacket all day.

Well, me beating Chevrolac and Lil didn't set well with Joe Tietjen and Gary Presley. I'd beaten their horses, shamed two grown cowboys and top rodeo hands in the Alaska rodeo circuit. But I had beaten their horses with kids riding them, so they wanted to see how I did against them, the horse owners, the *men*.

I was out of my clown outfit and back in the fully buttoned-up jacket. Awards had been given out. The crowds had gone home. Just rodeo participants hanging out. It was time for the main event!

For some reason, I had no say in the length of the race. The two men set the distance to favor their larger, long-legged quarter horses. This was back in the late sixties when quarter horses were still being bred much bigger than they are now.

Dusk was as nervous as I was. We danced and circled and pranced. I was priming him and he knew it. He could always sense when a race was getting ready to start. We both knew this was serious. But I didn't know what serious was till I looked at Joe and Gary. Now *there* was serious! They acted like they were defending horse pedigrees and cowboy honor and genealogy.

The hat dropped and we were off! Dusk shot out of there like a cannonball. I couldn't even see the other two who'd lined up, one on each side of me. Halfway to the finish line, there was a nose close to each of my knees. They were gaining. Could we hang on to our lead? They inched forward, one on each side, but I still had 'em by a head.

Those last fifty yards or so took an eternity, with Lil and Chevrolac creeping forward inch by slow inch on either side. When we crossed the finish line, it was Chevrolac by a neck, Lil in second by a head, and Dusk in third by a ... well, by a happy half-kid, half-man, half-hick, half-cowboy, half-honest, half-thieving delinquent. But a 100-percent total happy Atz, undaunted by the race I'd just lost.

Joe and Gary had redeemed their honor and I saw the rodeo queen I was sweet on smiling at me. Yes, she was also part of the Bar Five outfit, one of the Andersons. Life was good. Everyone was smiling.

It was a pivotal point in my life for many reasons. I still had years and miles to go to figure out who and what I was and to be comfortable with that, to become fully a man or a good human. But I never stole again. Something about having to hide that shirt all day and being in mortal fear that Gary would recognize the jacket or the cuffs protruding. Something about being around him all day, looking up to him as I always had, wanting his approval and acceptance. It cured me.

Edna was Presley by birth, married to Elton Anderson. He was the wild card, the "character" of the Bar Five bunch. He smoked, drank, and cussed. He had a voice like a mad brown bear crossed with a gravel pit. He was grouchy, sometimes scary. He was funny, full of jokes. He was kind and generous. He was a hard worker. Part homesteader, part cowboy, part construction worker. And he was one hell of a cook. Raised one fine and talented and diverse family. Of course, his wife, Edna, had a lot to do with that.

When Elton was close to the end of his life, in the terminal stages of cancer and dying, there was always family or a church friend with him. At one point, with many friends and relatives present, he made gestures and sounds indicating this could be the end, but he had something to say. People moved close with heads and ears bent low, and, in a gravelly whisper, he said, "It wasn't alcohol or cigarettes that took old Joe's last breath. It was a fly crawled up his ass and tickled him to death." And following that, he went into a spasm of raspy laughter.

Edna was like a second mother to me. I spent a lot of time at the Andersons' during those years. Jerry, the oldest son, was three or so years older than me, and I got to know him quite well. He dated and proposed to four of my sisters. Gotta give it to Jerry for nerve and persistence—the word "no" didn't seem to phase him. He was one of my earliest bad influences. He had an old blue Chevy that read "Navajo" on the hood in big letters. He had that dark Presley look and wore a black cowboy hat. He was one dashingly handsome dude.

Because he went through four of my sisters, he was around a lot. I loved him if for no other reason than he was there a lot to help with the farmwork. Plus, my dad was a bit mellower when he was around. He was a good bullshitter and knew how to shmooze my parents. My mom acted different around him too, sort of giggly and girlish. My parents also liked Jerry because he'd call before leaving Homer and almost always ended up bringing out groceries or a bag of chicken feed, packing it the mile and a half down our muddy or snow-covered road.

When he went to Germany for the army for two years, he left me his black cowboy hat—big mistake. It became a part of me, a part of my new cowboy persona, and I wore it out while he was gone.

Jerry was like an older brother and we had lots of good times together. He treated me as an equal and liked me.

The younger two, David and Andy, go together because it's hard to separate them in my mind after all these years. We went to school together, stayed over at each others' houses, played school sports together—wrestling, basketball, cross-country running, and track. Long bus rides to state meets, school dances after games, and later on, some drinking, general carousing, a car rollover, scrapes and bruises, and broken hearts. But my favorite times with them were of the cowboy kind.

We'd bought two mares from Elton Anderson. One palomino and one blue roan. The roan came with an Appaloosa filly. She'd been bred by the Andersons' stud called Apple, an Appaloosa. He was black but beginning to roan out, with a beautiful white blanket with black spots about the size of apples. I still remember the first time I saw him. I swore I'd have a horse like that some day!

Those two "cow ponies" were so different from our old work plugs that could hardly be beat into a trot. They were fast and quick. They were gentle but untrained. They were the first horses I trained. They were also a big part of that transforming period of my life.

My dad wanted Blue, the blue roan, to be bred back to Apple to see if we could get some more Appaloosa coloring. We had no horse trailer or pickup to get her to the stud, but it wouldn't be that hard for a guy like me. I'd ride her the fifteen miles to Homer, partly by beach, partly by road, along the Sterling Highway toward Anchor Point, then five or six miles to the Anderson homestead.

I headed out with her and the foal, and somewhere around mile eight we got a ride. The pickup had a sort of stock rack with sides and no back. Fortunately, the mare was used to pickups, but the foal had to be assisted. The men assured me the filly would stick to her mama and not bail out the back. I told them I was headed for the Anderson Ranch and they took me all the way to Anchor Point.

Once unloaded and remounted, I headed up the closest driveway toward a business with a residence attached. I knew the owners. It was dark and late but the lights were still on. The old man, who'd had a

This style of log cabin is held together by pegs placed into holes in the logs. Here, my dad stands on top of the cabin, driving wooden pegs into holes with a mallet he made.

My mom and three sisters taking a break from building the homestead cabin in 1946, just before I was born.

After cultured Swiss city life, my mother becomes a homestead huntress. We all adapt in life as we learn what needs to be done. Here, she holds up a spruce grouse that came too close to the cabin.

My mother, who is pregnant with me, and my sisters in the old fox cabin.

My mom and I re-creating the photo above.

My mother became pregnant with me in Alaska but traveled back to Switzerland to give birth in Basel. Here, she holds me in Switzerland in the early spring before returning to Alaska.

My mother and I in front of our newly built log cabin.

My four sisters, brother, parents, and I enjoying winter on the homestead in the early fifties.

My four sisters and I stand among summer flowers on the homestead in the early fifties.

My mom standing under the Swiss flag on Swiss Independence Day with my sister and a family dog. Notice the newer fox pens in the background that are still upright.

Me playing in the doghouse in front of the old fox cabin as my sisters play in the background. Notice the two large washtubs for laundry and bathing. The water for these was usually heated outdoors.

A cattle roundup scene at the head of the bay.

Mom and my three sisters looking out of the fox cabin window with the Swiss flag.

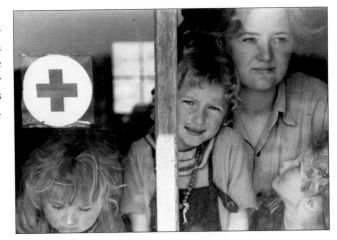

Mom, my sister Wurtila, and I re-creating the photo above.

My four sisters and I with our faithful dog, Bruno.

My mom used to carry me around the homestead in this old military rucksack. I've written several songs about the photograph on the right; it's one of my favorites. According to my mom, my early musical training began right there on her back as she sang to me.

In the next two photos, my mom and I revisited the location of the above photo in the late eighties.

There was always time for music. My father plays the accordian as we sit outside, celebrating the newly built cabin.

Me, in my mother's arms, with my three sisters in front of the log cabin my dad just built, circa 1948.

This is how we got to town in the winter in the old days. In this photo, my mother is riding in a homemade horse-drawn sled with a neighbor.

My father plowing
the virgin homestead
soil in the early days.

One of my favorite
early homesteading
photos. It says it
all—Mom and Dad
working side by side
to plow the ground
with shocks of hay in
the background.

My father and I on the homestead with one of my dad's many horses that he kept
tied around the cabin to serve as a lawn mower.

Above: The cowboy influence on my teenage years. We built this corral in the Fox River Valley. I sit on a horse on the far left.

Me standing with my Appaloosa stallion, Black Fog, at Swift Creek.

Why hang on to a trophy for fifty-one years, especially one with the horse missing? I've never displayed it, just drag it around in a box. I run across it every few years. I just can't throw it away. Keep thinking I'll have it renovated. Yep, that's what I'll do!

A view of the fox cabin through the fox pens, taken in the mideighties.

The old fox cabin with some of the old fox pens collapsed in the foreground. When my father felt we didn't have enough to do, he would have us pull rusty staples from those old pens.

Another view of the old fox cabin with the shed in the back, which I used to love to climb and sit on when I was a young boy.

This photo was taken when I was showing my children, Shane, Jewel, and Atz Lee, the fox farmer's cabin where I lived the first year of my life.

Here I am, passing on the stories of my roots to my children as we sit outside the fox cabin.

My young children and I hanging out at the homestead cabin with their Grandpa Yule. He demonstrates how to play a pushki flute, made from a dried pushki stalk.

These photos are all from the time my friend, Milton Lewis—one of the Bar Five crew—and I were hunting and roped a brown bear. Just another typical day, having fun in the wilderness. Milton was like an older brother to me in those days; I spent many of my teenage years with him and his family.

few shots, looked out the window and said to his wife, "Honey, there's an eight-foot-tall man coming up the driveway."

But they knew me, as well as the Andersons, and they let me sleep on their couch. The next morning, they hooked me up with the Clendenens who took me back to Eight-Mile Road, and I followed the tractor ruts to the Anderson spread. This was the first time I'd been out to their place, and it wouldn't be the last time I wore out my welcome by staying a few days.

The food was much different than the homestead fare I was used to. They ate chili with beans, breaded their meat before frying it, and introduced me to scones, tacos, enchiladas, and tamale pie. There also was no limit to the fresh, homemade butter like there was at our table of ten at home.

Years later, the Andersons reminded me of a holiday dinner I'd attended, probably self-invited. More and more people kept arriving unexpectedly, and every time someone else pulled up, Edna would add water to the soup, slice the bread thinner and cut pie slices in half, thinning down their feast. We were about ready to eat when yet another family came up the driveway, and apparently, that's when, according to local folklore, I said, "Let's hurry up and eat before anyone else comes!"

The thing I remember best about that first visit was the beauty of the Appaloosa stallion Apple. I decided right then I would someday have one that same color. There are many different Appaloosas, but I wanted one just like him: black with a spotted white blanket. That dream would come true but not for another thirty years.

Then there was Joyce, the daughter who I had a crush on as well. I had my share of teenage crushes on those Bar Five women, but this was different. The adults were more like movie-star crushes; out of the pages of my Western novels appeared these women in person. But Joyce was true love. I was sure of it. She was five years younger, but I was a very immature seventeen and she a very mature twelve. Lest you suspect I was deranged, I'm convinced had there been any personality or maturity tests, she would have scored far above me.

I even calculated how old I'd be before she would be old enough to get married. But every time my fantasies got out a little too far, I thought of Elton, her dad, and that sobered me right up.

Elton wasn't the stereotypical cowboy, more like an ambling brown bear: broad, big neck, and round face with a perpetual scowl like he was about to bite a teenager interested in his daughter. His most outstanding feature was the lack of any ears. Not only did it look odd, it made one conjure savage images of how he lost them. The rumors and stories ran rampant.

"He got into a drunken brawl and an Indian bit it off."

"It was a knife fight just outside of Gallup, got cut partway and ripped the rest of the way."

It all depended who you listened to and what stage of drink they were in when they told the tale. And that was just the story of the one ear. The second was more straightforward. Seems he had a rollover accident and a toolbox severed that one. He still had the lobe. I gave him a haircut—a one-time experience—no ears to get in the way.

All of his physical attributes as well as his raspy personality were multiplied if he was on or coming off of one of his benders. Yes, it definitely kept this moon-eyed teenager in check.

I am sure I never spoke any of my feelings to Joyce. Hell, I didn't learn to do that till I was in my fifties. I recall we did hold hands once, briefly. Been so long ago, I honestly can't remember, but it does seem there was a mutual spark there. Then again, as prone to fantasy as I was back then, I'll never know.

When I got out of the army at twenty-one, she was sixteen, old enough to date by her family's strict standard, and somehow I got word, possibly through a letter from Edna, that Elton recalled how and who and what he had been when he got out of the army, and there was no way in hell he was going to let his sixteen-year-old daughter go out with a returning-from-combat, testosterone-loaded soldier. It seemed a classic case of projection to me, but alas, I got back together with Nedra, the girl I had been dating before I shipped out, and the rest is history. Nedra and I married, and Joyce married a local farm boy, Alan Turkington. And here we are, and I've been married four times, and Joyce and Alan are close to forty years now. So, way to go—good match!

Love takes many forms, and changes shape with time. The love I feel for Joyce today goes way beyond that teenage crush. It is a love of family, of a sister, of a time and place long ago. It has spread to her entire family, her sons and daughters and her husband, who has always been there through the years when I needed advice on just about anything.

Years later, I had one of their daughters in my music class. She came up to me one day in third grade, smiling shyly, and said, "If you would have married my mom, Jewel would be my sister now."

What could I say but, "Yeah, I guess that's right." Too damn cute!

Yep, Alan, that old dog, got him a Bar Five girl. And his sister, Gayle, snagged her a Bar Five boy, one of the Presleys, Danny. Guess I wasn't the only kid in Homer enamored and taken with the Bar Five bunch.

But I gotta say, of all the Andersons, my strongest relationship was with Edna. I loved her like my own mother. She loved me and comforted me through alcohol and nicotine struggles that continued into adulthood. She held me as I cried out pains and conflicts with my dad and my sometimes-crazy family. She treated me like an adult, with dignity, always seeing my best. I reckon if she could see the good in Elton, it wasn't all that hard for her to see the good in me. She was a woman with love to give, and she was overflowing. I never had a Bar Five crush on her—it was pure love I felt for and from her. She was my *shama sani*, my grandmother, in Navajo. She made me want to be and do better. And I have.

Her grandson Charlie Anderson, son of my old friend Jerry, is like a son to me. He lives just up the road, and I often drop by unannounced, old school, like I did with his grandma Edna.

Time has slipped away. The original Bar Five siblings are no longer with us. Their kids range in age from seventysomething to forty, with grandkids and great-grandkids. But the beat goes on. And that Bar

Five magic is still alive for me today. It continues with some of the kids I was friends with back then. It continues with some of the kids that were too young at the time. It continues with some of the grandkids closing in on their thirties and forties.

I never pass through Ninilchik without trying to say hi to the Presley boys. Their family is as familiar to me as my own.

A month or so ago, we had a memorial for a lifelong friend and fellow cowboy, Bruce Willard, at the head of the bay. One of the cowboys attending the celebration of Bruce's life was Shirley Wilson. Yep, a cowgirl, who has no problem being called a cowboy. We needed to rope a calf while we were up there. No corrals, just out on the range like in the old days. It needed to be ear-tagged, and the best man for the job was a woman, an Alaskan woman, a Bar Five girl. She roped the calf on the first try, and my brother and I tagged it.

I still hear from Milton now and then. Had dinner with him at the Willards' a couple years back. This last year when I sang at the Grand Ole Opry, I had to call Milton. He and I used to sit in their small cabin and pick and grin when I was just a young teen, listening to the Grand Ole Opry on their battery-operated radio. I wanted to know that my old friend was listening from his ranch in Colorado.

I see Milton and Dorothy's two boys and daughter once in a while when they come up from Colorado. Fine kids they are, each carrying a piece of their dad and mom.

Down to the fourth generation, the Bar Five are carrying on part of their culture, a bit of the past, a few of the old stories. I wonder if they even realize I consider they're my family. I think they do.

Bar Five, I love you all, bar none.

# CHAPTER 11

# *Veterans Day*

What the hell is Veterans Day all about? How is it different from Memorial Day? Which world war are we talkin' about here? I'm a Vietnam vet, and I'm not sure. One is in the fall; the other is in the spring. They have something to do with World War I and World War II, and I think one or the other is sort of like Christmas—whatever we're commemorating really happened on a different date.

Sometimes I remember to say, "Happy Veterans Day" to a few vet friends, and sometimes one or two say it to me. Every year the greetings get fewer, both coming and going. My kids are probably the best to remember. Being honored by anyone feels good, having one of your kids take the time to remember, to reflect on something their parent did, and then actually take the time to say thanks, well, that's pretty damn special.

For some reason, my son Atz Lee has been the most consistent, ever since he was a teenager. What makes it even more memorable is that he says more than just, "Happy Veterans Day." He usually makes a statement. Only a few words, but he's able to convey his view of war in general, and that one in specific, and still thank and honor me. Of course, much of the cause of my amazement is the fact that he was mute in his early teen years. If he communicated with me at all back then, it was in nods of the head, grunts, or monosyllabic complaints. Other, less-endearing bodily gestures such as subtle eye rolling were common too.

But last year's phone message from him went much like this year's: "Happy Veterans Day, Dad. Thanks for what you did over there. I suppose thanking you might mean I agree with that war, which I don't, so maybe *thank you* is not the right word. Maybe it should be thanks for coming home, for enduring, not letting it take you down."

This year, he said, "Thanks for your brave years of war, I couldn't imagine the things you endured. You will always be my Zen hero. Jane says so too. Xoxo."

I have no clue what a Zen hero is, probably something from his artist-songwriter's mind. So, in my artistic mind, I interpreted it thusly: calm, accepting, centered, enduring, spiritual, trying to see everything as an opportunity for growth, for learning, for seeing the connectedness of all things.

Now, don't get me wrong—that is not how I would describe myself, but rather the picture that comes to mind for the term *Zen* hero. Of course, the word *hero* conjures up countless more images and definitions. And believe me, that ain't me neither.

The point here is that he chose those two words to describe me at that moment in time. Who am I to dispute it, question it, or intellectualize it? So, I basked in the warm glow of the energy of those words. I let 'em soak in, do their job. Wash, cleanse, heal, blow the dust off important memories, bury others in a deep layer of love and forgiveness.

It just so happens that this same son, Atz Lee, knowing I was a great reader of self-help books and maybe thinking I needed yet another one, or one of a different ilk, gave me a book on a Japanese approach to healing, self-growth, and awareness. It was called *Even in Summer the Ice Doesn't Melt*. The book was as different as its title.

The thing I remember about that book was a concept diametrically opposed to all I'd learned in my psychology and social-work training. I'd strived hard in my life up to that point to understand my feelings. I had tried hard to focus on who I was, not what I did; on being more of a human *being* instead of a human *doing*.

This very different book taught that to *be* different, to *feel* different, one needed to *do* different. If you want to be a kind person, feel kind, then get off your butt and do a bunch of kind deeds long enough until you are a kind person. Simple!

This was an especially bitter pill to swallow because my dear, very non-Zen dad used to say the same thing. Perhaps he had long before learned that it was in the doing that he felt the most at peace. Nonetheless, I incorporated that new and important belief of *doing* what you want to *be* into my ongoing search for meaning and happiness. And it made a difference.

A part of that difference was that this particular son, who lived with me the longest as a single dad and saw more of my very worst, un-Zen-like behavior, was drawn to this Zen book and gave it to me. This same son also said I was his Zen hero. Must be something wrong with that boy.

"Thanks for your brave years of war. I couldn't imagine the things you endured. You will always be my Zen hero."

Whew! Yeah. That's what I'm talkin' about. That's a whole lot of good stuff wrapped up in a very short message. For me, it goes to show how little it takes to make someone's day, how deeply mere words can take us to those places needing visited.

None of us who take the time to honor someone have any idea exactly what it leaves that person feeling, or how far it may take them. His words led me down a trail of long ago that started back when I got drafted.

I had turned nineteen in September of '66. I was drafted January of '67. Initially, I had lied to the draft board, telling them I was a sleepwalker. Seems they didn't want soldiers walking around in their sleep, so I got a medical deferment, a low classification. Since my brother actually was a sleepwalker, I knew what to say. I merely told them what I'd seen him do. "Well, Doc," I says, "according to my brother I got up one night and peed into the wood box. He had to jump up and stop me midstream. Another night, he said I was squatted down by our barrel woodstove trying to milk it like it was our cow." Oh, I had some good stories. I was convincing, and they were all true, except for one small detail.

I must have told the wrong person my little sleepwalking charade. Several months after receiving my deferment notice, I got a letter saying my status was changed to nonexempt and I was to report for the draft on January 9. I had two months to get used to the idea. And I was terrified.

After spending twenty-one months in the army, ten of those in Vietnam, I got out in October of '68—the twenty-first, to be exact. I got drafted for a two-year hitch, but I got an early discharge for a hardship. I elaborated on the truth a little. I also had a letter from a doctor attesting to my dad's poor health. My dad needed me to help with the fall harvest and cattle roundup.

So that's the short story. I didn't volunteer. I lied to get out of being drafted, got caught, and got drafted anyway. And then I stretched the truth to get out early. Does that sound like a Zen hero to you?

On this particular Veterans Day, instead of thinking back on my entire military experience, especially my time in Vietnam, I thought more about preparing to report for the draft.

Like most boys my age across America, I knew next to nothing about why we were involved in Vietnam. Nothing of the history or the politics. Most of us knew what we were told. The communists were invading, we had to help stop them, or they would get us next. Looking back, I suppose it wouldn't have been wise to educate all young men in all the reasons for our involvement, considering all the differing opinions. Yet still, I knew enough to be terrified.

And I was a tough scrapper. I was the kind of young man who was known to beat up a guy for looking at me or my girl wrong. What my dad dished out, I passed on to my younger brother and others. When knocked down, I came up swinging. I'd wrestled steers and broke horses. I was tough. And terrified.

I had killed many animals. Butchered farm animals, hunted wild critters. I'd done my share of needless killing of birds and small animals which my dad knew nothing about. I teased and beat up the less fortunate and less popular. I wasn't a nice guy. No great respect for the sanctity of life or people. Just out to survive. Not thinking much, and feeling even less. I was the abused, dysfunctional kid profile I'd come to know well later as a social worker for troubled youth. You'd think I'd have been the perfect candidate to run off and kill a bunch of so-called "gooks." But I was terrified in that deep place where the softness still lived. And it might have had something to do with most bullies being cowards underneath.

From the time I got my draft notice till I got drafted, I had a recurring nightmare. It didn't take Freud to figure it out. I'd always be out in the Joneses' corral, our closest homesteading neighbors to the northeast. There were no roads to get to the Joneses' place. In the summer and until the snow got too deep, they drove a tractor trail up the beach about ten miles past our homestead, then another trail up five miles or so to their place. In summer, I often walked or rode my horse using this route and I might combine a visit with checking our cows at the head of the bay.

Because of the steep bluff, in the winter, deep snow cut off access, leaving only skis or snowshoes for the overland route. Yep, we homesteaders were tough. Had to be.

So, what did we homestead-hick, wannabe cowboys do when I went visiting? Well, we didn't play Nintendo, watch television, or listen to iPods. We're talking Coleman lanterns, woodstove crackling, log cabin walls leaking heat out and cold in. We talked, played guitar sometimes, drank coffee, did chores like feeding cows and horses. We rode horses, chased cows, chopped ice at the water hole, hauled water to the house, played in the snow, maybe went hunting. Simple fun.

Sometimes we sat around and told jokes. I used to love it when one of them would ask, in their native Texan drawl, "Y'all got any good stout jokes we ain't heard yet?"

Being closer to town and attending public school long before they did, I tended to hear more "good stout jokes," but they knew their share as well. Still remember a few good ones too.

My favorite was a story they loved to tell about how to catch a polar bear. Even though the older Jones kids had come to Alaska very young, as teenagers, due to their secluded upbringing, they still had a heavy Texas drawl. I loved it. "Know hay-ow ta caych a poe-ler bay-er?" one would ask. "Well, ya go ta way-er there's a lotta ayce, and y'all sprinkle you a bunch o' frozen peas all around that hole ya just chopped in the ayce. An' then when the poe-ler bay-er comes to take a pea, ya kick 'im in the ayce hole."

Oh, my God, no matter how many times they told it we would roar with laughter as though it were the first time. Good times.

So, don't ask me why this nightmare of mine took place in the Joneses' corral where I had so much fun and formed so many bonding memories.

Like most, their corral had a holding pen in a long rectangular shape somewhat like an alley, which led to a chute. Once the gate they came in through was shut, the only way out was down the narrowing chute. It narrowed to the point where it was only wide enough for one cow to walk at a time. At that point, you would put boards or poles behind each cow to keep them from backing out.

At the end of the narrowing chute was a hinged metal gate called a squeeze chute. Once an animal stuck its head through that end gate, you quickly squeezed. The head would be out, the body still in. In this position they could work the cow.

In my nightmare, there would be a large group of us guys in that holding pen, the gate behind us locked. Men with rifles surrounded that holding pen and guarded the locked gate. There was no escape. The only way out was through the chute.

It is unbelievable how clear this image still is today, after forty-five years. Once the young men came out of the chute into the other part of the corral, they were mowed down by the men with machine guns. We never tried escaping over the sides of the holding pen, or back over the entrance gate. We followed those in front of us forward and into the chute as we watched the others in front of us being shot to pieces as they tried to run out of the far end.

As I write this now, after all these years, my heart beats hard and fast like I just ran a hundred-yard dash. Emotions course through my body. Basic, instinctual stuff of combat and survival. Stuff you have to learn to numb out so you don't go crazy. Of course, numbing makes you crazy too.

I always woke up before reaching that chute. I was always so thankful to wake up. Thought of that every morning I woke up in Vietnam. Every morning, I gave thanks. Terror is a pretty good word to describe that feeling. That feeling of facing that chute. Of facing another day in a war zone. At least until that terror is transformed, neatly tucked away to be dredged and sorted through another time. Or not. That's my definition of PTSD—the endless dredging up of bodily emotions you've tried to forcefully forget. The rekindling of cold and frozen cells, performing a million tiny CPRs on every one of them.

War—there's something unnatural about it. Nobody should have to learn how to shut down to that point. Ain't natural. Not even for a rough and tough homestead bully. Amazing how we adapt and survive in spite of it all.

So, I'm in Vietnam about six months when I get a letter from by brother, Otto. Since I've been gone from the homestead, Otto has blossomed, now out of my five-years-older shadow. To his mechanical fix-it skills, he has added cowboy skills, that turf which was once all mine. For some reason, he was never drawn to my screaming at and beating on the cows and horses. He chose not to learn at my feet, as I had at my dad's, all the subtleties and nuances of cowboy savvy and horsemanship. My absence was good for Otto.

Getting mail in Vietnam was a really big deal. No way to explain how big a deal it was. If you've never been in a war, hanging onto any shred of your past identity, you can't understand. One day, I got a letter from Otto. Thanks, Otto—not sure I ever told you how much your letters meant to me. Hope I did. If not, I should have. Thanks again.

In this letter, a puzzle slowly unfolded, or a piece of a puzzle. I've pondered over it ever since, but this is the first I've written about it. Or that I've come out, come clean.

It wasn't a long letter, yet it's stayed with me all my life. Otto told me how it was that my military draft classification suddenly changed and I got drafted. "I ran into old Glenn Williamson the other day," his letter read. "He told me that he wrote a letter to the draft board about your lying to them about being a sleepwalker." His letter went on to tell me why old Glenn had done this.

We used to hay Glenn's fields. As our cattle herd increased, we needed more hay than our homestead could produce. There were always neighboring homesteads or landowners who had no livestock and needed their fields cut. Sometimes we did it on shares, but most of the time we got all the hay. Old Glenn Williamson was one of those landowners whose hay we used to put up.

Glenn was an older gentleman, probably in his sixties or so. He walked with a limp. He'd been wounded in World War II. Well, over the years we put up his hay, we developed a type of friendship. This was often the case since we spent a lot of time cutting someone's hay, baling it, and hauling it home by wagon and tractor.

I once asked old Glenn what he had retired from, since I never saw him go to work. He told me that he lived off his pension check from the army. He'd been wounded in the war, and being the budding smart-ass I was, I said, "Boy, that must be nice."

He didn't react, at least not that I noticed. And I never thought about my comment again until that day I got Otto's letter. My comment had hurt him. When I came home from Anchorage having lied to the draft board, I'd stupidly bragged about it to him, and apparently that was the last straw for old Glenn. He relayed this to Otto with no small satisfaction. It wasn't so much a vindictive "I showed him." It was more like he was doing what was *right.*

Since then, my thoughts and feelings have changed many times. About what I told the draft board. About making fun of Glenn's easy money and belittling his service and sacrifice, not to mention the disability he lived with. About bragging to him how I was never going to go to war and get wounded and end up on a disability pension. About what he did in turn to make things right in his mind. Like an old pebble in the shoe, the thought has kept showing up and aggravating me. So, I've kept moving it around, trying to wear it down.

Of all the ways I've looked at it, interpreted it, and felt around it, the simple fact is this: it is done, and all I can do now is learn to accept it and try to learn from it and walk away a wiser person.

I can tell you, the lessons from that have been many, all rich and rewarding. Indeed, they *have* made me a better person. I have had to learn how to let go of the guilt and shame of lying to the draft board. Of making fun of old Glenn. Of being angry at him for "sending" me to Vietnam. I've had to learn to love and forgive that young Atz of long ago, all the hurtful, thoughtless things he did. And yes, perhaps the most difficult, I had to learn how to thank old Glenn for the important part he played in the life of a screwed-up homestead hick. I love who and where I am today. And old Glenn helped me get here. End of story.

I have strong feelings about war, when it is or is not justified in my mind. I have strong beliefs about where I draw the line and for which cause or country I am willing to lay down my life or the life of one of my children. In hindsight, Vietnam was very wrong. Hats off to those who volunteered or were drafted. Hats off to those who followed their hearts and conscience and went to Canada. Had I been smarter or braver or more of a coward, I might have gone there as well, or just hidden out in the deep, dark woods out by the Joneses' corral. Regardless, we all deserve to be welcomed home. From any war, however it started, whoever supported it, no matter how the passing of time exposes it all.

* * *

Recently, I was on a flight from Seattle returning to Alaska. In front of me was a veteran coming home from Iraq. Beside me was a civilian attorney who had spent a year helping the war effort in Iraq as well. Both went there to help our country, their country. They both came home with a very different view of our involvement there.

I listened to them both and then did what I always do. I looked them in the eye, shook their hand, and said, "Welcome home." And as I also always do at times like that, I contemplated war.

During my drive to Homer, the thought came to me that regardless of why we choose to fight or how we feel when we return, we all deserve to be welcomed home. I thought and wrote, wrote and thought, and sang my heart out. Nothing to write *on*, and nothing to record *with*, but by the time I reached Homer, it was memorized, deeply embedded in mind and soul.

*There were no flags waving,*
*Sure as hell weren't any marching bands,*
*I was just a boy of twenty-one when I got*
    *home from Vietnam,*
*Didn't know what I was expecting, I didn't*
    *know I'd feel so alone,*
*Didn't know there'd be no one there saying,*
    *"Soldier, welcome home."*

Chorus:
*Welcome home, my arms reach out to you,*
*Welcome home, I know what you've been*
    *through,*
*Welcome home mothers, fathers, all my*
    *daughters and sons,*
*Welcome home, welcome home, soldier,*
    *welcome home.*

*I've done what I've had to, to take away*
    *the pain,*
*And I've tried to do for others what I didn't*
    *get that day.*
*And it don't matter from which war, or how*
    *young or old,*
*I shake their hand and look 'em in the eye,*
    *say, "Soldier, welcome home."*

*You've been my flags a wavin', you've been*
*my marching band,*
*It isn't always easy living with this*
*wounded man,*
*Your gentle love has taken me to places I've*
*not known,*
*With your arms open wide saying, "Soldier,*
*welcome home."*

*There's a time for disagreement, there's a time*
*for debate,*
*Don't let the innocent feel your hate,*
*Sometimes we have no choice,*
*But we all deserve to hear that healing voice.*

*Welcome home, my arms reach out to you,*
*Welcome home, I know what you've been*
*through,*
*Welcome home mothers, fathers, all my*
*daughters and sons,*
*Welcome home, welcome home, soldier,*
*welcome home.*

So, to you my son, Atz Lee, who without fail remembers to say something to me on Veterans Day, as well as anyone else who remembers, you remember this: there is always so much more to the rest of the story. Saying something is such a gift to that vet, to help him dive into that deep, dark, scary water, perhaps for the first time, perhaps not, to explore that which lies below the surface, and to smooth those sharp rough edges, to move the cold ice to the surface and into the light. And then hopefully, to turn it back into water.

Zen hero? I don't think so. Far from it. I'm just taking tiny steps in that direction. One sharp, icy edge at a time.

# CHAPTER 12

## *Crazy Cow*

Dearest children,

The very first poem I read when Jewel sent me her poetry book was the one called "Crazy Cow." It was the title that made me pick that one over the others. Had I known what it was about, I might have waited. Reading it was the quintessential definition of bittersweet. I doubt if any of you could have imagined all it would bring up for me. In one short poem, she was able to capture a classic paradox, juxtaposing fear and admiration, love and hate, good and evil—your father. And holy shit! All of that was *me*—she was talking about *me*.

Jewel, you painted a dramatic life-and-death struggle. You brought readers right there to that rough-cut plank floor beside that hot barrel woodstove, where three young children are watching their father massage the ice-cold limbs of a half-frozen and near-dead calf with his strong, confident, and experienced hands. I felt I was right there beside you as those same hands you had feared "now seemed more powerful / and merciful than god's."

With mere words, you did more than create a picture. It was a video, a movie, a live interactive experience. I found myself breathing harder, my own heart beating faster, as I tried to help the father in your poem as you watched him "lean down and wrap his mouth / around the calf's tiny pink nose / fill its lungs," and breathe life back into the limp body.

I sat in deep thought and silence after I read the poem. Oh, how it hurt to read that my daughter feared my hands. It sounded so final, so condemning. Now the whole world would know.

And I cried.

After that, I wandered for hours down miles of old childhood cow trails before finding the courage to return to reality and that poem. The trails led me to all those places I knew so well but had never taken any of you kids. Those dusky forest meadows where the fear and love of my own father's hands and the joy and guilt of cows saved and lost now lay buried side by side. Had I taken you there years ago, when you were little and I was still a god in your eyes, maybe none of you would ever have grown to fear my hands. Maybe I would have understood better that old patterns were buried, and could be escaped. Had I talked it out, perhaps there would have been no need to act it out. It all may have turned out differently.

Oh, we've walked some of those old trails together, but as a single dad in his midthirties, we didn't walk or talk nearly enough. I still had too much figuring out of my own to do. I lacked the insight to tell my own inner boy or you young children what needed to be said. Other times, I said way too much, putting too much on your young shoulders.

But I need to go back to some of these trails with you now, my children. Hopefully you'll understand why I need to remember the things I lost, whether due to my carelessness or just plain ignorance. I need to know it isn't too late. And I want to see what might be recovered there.

There are many things I did to you children that I regret, that were wrong. Of everything I've done in my life (and I've had to deal with some pretty tough situations), going back to some of these places is the toughest, tougher even than the year I spent in Vietnam. But there's a good reason for going back. And it has to do with healing—mine and yours.

So, my dear children, maybe it's not too late. Let me take you there now. We can discover the way out of that fear together, and set it free once and for all. Jewel, someday, perhaps, you will elaborate on your poem, tell me of other memories. But for now, let me lead the way. Let me try and tell you all of my father's hands and heart. Let me tell you stories about cows.

We'll go down the cow trail below the sawmill, to the old watering hole. We'll sit under that towering old spruce, with our backs to its gnarly old trunk, just the way I did as a kid. I always felt so safe and protected there, cradled between ancient roots, next to the watering hole and surrounding swamp that nourished them. I never came away from there without feeling refreshed and cleansed, taller, and stronger.

Lean your little heads on my shoulders and listen. Morning chores are all done. We have all the time in the world.

It isn't strange at all that one of you should mention cows and a fear of my hands in the same passage. They are intertwined in my past as well. Having been around cows since birth, I saw at a much earlier age the love-hate relationship my dad had with cows and horses, which he passed on down to me. It was only as an adult, at his deathbed, that I finally let go of *my* fear of *his* hands.

I can't say exactly where these trails will lead us, kids, or what lies waiting to be explored. The hoofprints are clear and fresh. I know the trails so much better now. We won't get lost. We will return safely. All trails lead away from and back to this spring, to this wise old tree.

This particular spring we're looking at is like so many other things in my life, and like life in general. I've loved it and feared it at the same time. It has given life and taken it away. We can sit here and focus only on the frothy, rust-colored algae covering the surrounding sulfur-smelling bog, waiting to pull a cow to its death, or see the clear watering hole at the upper edge of the bog. New rain soft. Mountain stream sweet. It's all in where you walk, where you look, how you use it. Like so many other things, it is a paradox, both aspects are true, and need to be seen and considered.

Let's begin with Pansy. I'll never forget the old cow we called Pansy because of the pansy-like pattern on her face. But believe me, she was no pansy. She was big and her horns were long. As a calf, she used to crawl under the fence and eat all the hay she wanted. Nothing could keep her out once she found out she was stronger and smarter than barbed wire. It could be that she was a leader right from the start. The extra size she gained from getting all the hay she wanted also played a major factor. She reigned as queen for many years.

One year we dehorned all of our cows with dangerous horns. Pansy was one of the first to get her feathers clipped. When we were all done we heard one hell of a ruckus coming from the feedlot and adjoining spruce forest which served as a bedding ground. We ran to see what was going on. We couldn't believe our eyes at first. A cow much lower in the pecking order, now also dehorned but feeling much more equal, was mercilessly chasing Pansy. She was trying desperately to get a piece of her! What was amazing was that when she got tired of the chase, another cow with years of old scores to settle took over. Soon even younger stock with boosted confidence and the aid of short but sharp horns began giving chase to the ousted queen. There was no mercy in the barnyard for quite a few days. She ended up retiring quite a ways back in the herd.

I also learned a lot about confidence and trust. Most animals have a fear about putting their head in a place which does not allow them to see anything. Added to that, the cows had to get on their front knees in order to reach the water. If that wasn't making yourself vulnerable enough, you had to be willing to expose your very tender backside to the horns behind you. It took a lot of courage and faith, and of course thirst, to do all that.

Most cows, however, respected that vulnerable stance. Only the flagrant line breaker, who probably had been irritating others for days on end, would get punished when in that position. Sometimes it was the extremely weak who, even though they may have waited their turn, still got pushed in by a bossy cow coming back for seconds. There were definitely bossy, mean cows and more gentle ones. It wasn't always fair, but it was the way it was.

Which brings me to my next cow, Dogie. One night Dogie didn't come in for evening hay. The spring was the first place I went to look. His mama had died giving birth, so we raised him on a bottle, hence the super-creative name "Dogie"—an orphan cow. He was a yearling that long, cold winter, but he was small for his size and sort of scrawny. There is a saying among farmers that the skinny one of any litter "sucked hind teat," meaning they didn't get as much as the others. Well poor Dogie didn't even get hind teat, he got no teat. He was the runt of the feedlot, got pushed away from the good hay, and was picked on by the entire herd. Having been raised by us, he also lacked some basic animal and herd sense. He had picked up too much kindness and gentleness, easily mistaken for weakness by the herd. He was a good year behind in size. Only his horns told you his age. But he was much too gentle to use them to protect himself.

Sure enough, my worst fear, I found him in the spring. It was almost completely dark, and at first, I saw nothing. I put my face right down to the water. That's when I saw a slight movement, it was his eyes blinking. He looked like an alligator with only his nose and eyes out of the icy cold water. Jewel, you know how I felt right then. You felt that way the first time you found your horse Clear Water tangled and nearly dead at the end of his stake rope. At that moment, there is only you and this animal that needs you. The rest of the world disappears. You feel everything at once. In seconds you have to sort through all those emotions, keeping only those that will help you with the impossible task at hand. Soldiers feel it. I felt it many times myself in Vietnam. People who come upon the scene of a car wreck feel it. Parents feel it when their child is badly hurt or choking. From somewhere, you get the strength and wisdom to do what you gotta do.

It really doesn't matter at times like that whether you are saving a human or a scrawny dogie, the feeling is the same. Even though I get all kinds of strength, courage, and calmness at times like that, I always have a big lump in my throat. I remember being at the verge of tears back then. No time to run for help. It was well below zero. No telling how long he had been in there. He wasn't moving. Fortunately, the water temperature was warmer than the air. There was no time to lose!

"It's just me and you, little Dogie," I said to myself. "Your whole damn life has been one rough spot after another. We'll get through this one even though I don't have the foggiest idea how."

I couldn't tell you I remember this perfectly right after I did it, much less now after all these years. You know how it is. After a while you can't remember what you actually remember and what you're making up, but I think it went something like this.

Dogie weighed about, say, three hundred pounds soaking wet. Fortunately, he was still alive, and he was definitely soaking wet. If I remember correctly I was about fourteen, and weighed around one hundred and forty pounds. Another thing I had going against me was the lack of good footing. It was all snow and ice, with just a little cow manure. The fact that he wasn't floating told me that his feet must be stuck in the mud, holding him down.

I grabbed his horns and pulled upward with all my skinny arm strength. He struggled weakly to help. Part of his back was now showing. I pulled his head closer to the bank but kept slipping. I knew I didn't stand a chance if I had no footing. I broke a dead branch off the giant spruce we are sitting under, and used the jagged end to scrape some footholds in the ice. I took off my gloves and plunged my arm shoulder-deep into the water to get out some mud to put on the ice. It froze instantly giving me more traction.

His numb legs started helping me. I lifted and pulled him forward in the churning muddy water. His head was now on the ice shelf at my feet. It wasn't solid ground yet and I hoped it wouldn't break off. He didn't move. He knew better. He just blinked his eyes and looked up at me trustingly. I reached under him to grab a foot. I somehow got it up next to his nose. I rolled him to his side and somehow got his other front foot out. I pulled. I slipped. I swore like a full-grown man and cried like a baby. I reached over his back and found his tail.

"It's now or never," I shouted at him. I screamed my loudest Kilcher scream ever to that point. I leaned back, and as hard as I could, I pulled him by his tail. His tired cold back legs gave the very last strength they had and began churning the muddy bottom, also looking for a bit of traction. Somehow, we both ended up in a wet, muddy, frozen heap.

We lay there a moment, tangled and panting. A scrawny dogie and a skinny homestead boy.

When the day came, butchering Dogie was one of the hardest things my brother and I ever had to do. We said a few words, the way we imagined the American Indians would have done. We honored him with stories of his birth and life. And yes, how he survived the watering hole. We thanked him for his gift to us. We were at peace. We could never have done it otherwise. Like so many things there on the farm, it was hard, but you found a way to do it and live with it. We hung his long horns above our cabin door. They were weathered, scarred, and rough. Like the growth rings on a tree stump, those horns told a hard, sad tale. A glance told you he had lived an equally difficult life. We never said much when we looked at them but I never passed under them without thinking and feeling a lot of things. We kept them there for years.

Funny thing, I still think about him from time to time. I think there is more than a bit of him in me.

Not till I was an adult with a herd of my own, watching them drink right here, did I wonder why in the hell my father didn't have a safer watering situation. There were many options. I guess none of them were as viable as having your kids watch the herd as it drank and spend their spare time pulling them out. Any other options would have included thinking, planning, preparing, and maybe spending some money. No. It was far more complex than that. The answer to that question has only come to me recently, since dad's death, as I have questioned my own long-held beliefs and patterns and have been willing to explore my own blind spots. Willing to get help, to heal and recover.

Some we saved, some we lost. And that brings me to Daisy. Daisy was one cow who didn't make it.

I searched for days without a clue. Finally, I saw signs of where she went off the edge of the canyon. Generally, the first thing we did when a cow was lost was to look in the spring, check fence lines to see if they got hung up, or check the edge of bluffs and canyon for clues. You know that ridge down there where we go to pick those early spring nettles, well, she ended up down there, in the steep valley between the ridge and the canyon. The canyon isn't sheer bluff at that point, we've climbed down there before, but it's steep.

Had it been summer, and dry, chances are she would have walked right down and back up. But it was springtime, still icy under the dead leaves on the steep alder-covered canyon slope. She must have been trying to nibble the early grass along the edge, and slipped off. It looked like she rolled, walked, and dragged herself to the bottom.

When I found her, she had probably been there a couple of days. She was hungry. I had to get her some hay. There wasn't enough grass yet to amount to anything. If I took the long way, out to the beach road and up to the house it was about a mile. I could cut about half of that distance if I went up the canyon the same way she had come down. I didn't know at the time that I would be going up and down there many more times in the next few days, it soon became a trail. No amount of water grain or hay could entice her to stand up. We built a tripod and lifted her with a block and tackle. She could only stand on her front legs. We hoped for the best, that her back was only sprained and that she would soon regain the use of her back legs. I never left her side. I slept right there beside her, like a true cowboy.

The spring nights were clear and not too cool. It was probably late April with the Alaskan days stretching now from six in the morning to past nine at night. Chunks of coal I found in coal veins nearby kept my fire burning all through the night. I was happy, I had a purpose. Saving that cow became my mission. It was just me and my cow, and some simple food my mama prepared for me. I wasn't reading Zane Grey or Louis L'Amour now, I was living it. I was the story.

We finally had to admit that her back was broken. We had to butcher her. So, we did, right there on the very spot where we had spent days trying to save her. We discovered when we butchered her that she indeed did have a broken back. I still remember packing those heavy two hundred pound quarters out to the switchbacks of the beach road where we got it with the Jeep. It was only a hundred yards or so, but it was steep, slippery, and covered with devil's club and alder.

However, I remember that spot and that incident for a far more painful reason.

One night, while sleeping with Daisy, I caught my army sleeping bag on fire. Actually, it was the family sleeping bag. Either the fire was too hot, or I had gotten too close. I awoke in time to keep my feet from burning, and beat the flames out of the burning feathers and canvas. That and the burning coal made quite a stench. No telling how long I had been inhaling those fumes. Good thing I'm a light sleeper.

When my father came down to check on us later that day, he was in a foul mood. I knew I better be careful. I was fourteen or fifteen, and I had recently noticed a shift in how he treated me. He seemed more threatened by me. His anger was taking on a different flavor. It seemed to be more man to man. I became more cautious and frightened, learned to try to read him better. Those times when I did stand up to him, step between him and my mother, or "talk back," as he put it, his rage was scary, more severe.

I am sure that losing one of his prized Hereford purebred cows added to whatever else he was dealing with on an ongoing basis and on that particular day. He wasn't happy with how I had been caring for her. I had been wasting hay. Who knows what else he found to fuel his internal fire. Then he saw his favorite Swiss army sleeping bag. And that was the proverbial last straw. The smoldering embers leapt to flames. That peaceful canyon hideaway, where I lay and dreamed of being a real cowboy when I grew up, became the scene of another painful memory, a new kind of physical and emotional pain. He kicked me. When I was bent over and had my back turned to him. Oh, it hurt, but my inner hurt was far more severe and long lasting.

That was the end of something between my dad and me and the beginning of something else.

For years I would pass that spot, and still smell that stench of burning feathers and canvas, and feel the pain of that day, the anger.

Now, I feel sorrow for my father, who knew of no other way to deal with his demons than to turn them on his family. When I pass by there now, I have to chuckle to myself. I think of that father and that son and what they had to teach and learn and experience, how they somehow made it through, more or less sane and whole. It has taken me a while to get there.

I've pulled countless calves that could never have been born on their own. Some I pulled by hand, others needed a come-along tied off to a tree.[1] Once I had to tie the cow to a tree and pull the calf using the saddle horn of a horse. Sometimes the mother lived and the calf died, sometimes it was the other way around. Sometimes you saved them both or lost them both.

I have found many a cow in the early spring, poisoned on potent shoots of water hemlock. It isn't a pretty sight. Belly big and bloated, stretched tight and round as a huge beach ball. Legs stiff and pointing skyward. Eyes still open and glazed over.

Finding any dead animal in your care always conjures a deep sense of guilt. You can't help but feel there is something you could or should have done. Finding a dead milk cow or horse at the end of a rope that you tethered it to is especially traumatic.

I don't know if you will remember this or not, Shane, but it happened during one of my trips back to Anchorage to finish up my teaching certificate. You kids lived with me up there the year I had to do class work. After that I would occasionally leave you guys for a day or two here on the homestead. With your Grampa next door in case of emergencies, I was never worried, and it worked out fine. On that particular day, you called me sobbing. I knew immediately something very traumatic must have happened.

"I killed Ruski," you cried, over and over. "I killed her. It's my fault."

When I finally got you calmed down, the story came out. Ruski was a big black milk cow we had bought from a Russian up at the head of the bay. I had given her to you, my eldest son. Giving you that

1. A hand-operated winch used to assist in birthing.

cow had been very significant to me. My father had never given me a cow. Oh, he promised many to keep me motivated and from leaving the farm, but the promises never came to pass. I wanted you to feel that sense of ownership that I had never felt. It was also a way for you to make money, by selling her calves.

Well, pasture grass was getting low, and to have her closer for milking, you had staked her out in a fairly safe place below the house. Somehow Ruski had gotten tangled and had fallen down. You found her there dead at the end of her rope. She had choked to death. Perhaps a halter would have saved her. Maybe tying her in a perfectly flat place with no bushes would have helped. Had the cow been more experienced at being tethered, she also may have avoided falling and choking. You can "maybe" and "what-if" yourself to death at times like that.

You had gone to Grampa Yule for help. My poor father, who was driven by old and unconscious reactions most of his life, especially in times of crisis, began screaming before my heartbroken sobbing son could even finish his story. "You killed her. You goddamn son of a bitch, you killed her!"

I wanted to jump in my car, drive the four hours at breakneck speed, and choke my father. Every time he had ever taken out his frustrations on me, every time he had not been there when I needed him, all welled up inside of me. It took me a long time to calm down. I comforted you, Shane, and you comforted me. It ended up being a time of great father-son healing. Oh, but some gifts come in mighty hard and harsh wrapping.

My father's berating, swearing, and blaming had continued all the way down to the scene of the crime. By then, you were, indeed, feeling like a criminal. My father's should-haves, could-haves, and why-the-hell-didn't-yous rained down like harsh hailstones. From a distance, I pictured my impressionable and very responsible son going to his grampa for help or, perhaps, for comfort or even forgiveness for what he was already feeling was his fault. Instead he was made to feel like a killer. At the other end of the phone some two hundred miles away, I was livid. I felt a flood of strong emotions, the strongest and probably least important was anger.

But there are amazing emotional connections that can happen between kids and innocent animals. And I felt that early on.

I'll tell you kids about another one I'll never forget—a calf we called BahBah. Somehow, she became my sister Catkin's pet. If I recall correctly, it was also an orphan calf. She raised it on a bottle and they became very fond of each other. It's not every little girl who can run out the front door and shout, "BahBah, come BahBah," and have a small, soft, cuddly brown-and-white calf come running out of who knows where to nurse from her bottle. She fed it on bottle milk all summer and weaned it in the fall. She fussed over it all winter, giving it extra hay, and continuing to play mommy to it. Who needs a Barbie when you have your own pet calf to play real, live doll with? In the spring, the now-yearling BahBah went with the rest of the herd to the Fox River Valley for summer pasture. They would not return for almost six months.

A yearling almost doubles in size in those six summer months of sweet, rich valley grass. When BahBah returned we hardly recognized her. It was late fall. It was butchering time. I was around sixteen, my brother Otto was eleven, Catkin was six. By then, Otto and I were the chief butchers.

I swear that the older stock, who had witnessed many an autumn butchering scene, were aware of what was about to happen. It was in the air. The cows knew it. Little Catkin knew it. BahBah was a long yearling. It was his time to go.

Little Catty came to me with attempted calmness and maturity way beyond her years. She knew that only adult rationalism could save her BahBah. With quavering voice and trembling lips, she asked, "Are you going to butcher BahBah?"

"Yes," was my firm, sixteen-year-old chief-butcher answer. Her voice was quavering big time now, and her lip was jumping up and down. No tears yet. Her face remained amazingly calm. I see it today. "BahBah is grown now, not a baby anymore," I tried to say matter-of-factly, "besides that, it doesn't remember you. Look at them, they have all been in the wild for six months, you can't get close to any of them."

I was fishing desperately by now.

She looked up and straight into my eyes. With the resolve and firmness of the US Marine Corps colonel she became and is today, she asked, "If I call her and she comes to me, can we not butcher her?"

What's an older brother to say to his cute, blond, tears-held-back six-year-old baby sister with trembling lips? "Go ahead and try."

The cattle were all grazing in the meadow just below the house. I remember this scene so vividly. Little blond-haired Catty walking down into the herd of cattle. She held out her hand as though it still held that bottle. She called softly at first, "BahBah, come BahBah."

The cattle began spooking and turning away. Some began running from the approaching human. BahBah followed the herd without looking back. Little Catty's voice took on more confidence and urgency. We all knew that she was very aware that BahBah's life depended on her ability to make an old connection. "BahBah, come BahBah. Don't you remember me?"

That did it! Tears welled up in my eyes. BahBah stopped and turned. Little Catty just kept right on walking, calmly and steadily. She never stopped calling. Her invisible bottle held firmly in front of her, her eyes looking down in a nonthreatening stance. She reached BahBah. He nuzzled her outstretched hand and she scratched that itchy place in the hollow between his horns. She put her arm around his neck and faced us. She looked like a 4-H girl showing her prize calf to the judges at a state fair. There were tears running down her face now, but she made no sound. Her head was held high, her chin out proudly. She had won. We all won that day.

Catty is in her early forties now. At a recent family meeting of all eight of us Kilcher kids, we were discussing what to do with the over seven hundred acres we had inherited from our father. When Catty made a motion that no slaughtering be done on the headquarters sight by the old homestead cabin of our childhood where it had always taken place, she got some strange looks and reactions. It took me a while to understand too. Then I remembered little Catty walking out to save BahBah that day so long ago, and it all made sense. She remembered and honored an old pain. She was doing what needed doing, to heal from her past, as we all should.

That day, as well as that butchering day of long ago, was a good example for all of us. I don't think I could afford to remember all of my old pains. I have had to forget, shut them out, numb myself. It's not good for a young kid to have to do that, and to top it off, it gave me the reputation for being tough, being able to handle anything. I was the one delegated to do away with unwanted kittens or puppies. I developed quick and efficient ways to dispose of them.

When you are in a family, fighting for and starved for attention, you take it any way you can. Being able to do difficult things, hide my feelings, and do what others couldn't became my identity, gave me a sense of pride. I perfected it. It all came back to haunt me as an angry, aggressive teenager. It came back to me when I went to Vietnam. I've been unraveling all of that most of my adult life.

I was raised watching all of this killing. I think I was too young. I didn't understand the .22-caliber bullet between the eyes. Or the bone-crunching sledgehammer to the skull. Or the sharp knife to the jugular vein. I didn't know what to do with the high-pitched scream of the rabbits hanging with their back feet nailed to a tree before their necks were snapped. Or the honking cry of geese hanging upside down with cut throats leaking out their last life blood. Chopping heads off chickens and watching them jumping headless for several minutes was the least traumatic.

I realize my childhood on the farm was no different from that of many other farm boys. You learn early on about the life cycle from conception to death. You are forced to grow up fast and take on adult responsibilities early. Butchering was part of life, of staying alive, of eating or earning money to buy clothes. Hard work is the basic foundation to survival. All that is harsh, but it is bearable, even character-building. But surviving it well takes an important ingredient that was missing in my childhood, and that was parents who can help kids understand and make sense of it all.

Butchering always felt traumatic, tense, and cruel, and it was always accompanied by my father's anger and impatience. I only learned years later that it was merely his way of coping as best he could with the many feelings it brought up for him, feelings he had never learned to give voice to. I also learned later that what he expressed as anger was covering many more basic emotions. The biggest, of course, was fear. I never asked him, but it is true for me and I am certain that was the case for him.

Being around dead or dying animals or other animal crises quickly brought out my father's anger. As a young kid, I learned all I could about what triggered him. Driving in dangerous conditions, hauling coal, haying with rain approaching, horses on the loose, or, worse yet, in the garden or the newly planted fields. Getting stuck, getting lost, being asked questions he had no answers for, being asked too many questions even if he did have the answers, and feeling he was being challenged. And when he was feeling rushed or was simply in a bad mood, anything could trigger him. At times, there was simply no rhyme or reason.

On a farm, much of the time, several of the above situations come into play. Rain and muddy roads make for bad driving and getting stuck. Haying in Alaska means rain is always just over the horizon. Staying warm means hauling coal. And even with the best of fences, horses are going to get out. It comes with the turf. And no matter how hard you tried not to ask, asking questions is a pretty basic part of growing and learning. Fortunately, there were eight of us to share my father's anger. Maybe that diluted it a bit for each individual.

Those who did not confront him, kept their heads low, and stayed out of the way caught less of his wrath. I was one who stood up to him more. I describe my father so different now than I would have in the past. Abusive, angry, harsh, full of rage, or violent are all such simple yet loaded words. They conjure up different images for everyone yet they are all terms I have used.

It was only in the last few years of my father's life that I was able to describe my dad in a different light. Even then it was not always easy. It was a constant battle not to get caught up in his pain or fear.

Your Grampa Yule was one hell of a man! He was not a cruel or mean man, however. I thank him for my confidence in many areas. I thank him for my many talents, hobbies, and interests. I thank him for a fairly intelligent mind. I thank him for my adventuresome and inquisitive spirit. I thank him for my love of land, nature, and animals. I thank him for my ability and drive to improve myself, even if it means going back to school, leaving my hometown, or going to therapy. I thank him for the many domestic skills I acquired, even though this was taught by his chauvinistic attitude and not helping out much in the house. I thank him for music, for the entertainer in me, the showman, the storyteller, the writer. I have much to thank him for.

I remember a class I took in college when I was earning my master's degree in social work about the abuse cycle. I was terrified to learn that a very high percentage of parents from abusive homes become abusive parents themselves. Knowing that I was a prime candidate, I was worried; I stayed alert for early signs.

I decided early on, after spanking you kids a couple of times, that it brought up too much for me. I told your mom that if she wanted to discipline you kids by occasionally spanking you, that was up to her. I knew I could not. When she did—very rarely—spank, it was seldom in anger.

I remember that time I used my hand before I knew what I was doing. It happened during those single-parenting years when we were living at the old homestead where I was raised. I had gone to bed much too late again the night before, probably after consuming close to a half rack of beer, self-medicating after a long day in the trenches. My childhood had not prepared me to be a husband or a father, certainly not a single dad. Cooking, cleaning, laundry in town twelve miles away, shopping, notes to and from school, helping with homework, no hot water, no indoor bathroom, no steady income, trying to make it as a barroom balladeer. The job description went on and on.

Before your mother and I got divorced, I was a part-time marriage-and-family counselor with a private practice. I told countless single parents, usually mothers, the importance of taking time for themselves, replenishing their energy and strength. It was so easy to give that advice. I never dreamed that someday I would not only have trouble taking time for myself, I wouldn't even be able to find any. My only attempt at reenergizing myself was with wine and song after you kids went to bed. The guitar and songwriting helped, the booze didn't, of course. I never was one to stop after a glass or two.

On one such groggy morning, you were getting yourselves ready for school as you did in those days, depending on how late I had stayed up reenergizing myself the night before. I found that the mornings usually went better if I stayed out of the way. Shane, who was about thirteen at the time, fed the animals and milked the cow most mornings. Jewel was about ten and took care of breakfast. Little Atz Lee, age eight, got himself ready and tormented his sister, or vice versa.

My fatherly instinct did require, however, that all of you come up to my room to say goodbye every morning. Jewel, on that particular morning, you said something that triggered me. Before I knew it, my arm was flying through the air. It was like a reflex. I heard and felt my hand slap hard against your face. In an instant, I could see that your lip was bleeding. You were crying. The boys were scared.

Wide awake and clear-headed now, I saw that genetic demon had once again raised its abusive head. I don't remember the details after that, but I do know that I didn't try to say I was right or that you deserved it. I also remember feeling very bad about it. I remember lying in bed thinking about you for a very long time. I imagined you trudging the one and a half miles to the end of the road to catch the school bus, dripping blood into the snow. I had been a state social worker before the divorce; for God's sake, I knew what the teachers would say! But no calls came. You probably lied for me, I thought.

Atz Lee, remember when the school psychologist had you draw a picture of your home and family? You drew a picture of a man flipping hotcakes in the air by the stove. You said it was your father. When the school psychologist interpreted the picture for me, he commented on how the stove signified warmth, and the hotcakes, or food, represented feeling nurtured.

I think you were mostly impressed with my ability to flip hotcakes.

You kids used to raise your plates to protect yourselves from the flying saucers I launched toward the table. Not all mornings were bad. The good ones didn't teach you to fear my hands, though they didn't make up for all the others. I know that, and I regret it so. Who knows what story the rest of your pictures would have told.

Maybe you feared my hands most for their volatility; they were always loaded, ready to go off. You saw my muscles flinch. You sensed me fighting to control myself. Too many times my hands grabbed you roughly or held your face to make you look at me. Way too often, my finger shook inches from your eyes. But those were the least of my sins. Words were my real weapons. With them I could lash out, cause shame and guilt, deliver my anger. They were my hands in clever disguise. They left no marks. Oh, how they must have hurt you over the years. The name-calling, blaming, and labeling. All the orders and barked commands.

"Shut up! ... Sit still! ... If you want to sit and snivel, I'll damn well give you something to snivel about!"

You were forced to listen to endless tirades and lectures. It didn't matter how it started, it usually ended the same. Jewel, I recall how you would begin crying and nervously twitching and wringing your hands. It used to *infuriate* me! You couldn't just take your irrational scolding, you always had to go and start twitching! I was way too busy shouting my feelings at you to ever let it sink in that my job was to help *you* understand *your* feelings, not the other way around.

That has to be my single biggest regret. I am so sorry, to all of you.

No child should have to grow up fearing their father's hands. No father should have to feel the pain of seeing his many childhood vows of what he would never do to his own kids someday constantly being shattered and slipping farther and farther from his grasp. But it, indeed, seemed to be part of our script this time around.

My children, you know some of the things I endured as a boy and young man, many of which I repeated and passed on to you. You know some of the feelings I have harbored and fought to shed. You were there with me. So, when I say that what my father's hands gave me just before he died was a miracle, you know what I am talking about.

That day in the hospital, his hands lost their angry grip on me. That day in the hospital, as his gentle hands held mine and his soft kisses talked to my skin, my father gave me the greatest inheritance I could have hoped to receive.

And now I'd like to pass to you all the same feeling of total love and acceptance. Consider it part of your inheritance, my legacy to you to replace all the bad. Most of all, I hope you kids know I love you and I'm grateful I have more time to show you.

Shane, looking back, it's hard to understand how I could feel such rage at my father for not being there for you, for screaming at you, for shaming you at such a crucial moment, when I did far worse to you myself. I remember the time you flunked your science test. I don't know why it brought out such rage in me. I guess it made me feel like a failure as a single father. I grabbed you with both hands at the front of your shirt and screamed at you like I often did back then. And even though I saw your head rattling and your teeth clacking together, I didn't slow down. I kept ranting, kept raging. Have I told you how sorry I am for that—and for all the other times, as well? If not, let me tell you now: I am so sorry, Son. Please forgive me. I'm afraid, being the oldest son, you perhaps took the brunt of it all. I can relate. It brings joy and great comfort to my soul to see how gentle, calm, and patient a father you have been to your children. I am so glad the apple fell far from the old tree.

Atz Lee, with you my son, I travel down that old, snow-covered trail we'd use to get to our cabin. We'd been to see a *Peter Pan* movie because I thought that would be a good father-son bonding experience. You were fourteen and probably not the right age for *Peter Pan* or bonding experiments. I'd been touched by a certain scene and leaned over to tell you something tender, and you responded with something I interpreted as a typical teenager response, dismissing my comment or maybe making fun of it. And I was deeply hurt.

So, on the way home, down that snowy trail through the deep dark forest, we got into it. We ended up in the snow, with you lying on your back, and me straddling your chest. A big thigh and a snowshoe on either side of you, preventing your escape. You were wearing skis, and I could feel them thrashing the snow behind me. I was screaming angry words at your face and punctuating my sentences by pumping on your chest. It's an awful, horrifying memory.

We got to the cabin and you crawled up into your loft. I didn't know what to say. You played your Bob Dylan tape, the song about parents not understanding their children. And I lay there in my bed feeling awful and shameful but did not have the courage or the know-how to come up and apologize and comfort you. I hold you and comfort you now, my son. And again, I can only ask for your forgiveness.

I'm always filled with joy to watch you with your young children in the wilderness. I see your patience and helpfulness and concern for them. You're a good parent and you must've watched a good parenting video or something.

My young son, Nikos, I'm afraid you got off light. You won't have much damage to work through in your life or in your relationships with your children. Since I gave you up for adoption after your mother and I broke up and she remarried, we only knew each other briefly when you were a baby, and later you came to live with me when you were sixteen. I remember screaming and hollering at you a few times and making you cry, but I don't recall ever laying a hand on you. We didn't get to know each other till you came back to Homer as a young adult.

Did I do the right thing giving you up to an intact family? I don't know. I thought it was best at the time. And you've been fortunate to have a strong, loving, and caring mother who was always there for you. You suffered less abuse, even if I wasn't there for you. I have less shame and guilt with you, fewer boggy trails to go down. But I know your childhood had its challenges, as well. Like with the rest of my kids, I'm very proud of you and that you got whatever singing, songwriting, and yodeling genes I did.

And Jewel, I believe you when you say that you feared my hands. I also know we have both let it go. My first reaction to reading about your fear of my hands was *fear*—of what others might think my hands did to you. I also feared that you had unresolved issues, ones I thought we had dealt with. But then I realized the only way you *could* mention something like that was if you had no baggage about it.

I think your poem is a classic. My favorite by far. In one short poem, you speak of both the fear and the admiration or pride you felt for me as a child growing up. I acknowledge that both were present. Regrettably, there were too many times I gave you cause to fear my hands. Fortunately, I recall very few incidents of hitting you or being physical with my hands. Hopefully my memory is accurate.

I am glad you saw my hands gently strum my guitar. When I watch your hands on your own guitar now, it sends gentle healing music to my guilty soul. I am glad you saw my hands flip those hotcakes high into the air. When you come home to visit, it always warms me when you ask me to fix you some fresh nettles, a dandelion salad, or some *rösti*.

I am glad I have memories of washing your long honey-blond hair, and gently combing out the snarls with "no more tangles." I remember always starting at the ends, which were almost to your bottom, and then working my way up to your head, the way your mama always did. I thought about that when I was in your house in California watching your New York beautician getting you ready for an appearance. I am also so glad that I have memories of my hands gently bathing you until you were old enough to do it yourself. I did that even when your mother and I were still together.

I am thankful that you remember my hands bringing life back to Crazy Cow's calf. Thank you for your beautiful poem that brought back so much for me. Thank you for the courage to talk of your fears, old or new. May you always do so bravely. It really matters not what others think.

Of all your accomplishments, I am most proud of all the hard work you have done on your inner landscape, and how you have improved on the generations before you.

Keep up the good work, I love you all,

Dad

# CHAPTER 13

# My Last Castration

I had a horse I needed to get rid of. He was at the age where he needed more individual care. Winters were taking their toll on him and he needed a stable, extra hay, and grain. He needed and deserved to be not one in a herd of ten, but someone's pet, pampered and spoiled.

Clear Water was built like an Iditarod sled dog, lean, not an extra ounce of fat on him. No matter how well he ate all summer, he went into the winter lean, and came out looking a bit bony and malnourished. Other horses in the herd stayed roly-poly fat all winter. I can't say I ever tried to separate him and let him have all the hay he wanted, though I did give him vitamins and minerals. He was boss of the feedlot, so it wasn't that he was being pushed around. Clear Water simply needed a doting 4-H girl. So, I found him one.

She was a music student of mine. Her family had one horse already, and a few head of cows. I couldn't sell him for what he was worth to me—too much history, too many memories. I could write a book about all he lived through—and darn near died of. My daughter and I trained him. She rode him hard through her teen years, usually at a full gallop. Maybe that's what permanently wore off all his fat.

He and I rode many trails together, chasing countless cows. Since I couldn't sell him, I traded him for three cows. Somehow that made it easier, as well as knowing he was in the loving hands of a young girl who would adore and pamper him, the only girl in the whole world who now owned "Jewel's horse."

The cows were three head of cattle, one of them a yearling bull. To keep them with my brother's and sister's herds, which summer-ranged with the Cattlemen's Association cattle, meant castrating my nonregistered young bull.

Castrating was just one small part of my homestead upbringing. Many years of raising cattle helped me hone my ability to hit that emotional "off switch," allowing me to cut off scrotums, sever the testicles, cut throats of squawking geese and screaming rabbits as they hung upside down. I need only to close my eyes to see that crooked stump where they were tied and hear their high-pitched screams and gurgling honks.

I vividly remember watching my father butcher when I was old enough to be of help. Already I realized I had to hit that off switch.

I watched as he used the back of an ax or a small sledge to hit a calf, or even a yearling, between the eyes with a skull crushing thud, and then quickly "stick" them with a sharp long knife, severing the main aorta close to the heart. The goal was to stun them but keep their heart pumping to better bleed them for a cleaner product. For larger animals, a .22-caliber bullet was used, or sometimes a larger rifle.

I am not sure if it was to save money or to merely stun them, but my father's method often caused extreme anxiety and high tension. Animals getting back up and having to be hit or shot again, regaining consciousness and getting up while streaming blood. Or, worst of all, running off and having to be shot again, like a wild animal.

It was just one of the many things I never could understand about my father. He always did the bare minimum to get any job done. His lack of preparation left the good possibility for things to run amok, and often led him to be abusive. Anytime I was asked to help my dad with any task, especially butchering, I went into a numb fear. It wasn't that something *might* go wrong. I knew that sooner or later something *would* go wrong. There would be screaming and cursing and I would be berated for not being fast enough or smart enough, for not being able to read his mind, for not preventing things from going wrong. Or I would be hit.

After that emotional crescendo, he usually calmed down. It was his dance, the drummer he marched to. I memorized the steps and learned them well.

It all seemed normal because it is all we knew from infancy on. This goes for all children, only somewhere down the road with more information does one slowly compare and contrast one's childhood to others. This goes double for children raised as secluded and remote as we were. We were steeped in the way our family functioned, or dysfunctioned, and it was a long time before we saw how other families treated each other. We were more "well done" in the traditions of our small wilderness culture. Only decades and three wives later, after many addictions and abusive deeds of my own, would I come to realize the many damaging effects of my "normal" childhood.

However, somewhere deep down, I sensed in a knowing place that something was wrong.

Our wind-up phonograph and battery-run radio did not tell me that the loneliness, the hours crying while cradled in the roots of a giant spruce was not normal. I had no television to tell me that the fear of hearing my mother scream at night and seeing her bruised face the next day was not normal. I had no buddy, no uncles, no state social worker to tell me that being made to work without gloves in winter, or going way too long without eating or drinking because my father was driven to get the job done, was abusive and neglectful. Or that it wasn't my fault.

I had no loving aunt or grammas to tell me that my mother, though a helpless victim herself, was not doing her job by allowing those things to happen. Even before a road connected our homestead to the main road and we no longer traveled by horse and wagon, I knew something was wrong. Even before I started public school or before we traveled back to Switzerland to meet my relatives and I saw how other families and relatives functioned.

Even before all that, at age six or seven, I knew something was wrong, and a searching to learn the truth, to learn normalcy, to heal, to forgive and take responsibility was born. A journey I am still on at age sixty-two. I believe children know when something is wrong.

It was also as a young child that I knew I did not like killing or harming animals. I began to see a pattern with my father when it came to butchering. He became tense, argumentative, anxious, and angry. Killing a chicken for dinner was at one end of the butchering continuum. Killing ten head of cattle was at the other end, in the boiling-point red, where steam had to be released, and something exploded.

There was always a major blowup between him and whichever family member pissed him off, didn't jump fast or high enough, got in his way, asked him a question, made a mistake for *fear* of asking a question, tried to humor him, or tried to help him get going and quit stalling. These observations began about age ten or twelve.

It was, of course, not the ideal way to be introduced to the ancient, sacred, and necessary task of taking animal life to provide for your family. There were no ceremonies, no giving thanks, no calm talks between a father and his young son.

Instead, it was harsh, cold reality. A shout, a stinging slap to a cold cheek, a gunshot ripping through ears, bright red blood spurting, and icy feet standing in gut piles while nearly numb fingers hold a warm slippery hide as it's pulled away from the carcass, each blow of father's sledgehammer threatening to pull elbows and shoulders from sockets.

> *Heavy quarters carried on young but strong*
> *    shoulders.*
> *Fresh blood dripping,*
> *down goose-bumped neck and chest.*
> *Autumn light quickly fading.*
> *Lanterns and flashlights turned on.*
> *Hurry! Hurry!*
> *Moods watched, steps memorized.*

*Temperatures dropping!*
*Heavy quarters now hung,*
*wrapped with tarps to keep from freezing.*
*Hands washed with hot water from*
    *woodstove.*
*Fresh heart and liver sizzling in hot pan.*
*Cold hands and feet close to kitchen stove.*
*Slowly, warmth returns.*
*Toes and fingers and feelings*
*slowly begin to tingle*

*Pitch black outside now.*
*Another day of butchering is over.*

*A cow calls for her calf.*
*A young boy eats his heart,*
*to the pulse of a Coleman lantern.*
*The dimmer switch, to so many feelings,*
*is turned down yet another notch.*
*Another door closes,*
*another season gone by.*
*Survival.*

I believe there are many emotionally healthy and happy people who hunt or butcher domestic animals out of necessity or vocation. In my case, it was the act of killing, a dramatic and serious act in and of itself, taking life and all that goes with it, superimposed on a backdrop of intense unexplained emotions and emotional and physical abuse: too much expected way too young.

We had a cow we called Devil Cow. As you might guess, she was coal-black and had short, sharp devil-shaped horns. I had graduated to butchering by myself by then, with my younger brother, Otto, as my assistant and apprentice. I had inherited and learned many of my father's qualities by then and sadly, treated him similar to how my father treated me. I was on autopilot, switches off. We butchered together from about age fifteen or sixteen until I got my freedom by joining the army at nineteen. Since I was leaving, my dad cut his herd way down. We butchered about thirty head that fall. I bet Otto was mighty glad to see me leave.

I was helping him butcher just yesterday; now he is fifty-seven and I am sixty-two. He mentioned several incidents of that period long ago, incidents where I, as the older brother, had treated him much like my dad used to treat me. Once again, I told him I was so sorry. He assured me there was no need to apologize. I told him that even if he did not need the apology, it did my own soul good.

I help him now partly because he needs help and I am a pretty good hand. He also gives me beef in trade. But mostly I do it as a sort of atonement. It does me good to be his helper now, to do things his way. I don't shoot or bleed them. I don't even hook up the chain to their hind legs to hang them up as they bleed. Instead of turning off, I keep my feelings on. I feel what there is to feel and process it. It is healing, and when I need to, I take a break.[1]

Just so happened that my own thirty-three-year-old son, Atz Lee, and Otto's twenty-six-year-old son, Eivin, were also helping with the butchering. I believe both our sons have been spared what Otto and I went through during butchering at the hands of father and older brother. Thank God.

We used to lure the cows to the butchering tree with a little grain poured on the ground directly under the block and tackle—tied to a strong log pole suspended between two spruce trees. Once the critter we wanted to butcher was in place, shot and stuck, we used our ford

---

1. While I was helping him, he reminded me of a time our dad was helping him. My dad was in his late sixties at the time, still healthy and strong, but still, getting older with some shoulder issues. Otto had our dad hang onto the hide as he pounded it off with a sledgehammer. He cut slits in the edge of the hide for my dad to put his hands in, just like dad used to do for us. After my dad had been having his arms stretched and his shoulders yanked every time Otto pounded on the hide, he asked Otto to stop for a minute. "You know, Otto," he said, "this is really hard on the hands, arms, and shoulders." Otto didn't cut him much slack. "Yeah," he said. "I know. I remember!"

tractor to raise the beef for proper bleeding, gutting, and skinning. If we could get close enough, we used a .22 to drop them. If the animal was skittish and we couldn't get close enough, we used a 30.06 rifle, or an old army 30.40 Krag rifle.

Devil Cow was of the skittish variety. I learned over the years the importance of a bullet hitting its mark on the first shot. A poorly placed shot, even in the head, can merely wound the animal, causing it to take off running, blind and crazed, or lock and spread its legs and remain standing on pure adrenalin and survival instinct.

I made a poor shot. She locked her legs and spread them wide. Two more shots from my .06 couldn't drop her. Then my rifle jammed and I shouted at Otto to sprint for the house a couple hundred yards away to get my dad's .44 magnum pistol. Two or three shots later, with eyes glazed, blood draining from nostrils, mouth, and bullet holes, steam rising from the red snow, a mere spark of life commanding her to stand, we pushed her over to bleed her, though there wasn't much blood left.

> *Pure white snow soiled.*
> *Spreading stain of crimson.*
> *Gurgling breath, gushing spurting blood.*
> *Hot steam rising.*

Coulda used a father's hand on my shoulder right about then. Some calm reassurance. Some help from a wise elder.

That story was repeated many times. We hoorahed and laughed and slapped our legs. It was my way of feeling accepted, being one of the boys. It was also my way of letting go, revising it to a funny experience and distancing myself.

"You shoulda' seen 'er," I would say. "Man, she just wouldn't go down. Little devil horns just a-pointin' straight up ... steam like smoke and blood just a-squirtin' out of her mouth and nose. Three more blasts from the .44. Blam, blam, blam!" The story got better over the years. "Sure hope that devil cow went to hell, 'cuz I don't want to run into her in heaven, ha-ha-ha."

Butchering those cows, I had to turn the dimmer switch on my feelings way down. They all blur together, dim hazy memories. But Devil Cow, I see as clearly forty years ago as if it were yesterday.

The names of most have faded, as have many of the memories. I do remember Pansy, Quarter Moon, Pepper, Daisy. The hardest to kill were the old cows I grew up with, fed through many winters, pulled out of bogs, pulled calves from, nursed through sickness and many near-death experiences. Take old Quarter Moon just for one of so many examples.

Because our homestead borders Kachemak Bay on the south and there's a near-vertical two-hundred-foot cliff that drops off to the beach, we never put a fence along that bluff because it's a fence of its own. Same holds true with our west boundary.[2]

One day my dad was walking along the beach, and at the bottom of a mudslide that had come down one of the many ravines, he saw something blinking. It was an eye. Upon closer inspection, it belonged to Quarter Moon, whose entire remaining body parts were buried under mud. He dug her out as best he could and raced the two miles up to the house to get help. We went back down and there she lay, still alive.

After the tumbling, rolling fall she took, we had no idea how many bones were broken or if she could even stand. We coaxed and prodded and helped her to her feet. It was obvious that a hip was broken or seriously injured. Step by slow step, which I am sure were very painful, she walked the two miles back up to the haystack, where we made her a bed of hay and into which she quickly collapsed.

Over the next several months she got stronger. At first, she would eat and drink while lying down, but soon she got strong enough to stand and lay back down on her own. Miracle of miracles, when early June rolled around, she had a beautiful bull calf.

---

2. Of course, if we added up the value of all the horses and cattle lost over those cliffs, plus our time and energy in looking for them, once in a while helping one back up or, in the case of one cow, finding her with a broken back and butchering her and carrying the meat out, we could have built a mighty fine fence.

Yep, when it came time to butcher *her*, it took some doing. But you did what needed doing.

When the standard line became, "Guess I lost too many brain cells in the sixties," I've always thought, "Not me. I was hanging out in the breathtaking Alaskan wilderness, living the good life on a remote homestead and losing heart cells, soul cells, and numbing out nerve endings."

There was a two-year-old steer once who wouldn't go down. He took off at a slow run, partly dazed from the first .22 shot between his eyes. Running along beside him, I shot him in the side of the head as fast as I could reload the single shot rifle. Five or six shots later he was still moving. By now he had crossed the hay field and was stumbling through the brush and crashing blindly into trees, falling over dead logs, getting up, and staggering again. Finally, he fell and stayed down.

Another three-year-old bull we shot years later wouldn't go down. This was after we'd built a corral.[3] The second shot didn't drop him either. So as not to waste more ammo and take a chance on hitting another critter, I went to cut his throat. He stood glassy-eyed, legs spread, hot blood spurting out of his mouth and nose. I'd never cut the throat of a standing animal before, but I gave it a go, and it wasn't going well. It took forever and his hide was tough. Once the blood started flowing from his jugular, he slowly sank to the ground. And as I walked away, I noticed some feelings coming up, regret and sadness, and I thought, *I must be getting soft.*

But maybe some things should never be easy.

---

3. Why we'd never built one sooner, heaven only knows. It probably comes down to the same reason we did so many things the hard way in those early homesteading days: it was how my dad did things. We'd started using heavier caliber rifles, having abandoned my dad's theory that they had to be merely stunned so their heart would keep pumping out the blood. After they dropped, we picked them up with the front-end loader of a tractor and bled them. Once they were bled, we took them out of the corral and let them down to be skinned. And after skinning, we picked them back up to saw them in half and quarter them. Those that we sold by the quarter or half, we hung in our barn to age. For those customers who wanted it cut and wrapped, we took it directly to the butcher up the road.

Well it's time to get back to my last castration, where this whole thing started.

Compared to butchering or slaughtering, castrating is really nothing. I have lots of happy memories of cattle roundups in the spring at the head of the bay. It was always a time of cowboy camaraderie, laughing, joking, good food, and hard work. It was also a chance as a young teenager to see other male role models and how they did things.

All the cowboys would gather up the cows in the spring. The cows had already been turned out to the summer range with the calves still unbranded, the little bull calves still intact. Once we gathered all the cows together up in the valley, we drove them to the Lewis ranch. One herd at a time was separated out to be "worked" in the corral. All the older animals were already branded and easy to identify.

I also learned to castrate by watching the older guys.[4] With a razor-sharp, sterilized pocketknife, you would cut off the bottom one-third of the scrotum. Next, you pulled out one testicle at a time, and severed the cord with a sawing motion. Then you sloshed some disinfectant over the site of surgery, and the calf ran to its mother. They never bawled during the procedure like they did when they were branded, which led the old cowboys to say that it didn't hurt. I was never convinced of that, and I'm sure no one ever asked one of the bulls.

The hardest part of a branding was the embarrassment if girls were watching and the older guys pretended you could be the next patient to lose his balls. Otherwise, it was a fun time, with lots of good food and laughter. Of course, it helped to have already learned how to turn off those emotional switches.

So, when the time came for me to put my yearling bull and two cows up with the other cattle and I had to castrate the bull, it had probably been twenty or thirty years since my last castration. I last

---

4. We'd never castrated at home when I was younger. We usually butchered our bull calves before they were old enough to breed. If we did castrate, it was by putting a strong rubber band around the scrotum of the young bull calf. Eventually the entire scrotum and its valuable contents shriveled and fell off.

castrated a horse in Utah when I was going to college in 1972.[5] Even though it had been a few years, I wasn't worried about castrating my little bull. Castrating a horse is more difficult and more things can go wrong. A bull is relatively easy.

All three head were at my sister Mossy's Swift Creek cabin where they were pasturing till I put them with the rest of the herd. My son Atz Lee and his two friends James and Johnny were going to help, or watch, whichever. It was sort of an outing for us—no better way to introduce my son's two friends to the wilds of Alaska than have them watch a bull lose his balls in the beauty of a spring meadow.

The boys were already there, camped out on the beach from the night before. I brought everything I would need: ropes, disinfectant, sharp knife, a container to put the testicles in, and a frying pan. You see, it's a tradition at roundup time to eat the fresh "Rocky Mountain oysters." Of course, it's also part of the tradition not to tell newcomers to the sport what they're eating till after they eat it. How they never guessed, even at the table, with the breaded oysters heaped high on a plate, I don't know. But we all used to try hard not to let out the secret.[6] My son and I decided to tell James and Johnny ahead of time because they were special friends and we didn't want to pull a teenage prank on them. They both were down for at least trying them.

I had stopped at our favorite local neighborhood bakery, Fritz Creek General Store, and bought a whole cake. It was an angel-something cake, with yellow lemon frosting. Never before, to my knowledge, had a castration been celebrated in this fashion to welcome young men to Alaska. We were all stoked. James and Johnny were all smiles and big eyes, trying to look calm and cool.

5. I had felt a sense of not doing enough just going to college and working two part-time jobs, so I acquired a horse, a goat, and a bunch of pigs. Having chores to do morning and night made me feel more at home.

6. Actually, Rocky Mountain oysters are delicious. They taste like the best boiled egg you have ever eaten. My favorite is to bread them and fry them crisp. The fun, of course, was to watch the faces of the initiates once they were told, or it dawned on them, what they had just eaten.

By the time we had the bull on the ground and hog-tied, it was all coming back to me, just like riding a bicycle. I whopped of the scrotum, cut off the nuts, put 'em in the ziplock, spurted some disinfectant blood coagulant on the wound, and let him up. Then, of course, I winked at Atz Lee, and we grabbed Johnny and acted like we were going to hog-tie him. We all laughed and headed for the cabin with cake and fresh nuts in tow.

Johnny and James were blown away. I can't remember now which one said it, but it made me realize how something like this must look and feel to a newcomer to Alaska, to the wilderness, to throwing wild critters down and lopping off their nuts without blinking an eye. "Man, I just totally respect you for knowing how to do that. I can't believe what I just saw. You just threw him down and, before I knew it, you were done. Amazing!"

Then a strange thing happens. At this point in my life, I am good at numbing myself out when necessary. I also have a strong stomach, which comes from eating Rocky Mountain oysters. But strangely, I start feeling sick to my stomach, a little dizzy, and then I feel like crying. Damn that Johnny with his, "I really respect you, man," California bullshit!

I suggest we eat the cake on the grass in the sunshine. I tell them I don't feel like cow balls for lunch. I get no resistance. I tuck the ziplock with the nuts into a bag, and I tuck the flood of incoming feelings away also, to be understood and dealt with later.

On the way home, I wander down a lot of old trails, some of which I've taken you on, plus a whole lot more. When I get home, I know what I need to do. I don't even think about it.

I go down to the cliff in front of my cabin. I have no clue what I am going to do, yet I feel like I've been rehearsing for this moment for a long, long time.

A ceremony starts to take shape. I stand there, baggy in hand, and I close my eyes.

I am up to my knees in the early spring barnyard of my youth. It seems to have no bottom. It is slimy, brown, runny, churning, bubbling, foaming just like that old spring of ours. Everything is bubbling to the surface.

*Feelings, memories, images, sounds.*
*Pent up, pressurized, pushed way down.*
*Frozen, turned off.*
*All jumbled together.*

*Anger, ice-cold hurting hands,*
*screaming, swearing.*
*Hard slap to cold ear,*
*already ringing from rifle shot.*

*The last moos and bleats*
*and honks and squeals*
*and spurts and gurgles.*

*Poisonous weeds blooming,*
*bloated bellies.*
*Bulging strangled eyes,*
*at rope's end.*
*Tangled body,*
*at base of cliff.*
*Frozen nose and last breath,*
*protruding from ice,*
*Struggle of death.*

*Bleeding, wounded,*
*running blind,*
*stumbling.*

*I am drunk,*
*stumbling,*
*overwhelmed.*

*I am young.*
*For some deaths,*
*there are no excuses.*

My whole life isn't flashing before my eyes, just the part to do with animals and neglect, perhaps cruelty.

The brown goo is boiling. Damn that Johnny, anyway! He had to go and ruin a perfectly nice bonding experience, a pleasant lunch of mountain oysters and cake. It's time to review, time to sort things out, to take another step toward higher ground.

It's always taken me forever to sort things out, physical or emotional. It's just the way I'm built. I was raised in a rush. I've become allergic to it, so I've learned to take my time. Since I'm sorting out things to do with animals, I'm gonna move extra slow. Let me tell you why.

You have a herd of cows gathered up out in the middle of nowhere. There's no corral, no fences, just horses and cowboys. You have three or four cowboys circled around the outside of the herd. The cowboys become a moving fence, the cows soon think they're surrounded and stay in their bunch. One person or two go into the herd and start sorting out the ones they want, say, all the yearling steers. Together they work the steer, by itself or in a group of two or three, to the edge of the herd. The perimeter cowboys separate, like opening a gate to freedom, and the steers are pushed out of the herd.

Now the perimeter cowboys are not only keeping the big bunch of cows together, but they have to keep the steers that were cut out from reentering the herd, following their instincts back to safety and protection. The number one cardinal rule is staying calm, moving slow, not getting the animals stirred up. Once they get excited, they will run right over and through the perimeter cowboys; even a fence won't hold cows that are riled up. Put a brown bear behind them, and the most docile cow will try to go through or over anything.

The further along in the sorting process, the calmer everyone has to be. Now the yearling group is getting bigger on the outside, and cows from the main herd want to join them in their freedom, especially if they are wandering off. The last step is keeping them separated as you drive off the ones you cut out. Many times, members of the big herd who see their friends leaving will try to follow. They don't realize where those steers are going—to become chuck, London broil, lean ground.

Sorting is about knowing what you want to sort out. It never went well helping my dad. He used to scream, "You have to be smarter than the cow!" And I would think to myself, *Well, Pops, it would help if we weren't all trying to get away from a screaming maniac.*[7]

Standing there on the edge of that cliff, I've got some sorting to do. And it don't matter how long it takes, it's time to get 'er done!

I can see clearly that my trouble didn't come from things like earmarking, dehorning, or castrating. There was some pain and blood involved in all of those, but it was part of ranching. It didn't bother me finding animals dead due to natural or unavoidable causes. It wasn't even the slaughtering when humane methods were used, when it was calm, or there was a feeling of thankfulness for the sanctity of life, of oneness with the circle of life. It was none of that.

The more the barnyard cauldron churned and boiled down to its essence, all that was left, what I finally had to get rid of, to *forgive*—oh yes, cowboy, it does mean forgiving—were only two things. One was all the anger, fear, and pure horror I experienced too many times helping my dad do normal ranching things, whether butchering, working cows, or finding dead ones. Those were his issues, which he just kept dumping on me as long as I would take them. But the other was the needless suffering and death we caused by what we did or neglected to do. This was the story of a big part of my childhood, doing things in a rush, not spending the time or money, and accepting "good enough for now" because he was too impatient to do it right.

---

7. To this day, get me around anyone the least bit tense or impatient, and I go real calm and slow, which inevitably pisses off that impatient person to no end. Of course, get me around cows or horses, or around certain folks, and I'm liable to become that tense, impatient person others are trying to get away from.

My dad and I did the very best we could at the time, as wrong or bad as that might have been. I believe that. But the saddest of all this and hardest to forgive was that when left on my own with my brother or with my own kids, I didn't do much better.

The salty sea breeze is in my face. I feel clean and fresh. I hold those yearling testicles in my hand and look at them long and hard. Never was so much wrapped up in one pair of balls.

I give silent thanks for the unexpected gift they brought me today, and I throw them as far down the cliff as I can.

It's time to let go. It's time to move on. To *be* different, one must *do* different. It's time to start *doing* different.

Time to start putting some new memories into my old saddlebags.

# CHAPTER 14

## *Skiing*

Not too long ago someone asked me when I started skiing. I thought for a moment and then realized that I never thought about it before, had never been asked that question. The question I *had* been asked over and over again was when I started singing. The answer to that question is that in our family of origin, we always sang. I couldn't remember not singing. As I contemplated when I had started skiing, I realized it was the same as singing.

As infants, we were put on sleds or toboggans or packed on the back of a skiing parent. I remember my younger sisters stumbling around on skis about the same time they learned to walk. I don't think it was so much that our parents taught us as it was that skis were always around. Skiing was constantly being role modeled, and the younger kids were always trying to copy the older ones.

So, the answer to my fellow skier was that I didn't remember exactly, but I imagined I began about the same time I started walking.

What I do remember quite clearly is the first cross-country race I won. In fact, it took place not too far from where our men's group was skiing the day my friend asked me that question, up at Ohlson Mountain.

I was around six years old. I had a pair of those skis with cable bindings and the bamboo poles of the time. My dad had been a national ski champion back in his day in Switzerland, so he did a good job of keeping all his eight kids in fairly good ski equipment. I can't imagine how hard it must have been keeping us all in skis. I am sure it was partly for transportation, getting out to the main road, or going ptarmigan hunting in the winter. Many, if not most, of the old timers in those days skied to get around in the winter. But mostly, I just remember skis being a big source of fun. I loved it then, and I still love it now.

I had never been in any kind of an official race up until this point. At home when we raced, everyone started out at the same time, and the first one there was the winner. Is there any other way to race? I don't need to tell you I was very confused, and not at all happy about the way this, my first ski race, started.

We all lined up one behind the other, but they let one kid take off at a time. Well that might be great for that kid who got to leave first, but I happened to be the very last one to take off. By the time I got to the starting line and they said, "Go," I was very unhappy. But I was no quitter. I was a homestead kid. I turned my anger into energy.

My dad gave me some advice just before I started. He told me that if I came up behind someone and wanted to pass, all I had to do was holler, "Trail!" The kid in front of me would quickly step off the trail, while still trying to ski alongside as best he could, while I passed staying in the trail. The trail in those classic skiing days consisted of a single track. If there was time there might be a set of ski tracks on either side of the trail for your poles. Most of the time your poles were just planted in the deep undisturbed snow. That's the way it was then, so being last, at least I had the advantage of a somewhat packed pole-planting track.

I took off as fast and as hard as I could. I didn't know anything about pacing. All of the races against my siblings on the homestead were all-out, go-as-hard-as-you-can-all-the-way. That was the only strategy I knew. And now I had a whole slew of kids to catch up to and pass, so I put my strategy to work!

My dad also told me that if any kid didn't get out of my way after I hollered "Trail!" I should just hit him over the head with my ski pole. Did my dad say, "I'm just joking, Son"? Hell, no! He said it dead seriously and I took it that way. Says something right there, doesn't it? A young kid actually believing that it was all right to whop another kid over the head with a hard ski pole?

Well, I was whistling along pretty good, hollerin' "Trail!" every few seconds. Seemed like I was hollerin' more than I was breathin'. All the kids, who had probably been properly coached by their parents, quickly got out of the trail. Except for Marvin Bellamy.

I think I hollered a couple of times. I hope I did, anyway. But old Marvin just kept on a-skiin'. He may not have heard me through his winter gear. Maybe he was trying to ignore me. But I had somewhere to get to, and I had gotten a late start, so I had no time to poke along speculatin'. So … I bopped him over the head a real good whomp with my bamboo ski pole. That got Marvin's attention! Marvin moved!

I was on a roll now. Only a few kids ahead of me. I passed 'em all but one. He got to the finish line just ahead of me. I was so dejected. Not so much from losing, but from the unfairness of it all!

No matter how many times my mom and dad told me I had won, I knew I hadn't. Apparently they had not seen that other kid cross the finish line ahead of me.

When they handed out the prizes and gave me a stick of wax and announced I was the winner, I still didn't understand. How stupid could a whole bunch of adults be for not seeing that other kid beat me?

On the way home, the concept of interval starts was explained to me. But believe me, the light came on very slowly. Perhaps that's one of the reasons that very first victory has never been forgotten. It was a whole lot more than just a race. It was an education.

Poor Marvin. He was a part of my learning curve. I have apologized to him several times. He says he doesn't remember it. I'm glad it didn't have a traumatic effect on him.

I've raced many a race since that first one fifty-seven years ago, and I love 'em all. But I gotta say, when I hear it's gonna be a mass start race, I say to myself, "Now that's a *real* race!"

Fast-forward to another first victory in '65. I'm seventeen, and although I've been skiing in between, I've never competed. As a junior, I went out for the ski team and I was the number two skier. The two or three races I participated in I placed somewhere midpack.

I'm on skis my dad used in Switzerland, and they're great compared to those old cable bindings I've been skiing on. My dad won his big National Swiss race on these and I've merely looked at them all those growing-up years. Now he's letting me use them! They look sleek and modern to me, but they're heavy and not much wider than my old ones. Coach gives me some newer gear to race on.

I'm not thinking at all about how I look—my differentness as a homestead hick is normal to me by now—but when we get to the resort where the race is, the ski teams from all over the state are decked out in the sleekest-looking outfits, some even with matching hats. I look down at my jeans tucked into the pathetic striped socks. They aren't even ski socks!

Suddenly, I never want to look up again. I realize I now know what public humiliation feels like. Being teased for wearing a cowboy hat to school didn't bother me. But this is different. My head hanging, I'm totally out of my league, whatever league that is. I want to head back to the hills, back to my log home on the homestead.

Fortunately, soon the butterflies set in and I forget about my outfit. It's an interval start and I take off somewhere in the middle. I don't know anyone just ahead or behind me, so I can't gauge how I'm doing. My teammate and friend Ray Martin, who is in the running to win the race, is seeded toward the front.

The underdog, that's me. No one knows who the hick is. So, what else can I do? I go like hell!

*I'll show 'em.*

That six-year-old kid at Ohlson mountain comes to me, the one they made start last. *I showed 'em then; I'll show 'em now.*

If it's possible to ski your heart out, I'm going to try. I go full-out, fast as I can the whole way. No pacing—for me it's a sprint. I have five kilometers to prove myself.

I pant across the finish, no clue how I did. I rush into the lodge and head downstairs to the big chalkboard. I meet a group of skiers in fancy racing uniforms coming up. As they go by, I hear bits of their conversation, one bit in particular.

"I have no idea … never heard of him … from Homer … named Atz Kilcher."

*Atz Kilcher! Holy shmoly!*

I fly down the rest of those stairs with dangerous leaps. I push my way through the skiers.

*No … YES!* There it is at the top of that huge chalkboard. First place for the whole state of Alaska. My name: Atz Kilcher!

That moment, that precise moment, is still a part of who I am. It opened new horizons and gave me a glimpse of what I could be, of who I really was. And in some way, it forever aligned me with the underdogs, the ones who can't afford the best but somehow make it work, all the ragamuffins out there without much more than a hope and dream.

Well, when my daddy, who was playing state senator down in Juneau, found out, he was ecstatic! I had seldom heard such excitement in his voice. At last I had done something he was truly proud of. The cheering crowds I had managed to work into my life to boost my ego were nothing compared to the excitement I heard in his voice.

"So, my old skis won another race!" he shouted over the phone.

"No, Father. I used a pair coach let me have."

"Well then at least my old ski boots won another race!"

No again, I said, and handed him off to my mom whose eyes were mirroring my pain and disappointment.

Can you believe that? Well, sure, it *would* have been a real kick if the equipment he'd used thirty years prior had won again. But give me a break already! What a piece of work. You gotta love him. He was a hell of a skier, and without him, I may never have gotten into skiing.

When someone asks me, "What do you do?" skiing is right there at the top of my list of things I do. I know they mean my profession. I don't feel much like a retired teacher or social worker, hardly defines what I'm doing today, who I *am*. "I ski, make baskets, sing, and write songs," I say.

And then they walk off thinking I avoided their question. Which maybe I did.

* * *

Some people are part of a church group or a social organization such as the Elks or Lions. I consider myself a member of the world-wide ski association. Wherever you are, when you meet a fellow cross-country skier, you've met a member of your larger family. And invariably, as you talk, you have friends in common.

Who in my age range who knows anything about Alaskan skiing doesn't remember Tom Besh, my senior-year nemesis? If they don't remember two-time Olympian Larry Martin, they're not a real skier. If skiers my age or older who've been on the National Masters or World Masters circuit haven't heard of multi-gold-medalist Richard Mize, well, I don't even talk to 'em. Yep, in the skiing circles, I don't ask people if they've heard of Jewel. If I want to find common ground, I ask if they knew Tom Besh, Larry Martin, or Dick Mize.

When it came time to choose the Junior National team to represent Alaska, there was a bit of a problem. It seemed I hadn't raced enough races to qualify. They thought I just had a fluke race, a good day. I'm not sure if they had any rule about it, but my win only made them scratch their heads. Makes sense, I guess. I sure didn't believe it at the time.

When the next year rolled around, I trained hard. I started the year with cross-country running, then basketball and wrestling came next. I squeezed skiing in during wrestling or basketball. I skied at home, as well as to and from the bus stop, and I also had to work out with the team a couple of times a week.

Needless to say, I was pretty pumped from my win of the year before, and now that I knew I might get to go to the lower forty-eight for the Junior Nationals, I skied my butt off. No heart monitors in those days to help you train, so except for the two days a week I worked out with the team, it was just me skiing out our road and in the hay meadows.

I took second place throughout the state pretty much all season. I was ten or twenty seconds behind the first-place guy and I hated him! Till I got to know him, of course. Name was Tom Besh, as fine a fellow as you'd want to meet. He was fiercely competitive, but low-key, humble, a bit bashful, and very friendly. My claim to fame is that I *did* beat him in one short race, maybe a three kilometer up at Ohlson Mountain. One other race in Anchorage, I went by him as he was having ski trouble. I didn't see blood, so kept cruising. I had first place in the bag, but a kid I'd been beating all year had a good race that day and beat me. So, no first place for me. But that's how it goes.

I qualified for the Junior National team that year and it was a highlight of my life. It was one thing to win a local or state race, but to get to go *outside?* Dude, now that's something. Miss school for at least a week, see people and places I'd never seen, including *girls.* Oh, yes, and get to compete against the whole United States.

I was as proud of the fact that half of our eight men on the men's team were from Homer. Winter Park, Colorado, was where we were headed, and I needed a suit and money. Coach Schroer came to my rescue once again, this time with one of his suits, which fit me perfectly. He also gave me some spending money. And my mom managed to sneak me some of her grocery money.

The motel where we spent our first night in Denver didn't know what hit 'em. Close to midnight, all the boys on the team jumped in the cold pool in our underwear. It was only March, but we were from Alaska, and far from home!

In Winter Park, it took a few days to get used to the altitude. I'll never forget that feeling of fatigue after barely starting a workout. We didn't think there was any way we'd be ready.

Back in Homer, I wore a cowboy hat to the starting gate at most races, and once the official gave the ten second warning, I'd ceremoniously hand it to one of my teammates. I thought I was pretty cool. But when it came time to leave Homer, they took me aside.

"Look, Kilcher. We don't want anyone outside thinking we're a bunch of hicks, so leave that cowboy hat and your boots at home."

I understood. Compared to where we were going, my need for my cowboy identity was no big deal. I'd go as a normal person in a suit and tie. But I felt naked.

And wouldn't you know it, the first night out was for the welcoming ceremony, and the theme of the Junior Nationals was cowboys. Everyone was wearing cowboy hats and boots. Gorgeous ski babes from across the United States all wearing cowboy hats and boots, and for the first time in my sorry life, I could have fit right in. And all my authentic cowboy gear was back at home in Homer.

The first race was a ten-kilometer race. I didn't have a good day. I think I finished about thirtieth out of sixty-some. Then came the relay, four to a team. I was the anchor man.

I should have taken what had happened to me earlier that day as an omen. Dick Mize, our cross-country coach, asks me to go and get him a pair of practice skis, and while I'm running with them, I cross a snow berm, dig in a tip, and break it. Little do I know, that's not the worst trouble we're going to have.

The race starts and by the time the third man on our team tags me in the starting area, we're in second place. I'm sure I can catch and pass the first place man because he doesn't have a big lead. Each leg is only five kilometers. After two or three, I can see him. Sure enough, I'm gaining.

Then *crack!* I break my tip. Darn wooden skis back then. I'm wearing a plastic slip-on tip around my waist, I stop and whip it on. But now I've lost time and need to make it up. I know I can still do it! I can win this race for Alaska, for Homer, for our team. This isn't some Swiss-mountain-village fantasy, this is Winter Park! This is the Junior Nationals. This is *real!*

Suddenly, I fall, *crack!* I break the same ski, this time just in front of my binding. I hop along as best I can, asking all the bystanders if they have my size boot so I can use their ski. No match for my size forty-six. The rules say you have to finish on at least one of your own skis.

At this point, there's maybe one kilometer left. Having to hop with that broken ski to keep in from digging into the snow is not going to work, so I take it off. Now I'm a scooter. I'm kicking once in a while with my boot, but mostly I'm poling to beat the band and balancing on my one remaining ski. It's a slight downhill and the finish line is in sight.

At this point I'm just hoping I have enough of a lead on the third-place man that I can hold on to second. The crowd is roaring. What a noise. I might not be winning, but I'm making one hell of a spectacular finish.

I have only yards to go! I hear the announcer saying, "And here comes the last skier for the Alaska team still holding on to second place! It looks like he's finishing the race on just one—"

*Crack!* My one remaining ski breaks.

"On … *half a ski!*"

I fall when it breaks, just in front of the finish line and crawl across. Not exactly the finish I had in mind. Four breaks in one day! That has to be some kind of a record. But I did finish on one ski, sort of, so our team was officially second.

I got back to Homer without winning any races. I hadn't even done that well. But it was another experience that stayed with me, shaped me. No, it wasn't the Olympics, but I was out there competing against the country's best. Experiences like that stay with you. Winter Park, Colorado. I'll have to go back there someday.

When I got out of college and moved back to Alaska I did some racing. In Anchorage, back in the late '70s and '80s, they had a Tuesday-night race series. I usually placed third in my age group. I was in the thirty-five-to-forty-year-old age bracket. I'll never forget one race. Back then we were still classic-skiing, skate-skiing still hadn't been sanctioned. It was a good old mass start on a lake. Lots of room to spread out. And yes, lots of us skated across the lake till we hit the classic trail.

And there on the starting line was … Tom Besh. I had lost touch with him over the years. We took off. It was just me and Tom. Just like the old days. He pulled out front and I was right behind him for the first three hundred yards or so, then he pulled away, and a whole slew of younger and fitter skiers blew by me. Tom did really well. I didn't. But when the paper came out, there we were on the front of the sports page. Out front. Me and Tom. I saved that paper for a while.

I kept skiing on and off, competing once in a while. I always did fairly well even though I was never in top shape. I kept telling myself that if I ever trained really hard again, I could be at the top of my age group. I figured I was at the top of the pile back in high school, no reason why I couldn't be there again.

I have done a lot of things over the years to stay in shape. Aside from just living an active lifestyle, I also run, bike, hike, and swim. I try to throw in a bunch of sit-ups and push-ups and other floor exercises even though I hate them. As I age and my active lifestyle isn't as active, I find myself having to do more on the old floor. But skiing is a whole other thing. Although I do it to race and do it to stay in shape, I mostly do it because I love it.

Back in '07, I spent a winter in Bend, Oregon, doing some hard cross-country skiing, racing almost every week, and getting some top-level coaching. I have done a lot of coaching in my day, and I have been coached by many people, but I learned tricks and techniques from this coach I had never known.

Every year, National Masters ski competitions are held. This is a chance for skiers of any age to compete against other skiers in their age bracket. Since I was fifty-nine, I was in the fifty-five-to-fifty-nine age bracket. That year, the National Masters was held in Bend, and I competed. I didn't do all that well, taking fifth.

The following summer, I roller-skated all summer. So, by the time the snow hit I was in pretty good shape. I returned to Alaska and kept skiing and racing. In 2009 and 2014, the Masters races were held in Anchorage. I won both of those. Although I was proud of my accomplishments, I also realized that some of the best skiers in the US were not competing.

When I am skiing, I am in the zone. I feel young and strong. I feel like I am back in high school. Until I fall down. Last winter, I was out skiing by myself in a blinding blizzard. I missed a turn and fell down in the deep snow off the trail. It was hilarious. I damn near couldn't get up and out of there. And I was too proud to take off my skis. The rule of thumb for guys my age is: don't fall! Oh, yes—also, don't go out skiing by yourself.

Well, it's about time to call it a day out here on the ski trail for now. Just one more little side trail, and we'll be at the finish line. I promise I saved the best for last.

For some reason, my dad was never at the start or the finish line of any of my races. In high school, I quit expecting it. When I was a frazzled dad with kids of my own, I found out how hard it was to get to all my kids' functions. Regardless, any kid wishes to have their parents there to cheer them on. To be proud of them. To compliment them on their hard training.

As I mentioned earlier, my dad had been a cross-country ski champion in Switzerland. He knew about training and racing. Throughout my adult life when he saw me out running or skiing he would ask me, "What are you training for?" When I answered him that I was not training for a race, just running for exercise, he would shake his head and walk away. He was of the old school that believed if a man had enough energy to waste it exercising, he wasn't working hard enough.

When I was forty-five, I raced in the forty-two-kilometer Homer Marathon. It started at Lookout Mountain and ended close to Homer. Remember—where I won my first ski race? Right! So, I tell my dad the race is starting up where he used to take us skiing, and I ask him to come to the start. Somehow, I still hadn't given up on my dad seeing me race. I could have told him just to come to the finish, but for some reason, I didn't want to make it too easy on him. To get to the Lookout ski trails he'd have to drive ten miles in toward Homer on East End road, then another ten miles up a steep, winding, icy, and snow-covered road. All of this in his old, beat-up, rusty Subaru. Once there, he'd still have to walk fifty yards through deep snow to get to the starting line.

I already know he's not going to show up. But something in me can't help but keep an eye out and ear tuned.

The thing was, I'd know if he was there. My dad always stood out, even when he was younger. As an elderly gentleman, he stood out even more. He sported a neatly trimmed gray beard and brown mustache. The mustache never did turn gray. Unless it got bitter cold and he needed something warmer, he always wore a beret. He looked like a poet or an artist. In winter, he wore shoepacs which were usually unlaced, a baggy down coat, and baggy wool trousers.

He was well loved and well known around town. He was a fixture at the post office, where he stood reading his mail and visiting with friends. He was an avid chess player and never missed a chance to stop at several of the local cafés to play chess with his chess buddies.

In part, he was known for being the head of the musical Kilcher clan. He was, of course, also famous for his political contributions to the state. Many people had seen or heard of his rare color documentary film on early homesteading. He always had a sparkly eyed, friendly nod for everyone.

But the skiing community knew and respected him for a different reason. He was one of those rare old-timers who used to get around on skis. He relied on them for transportation.[1]

At the start of the race, I hear them give the ten-minute warning. I do a few more warm-up laps, use the port-a-can a couple more times, jump up and down and swing my arms to keep my hands warm. It's time to get to the starting line. Skiers start to gather.

The excited prerace chatter dies. Spectators and even some skiers start moving toward the road. Noticing a shift in the energy, I look in that direction. And there, a ski babe under each of his arms, comes my daddy! Every few steps he sinks in past his knees and they pull him back up to the surface. He takes a couple more steps and sinks again, all the time smiling and hanging on to his gorgeous guides.

---

1. In fact, he and his big wide boards were honored and featured at the end of one of the recent Homer Marathon races. There was a write-up and some old photographs on a bulletin board at the finish line.

His shoepacs are unlaced and filling up fast with snow. Now he's surrounded with friends, many hands reaching out to help him. Young friends are helping the old pioneer across the snowfield; fellow skiers have gathered to help the old ski-meister to the starting line. He's all smiles, his cheeks red and face aglow.

I'm too moved to move. I'd been smiling so long it feels frozen in place. I can't stop nodding my head up and down.

*Well I'll be darned. He finally made it!*

The scene of my eighty-year-old, pioneering, homesteading, skiing dad slowly making his faltering but steady way to that starting line, was just too precious to me. He was loved by all and as more than a friend. He was a father figure, a grandfather. And I think he was filling more than just my void that day.

The crowd around him slowly fades and I can see only him. My daddy. Coming to watch me for the first time … since I won my first race not too far from here when I was only six.

He's barely made it. But he smiles and waves and I smile back and raise my ski pole in salute. Many other ski poles go up as well. We all get ready and the gun goes off.

I'm in heaven the whole race. I don't even care anymore how well I do. I just want to get to the finish line and see if he makes it there. That might be asking a little too much, but what the heck? It could be my day.

I race hard and get to the finish line. No dad. I hang out watching the other racers come in and visit with friends. Still no dad. Slowly I'm having to admit he's not going to show up. Oh well, he was there for the start. But the little boy in me just can't leave. And it pays off! I look up and there he is! *Glory be!*

I go to him and ask if he found his way okay.

"Ya, ya," he says in his Swiss accent. "I stopped by Latitude 59 and got in a chess game and lost track of time. How long ago did you get here?"

I smiled. My anxiety and annoyance disappeared. It didn't matter. He'd come to the start and the finish. He'd come a long, long way. We'd both come a long way that day.

Skiing is seldom about winning great races, or winning at all. It's all about adding up a thousand-and-one little moments, making lasting memories like that one with my dad. Little moments, like twenty-five-year-old Megan passing me one year during the Homer Marathon. She passed me just before the finish line, in a big muskeg. The very same area where I taught her how to skate ski when she was a gangly fourth grader. It was the first time she'd ever beaten me. Today, she is one of the top skiers in the state in her age group, married to the man who is now *my* coach. Little moments, like crossing a highway in another marathon and seeing my son Atz Lee there nestled in the snow bank with my grandson Etienne. He'd brought Etienne to watch Grandpa race. Little moments, like my son Nikos coming out to yesterday's Homer Marathon to cheer me on, taking time out of his life and day for me. Little moments, like betting my twenty-eight-year-old stepdaughter Hanni a dinner that I could beat her—which I did, barely. Little moments, like crust skiing in the spring with my wife, kids, and friends.

Little moments, skiing up the partially snow-covered ice of the Bradley River.

*Sometimes skate skiing,*
*sometimes ice skating with skis,*
*steering with ski pole tips.*
*Spring sun reflecting and dancing,*
*off crystal clear ice.*
*Blinding, dazzling!*
*Gorge narrowing, more open water now.*
*Cliffs closing in,*
*river narrower,*
*Water swifter.*
*Careful!*
*I'm all alone.*

*Many animals pass this way.*
*The wolf left his sign,*

*his message was clear.*
*This is his river.*
*He came shopping,*
*for something hopping,*
*or sliding.*

*The rabbit, who does not swim,*
*can finally visit relatives,*
*on the poor side of the tracks.*

*Only Mr. River Otter lives here.*
*Summer and winter,*
*Above and beneath.*
*He leaves running paw prints*
*and the long sliding glide marks,*
*of his belly.*
*He speaks to me*
*through the Morse code*
*of his dots and dashes.*
*He likes to play here also,*
*within these canyon walls*
*of this outdoor church.*

*Out of ice, only open water ahead.*
*Time to leave*
*the green and blue colors*
*of icicle-covered cliffs.*
*Time to leave*
*this gurgling, giggling wilderness playground.*

*Time to leave*
*my tracks*
*with theirs.*

*Time to return*
*to reality,*
*to my home.*
*To plan*
*and prepare to return.*
*Here.*

My cell phone rings. To my great delight, it is Dick Mize, my Alaska team Nordic coach from '66. He still skis, and he still competes. He has attended numerous World Masters competitions. He beat them all. Many times. We're talking world gold! Talk about good timing. He reached me on my cell phone just before I disappeared up the gorge and lost service. So, his spirit is with me as well on my solo icy heroes journey.

Two weeks later, I took my nephew Eivin up there. Now he knows the way. Now he can take *his* kids and nephews there someday. These are the kind of moments I'm talking about. Some you can plan, but most just happen.

Skiing, to me, is more about staying in touch with something greater, more about enjoying life, the out-of-doors, your body and your health. Skiing isn't just a lifetime sport, it's a social network, a family, a way of life.

My dear old daddy, rest his soul, can shake his head all he wants, but it's all his fault, this skiing business I've been involved with all my life and still am. He was my first ski coach. And it was being carried on his strong back that I first saw the snow fly by while gliding on cross-country skis through the forest.

# COMING HOME

# CHAPTER 15

## *He's Still Screaming*

He can't remember for sure how old he was. It doesn't really matter. He was young. He sees his three older sisters more clearly in his memory, and guesses his age to be somewhere between five and seven.

In his mind's eye, he is on a hayrack being pulled by an old Ford tractor his father is driving. His three sisters are running alongside. They're heading out to get more hay. The sisters are quickly being left behind, laughing and playing as they run to catch up. He's by himself back there hanging on for dear life behind that noisy tractor. Dad seldom looks back when he's in a hurry or working hard or in a bad mood.

He is not sure why he has to revisit that scene of long ago yet one more time. Maybe he's like an archaeologist returning to the site of a dig, hoping his careful screening will turn up a crucial artifact missed earlier, a missing piece to the puzzle to help him better understand what once took place there.

The hay, which was used to feed the cows and horses on the homestead in those days, was usually put up long, mowed and raked with a team of horses. Otherwise it was worked with a pitchfork. When it was dry, it was either stacked in the field to be hauled in over the snow with a team of horses during the winter or with the tractor and the hayrack as soon as it was dry.

Picture a big raft made out of small, crisscrossing spruce poles, roughly fourteen feet long and ten feet wide. A true homestead invention. The amount of hay on this rack was as high as we could throw it with our pitchforks. The kids usually clambered up, trying not to pull off any hay, and rode back to the haystack on top of the pile. Going back out to the field for another load, sometimes they rode on the empty rack, but it was dangerous. No one had to be told; the older kids helped the younger ones. But this time, the youngest one, being easy to lose track of, sort of fell through the cracks.

He was barefoot, as were all the kids during those early homestead summers. He remembers many autumns only begrudgingly returning to his shoes after the first snowfall. His soles were as tough as leather.

As the tractor pulled out of the yard, heading back up the hill for another load of hay, he decided last minute to jump on the hayrack. Some of the older kids could stand on the rack and keep their balance, sort of like surfing. He always sat securely on a cross pole, with feet firmly braced and hands hanging on for dear life. Usually his sisters were there to hold him. The ground was a green blur as his father put that old Ford tractor into fourth gear, and bumped his way across the rough hay meadow.

How exactly it happened he doesn't know. But it doesn't really matter. It happened. His foot slipped through the rack while flying over a bump. When that heavy spruce pole rack came back to earth it landed on top of his young, tender ankle.

The pain is intense, but he does not cry out. He is sure his ankle is broken. But he knows that if he cries out, something bad will happen. His hands tighten their grip to keep him from being pulled farther under the rack. He is in full survival mode. He is doing everything he can do, holding on with all his strength, telling himself over and over again that they will soon come to a stop. He is thankful that his ankle has gone numb. He is thankful that the rest of him has gone numb as well. All of his energy, all of his will, all of his thoughts are focused on hanging on. Even at that age, he is a veteran of enduring. Without complaining. Without crying for help. Without screaming.

At least, not out loud.

The tractor comes to a stop. The young boy quickly pulls his leg out from under the sled. His father doesn't notice. His sisters catch up. They do not notice. A fine actor he has already become, still screaming silently, with a frozen smile on his face.

Now, years later, for the life of him, he can find no new clues during this visit to the old memory. No new evidence to answer the mystery as to why he would not scream out loud. What would cause such a vitally natural and important reflex to be so completely silenced? Extinguished? What pain did he fear would befall him greater than the pain in his ankle if he screamed for help?

As he sits there on that hillside all these years later, he closes his eyes in the warm autumn sun. The better to see into the past. The better to feel what that young boy felt. The better to hear the far-reaching effect of that silent scream that day. And sitting there, he realizes he has found the clues.

It is really quite simple. He has been screaming silently all his life. Always that scream, always that anger, right there under the surface. The fear to scream for help. The fear of being weak. The fear of not being strong enough or good enough. The anger and pain of the knowledge that admitting your pain and asking for help is simply not an option. In fact, he knows that revealing his pain to his father will cause him a much more serious pain. He realizes how early that must've begun. Somehow, because of the pain and fear a child's pain brought up for his father, the father had to punish, had to silence the pain of his children.

The movie of the boy's life runs. He watches in more detail than he ever has, and understands on a higher level. The boy on the sled learned his lessons well, as all survivors of such childhoods do. The trick is unlearning. But when you learn hard lessons young, they stay with you. They are imprinted deeply. It can take a lifetime to unlearn them.

He sees wives and children. He sees his sisters and brother. He sees close friends and coworkers. And he watches scene after scene of how that silent scream that once served to keep him safe from further injury has become his lifelong enemy.

Other little clues begin emerging. He recalls the first time he went to marriage counseling with wife number one. After several sessions, the therapist looked at him and said, "You are a very angry person." If she truly saw all that anger beneath the surface, she must've been very brave to confront him so matter-of-factly with no fear that he would go into a rage. Age thirty-five. He had never seen himself as an angry person.

He fast-forwards through the scenes where he slaps his first wife for the first and only time. The beginning of the end. The realization that the die is cast—he is becoming his father. He forces himself to put the movie back to normal speed and watch. He came here to learn.

He sees another wife grabbed roughly by her arm to pull her out of his space because he knows of no other way to get what he needs. A few years later, another wife poked that sleeping screaming monster. He throws her to the ground, away from the entrance to that cave where the demon lives.

He watches scenes between him and his brother, now in their thirties. Hardest to watch are those scenes with his father, the man who gave him life, the man who should be revered, respected, and looked up to. He sees so clearly how that silent scream held in too long could only be released through physical anger. Yet he also can see that anger now for what it was: an attempt to give something back to the owner, the source. To give back what he should never have been given.

He came here to dig and dig he must. In places where he has never dug before and in places where he has, always looking for finer pieces. For the final pieces. Acceptance and forgiveness are his tools. And, of course, courage. For without courage he would not have come back to these ancient ruins.

That was someone else, he tells himself. I am not that person anymore. That allows him to continue excavating, allows him to chuckle, to ponder what happened back there in another time.

He raises his head and gazes across beautiful meadows gently rolling toward the water, the ones he and his sister and his brother helped clear by hand. Thousands of roots and sticks were pulled from the soil, piled, and burned. Hundreds of pounds of grass seeds had been sown by hand, walking around and around and around those ten- and twenty-acre meadows. Hard work pulling sticks and roots. Easy to forget, to take for granted these lush green hay meadows. But it's so important to think back on what they were, what it took to bring them to where they are now. Hard work—a gift, a skill he thanks his pioneer parents for.

He hears his father's voice, as he often does since he passed away. "I may have given you some tough grounds, Son, but I also gave you the tools you would need to work it."

He bows his head once again and goes back to work. One of the last reels in his collection of family movies, the title written in his mind with a Sharpie on a piece of masking tape, "Young Father."

He sees the young father smack his children around a time or two. He sees himself spanking a young child's bare bottom until it is red to stop her from screaming. It doesn't work. She keeps screaming. He stops. He makes a vow never to spank again because he feels a monster in his hand and arm leading to the cave.

Instead, he grabs his children by their shirt or coat front and shakes them while screaming in their faces. He sees and hears the belittling, the shaming, the blaming. All to hold back that silent scream. He knows no other way.

That reel has run out, thank God.

Thank God, he is still able to accept and forgive that younger version of himself. It is becoming clearer to him how that silent scream has affected his entire life.

He turns his head and glances across the field of wildflowers toward his father's grave. He directs that same gentle acceptance and forgiveness he's received for himself in that direction. And now he realizes, after having traveled all this way, there is still more digging to do.

His memory drifts back. It slips and slides down that steep muddy and narrow canyon road leading to the beach. Back then it was barely wide enough for a small farm tractor. The higher you climbed up the canyon wall, the steeper and farther was the sheer drop off to the canyon creek below.

The old Ford tractor had a box built on the back hanging off the back axles. In that box his father would pile heavy chunks of natural coal gathered from the beach. That coal heated the log cabin. That coal cooked the food. Gathering that coal was a high priority on the list of tools for surviving in the wilderness.

There was one major problem with putting too much coal in that box. It caused the front wheels used for steering to come off the ground. When that happened there was no steering; the front of the tractor went wherever it chose. It could rear up like a wild bucking bronco. One wrong move and it could lurch over the edge of the cliff before it could be stopped.

The fix that was eventually added was easy. A box was built sticking out from the front of the tractor, which was also loaded down with coal. But that was only thought of years later. In the meantime, the weight of young children's bodies precariously perched on the hood of the tractor would have to be enough to keep the steering wheels on the ground. If you have enough kids equaling enough weight, no need for a box.

Thinking back, he shakes his head. He's not sure if his dad was just lazy, chose a quickest solution at the time, or had no clue the terror he was putting his young son through.

He doesn't have to close his eyes very hard and he is right back there hanging onto the hood of that tractor. His bare heels are tucked under the hood on each side. If he sticks them under too far, his heels get hit by the whirring fan blade. If he moves his feet too far from the fan, they get burned by the exhaust. If he slides back too far going up the steep side road on the cliff, his back comes in contact with the red-hot exhaust pipe going straight up out of the tractor hood.

So, rather than tucking his feet under too far, he squeezes with his calves as hard as he can against the hood. He hangs on for dear life, one hand on the radiator cap, which is also getting hot, and the other hand reaching to the front of the hood, fingers digging into the grate of the radiator grill.

His feet and back are hot. His calves are burning from exertion. His hand and fingers and arm muscles ache. But all that is nothing. It's managing his fear that he has most trouble with. Holding in that scream for help. That cry that wants to say, "Daddy, I can't do this. Please, don't make me."

It's only him on the hood this time. Not very old, not much weight, not much good. The tractor comes off the ground with its front end. Swings to the left toward the bank, comes back down. His dad straightens it back out. Another bump and it comes back off the ground. This time it bucks toward the edge of the cliff. His dad quickly steps on the clutch and the brakes to stop the tractor. The young boy begins breathing again. Then it all starts over as the tractor continues up the canyon.

Sitting there on that graveside hillside all those years later, he finds that going back to that steep road was a tougher journey than he had planned for. He is crying. Trying to find that place of forgiveness for his father. Trying not to feel the pain of that young boy on the hood of that old Ford tractor, desperately hanging on for dear life. That young boy somehow believing it is his fault. He is not heavy enough.

He is not good enough.

It becomes so much clearer. His father was battling his own demons. In the middle of the wilderness with a wife and children who depended on him. Perhaps he too had trouble asking for help. Perhaps there was no one close by to ask.

Puzzle pieces finally come together. The old family movies become more current ones. He watches his journey through years of therapy, through years of reading self-help books, through years of studying psychology and social work, years of trying legal and illegal drugs, painkillers and medications. A long, steep road. A rough homestead meadow full of roots and sticks and stumps and stones. But he keeps working. With old tools his parents gave him. With new tools he has gathered along the way.

He sees his life like a car being driven too fast down a snow-covered country road. High berms of snow on each side of the road. The car is careening and bouncing from snowbank to snowbank in a zigzagging pattern but somehow manages to keep going.

Bouncing from one extreme to the other. Trying on one hand to keep it all in, to say nothing, to remain silent, not asking for help. He realizes it was as much a matter of not realizing he needed help as it was not wanting to ask—or knowing how to ask.

Held in too long, keeping that scream silent too long, inevitably always resulted in the same thing. Anger, screaming, and blaming. When you are hurting that badly, so afraid to ask for help, there *has* to be someone to blame. There *has* to be someone or something causing that pain. Someone else *has* to be responsible.

Of course, there was another option besides anger and blaming. Get drunk. Get stoned. Go numb. He tried them all and none of them worked too well. It could be argued that those options were even worse than the screaming.

He glances again toward his father's grave. This is a perfect place to be doing this work. Exhausting work! Thankfully, he is almost done. He finds the last piece. He's down to the last memory reel.

This one is titled "Vulnerability." A couple of his less-educated, more country-bumpkin inner selves put their hands over their mouths and chuckle cynically. He can hear them whisper, "Oh, boy, this one's gonna be fun. Looks like some good new age psychobabble, foo-foo bullshit coming up here! Good thing he's running out of old home movies or there would be one on yoga or veganism. Let's get out of here and go play a game of horseshoes."

That's a good place for them. He lets them go.

He can't help but think of that expression, "It was like pulling nails." He replaces that worn-out phrase with, "It was harder than pulling roots." Thinking about vulnerability as he closes his eyes, he sees one of those now perfectly smooth meadows that once had the deepest, hardest roots to pull. Stumps that were anchored far below the surface of the ground. Stumps that had to be blasted out with dynamite. Stumps that had to be pulled out with teams of horses. Stumps that had to be dug out with picks and shovels. Those were the old-school tools used by pioneers. Tools used to make back-breaking work easier.

Vulnerability. A most necessary tool for excavating. For digging out and extracting old pains and memories. For smoothing and planting fertile fields. Fields that would nourish and heal his soul. New frontiers with room for his children to grow safely.

The hardest tool he has ever had to learn how to use. Because to use it, meant asking for help. It meant getting over deep-seated fears. It meant that showing someone who you really were would not hurt you, but help you. A very foreign and difficult concept to grasp.

He marvels in disbelief at how far he was able to come without this vital tool. He is thankful for those teachers, those books, but mostly his children, who have helped him develop the courage to become vulnerable. He is thankful for that voice from one of his greatest teachers, saying, "That wasn't you, you're someone else now." He is thankful for his wife who loves him strongest when he is most vulnerable, more willing to admit he's lost, doesn't have a clue.

He is the son of a homesteader. It is hard to give up. It is hard not to try to salvage that old building. It is hard to believe that starting over, sometimes from scratch, admitting you do not know how to build and need help, is the only way to rebuild yourself. The only way to reclaim yourself, to remember who you really were meant to be.

He has grown, and his progress can be summed up in three steps or stages. First, he saw the unhealthy pattern of blaming others for his pain and fear. Then, as he became more conscious of it, he began to blame less often. Finally, he learned to fight the demon inside instead. Instead of punishing others for hurting him, he began to take on that deeply entrenched demon.

He knows his progress can seem small. He still feels the desire to fight. But there is a difference between feeling and doing. It is big progress. Any former abuser who can say, "Right now, I am battling being a real schmuck. Please give me a little time to find my center," is making progress. That's real relationship work, some of the toughest there is.

He's tired. It's been a long day. But like many hard-working days here on this homestead where he was raised, he sees the fruits of his labor. Not piles of hay this time. Not stacks of wood or coal. Not miles of fences built. But a growing inner peace. A gentle sense of self-acceptance and forgiveness. A growing belief that in spite of his failed vows to be the perfect father, he is worthy of his children's love, forgiveness, and acceptance as well.

> *We are warriors, we are warriors, the first*
> *    syllable is war,*
> *Four generations of fighters, tell me what*
> *    have we been fighting for?*
> *We are warriors, we are warriors, but we*
> *    can fight no more, It is time to lay*
> *    down and surrender our samurai*
> *    swords.*

# CHAPTER 16

# Final Truce

My mother came to visit last month. It was her third trip back to Alaska since she and my dad divorced back in '69. They emigrated from Switzerland in the late thirties and had homesteaded twelve miles east of Homer. They had been married almost thirty years.

Yule, with Ruth at his side, cleared land by hand, traveled by horse and wagon, and raised eight children. They lived a remote subsistence lifestyle. What they couldn't raise on their farm came from the wilderness. The forest, swamps, and meadows gave mushrooms and berries, moose and black bear, fiddlehead ferns and wild teas. The ocean and rivers were rich with salmon and trout, shrimp and crab.

Because my father was a constitutional delegate for the state of Alaska, he helped draw up the constitution for the forty-ninth state. When he later went on to spend one term as state senator, all of this, along with having made the only early color film documenting pioneering in Alaska, gave us a high-profile life.

My mother was active in community and civic affairs. She was well known for her beautiful voice, her writing and poetry, and her knowledge of wild mushrooms. She wrote for the *Homer News* and the *Anchorage Daily News*. She was also on the local school board. They were not the ordinary pioneers of that era.

Our family performed on radio and on the stage in Alaska and Europe. Our faces were on postcards sold during intermission on my father's lecture and film tours. Our entries of homemade bread, vegetables, and livestock won blue ribbons at state fairs. We entertained governors and senators at our log cabin table, with feasts prepared by my mother. We posed for countless publicity and political photos.

The public could not understand why my mother wanted out of this high-profile, idyllic, and close-knit wilderness family. The judge who presided over the divorce called it one of the most tragic he had ever been involved with. Few townspeople knew the truth, maybe one or two close friends. My mother was not one to complain to others. But the family knew. We saw and heard what happened within the four walls of our small two-room log cabin. But my mother experienced it, she felt it. Only she knew when it was time to go.

My view of the tragedy was different than that of the public. I was genuinely happy that she had decided she was through being a victim, that she was ready to start a new life. It was a warm and satisfying feeling to know that there was another man in her life who appreciated her many wonderful qualities, a man who finally treated her gently and lovingly. For me, the tragedy was that my mother walked away without a single dime or acre of land. She wanted out and she was willing to pay the highest price.

She had left it all behind one other time. At the rise of Hitler, she had left Switzerland for the freedom of America, taking along only one suitcase. This time, less idyllic, older, and wiser, she was escaping a thirty-year war with my father to a freedom far from the Alaskan homestead. This time again, taking only a few earthly possessions.

She didn't need much, and her folders of writing took up little room. There was poetry in her heart, waiting to be written, needing only a softer page. There were love songs on her lips, long since silent; she heeded their welcoming stirring melodies. These she took with her. With these she had come to him, something he had not been able to take away from her.

She walked away from the smokehouse where she had smoked thirty years of moose, bear, and fish. She walked away from the dirt cellar where she had stored tons of canned and bottled meats, vegetables, and jellies. She walked away from the meadows and forests where she had hunted and gathered. Where she had shot the moose, picked the low-bush cranberries and mushrooms in the fall, the dandelions and nettles in the spring. She walked away from the rolling hay fields she had helped clear and plant, and the tons of hay she had helped cut with the hand scythe and later the horse mower.

She walked away from the log house she had helped build with broadax and crosscut saw, where she conceived and raised eight children, the table where she homeschooled them and taught them poetry and music. She walked away from the kitchen and woodstove where she had made home brew and homemade bread, pastries, and desserts from the dozens of eggs she had gathered and the gallons of rich cream she had separated and the pounds of butter she had churned. She walked away from her greenhouse and driftwood-bordered flower gardens that were her source of pride and inspiration. They were never replanted. She walked away and vowed never to set foot in that house again, a vow she kept with pioneer determination.

The first time she came back, she stayed with my sister Mossy in Homer. She and her husband, Rod, drove out the old dirt road toward the homestead, but she had him stop a quarter of a mile from the house. That was as close as she wanted to go.

My father heard that she was in town and reacted with hurt and panic. No one had told him! Mother did not want him to know. But it is a small town and word got to him. He jumped in his car and drove like a madman out the dirt road toward Mossy's house. A friend met him racing out the road. Hearing where he was headed, he ran to a phone to tip us off.

My mother reacted with surprising speed and exterior calmness. "Take me to von off yor cabins so I can hide," she stated curtly and firmly, "I don't vant to see him." It seemed a bit dramatic yet also very familiar, we all fell into our old family roles. I walked her, as quickly as she could go, up to a guest cabin. Her eyes were focused on the safety ahead. Her face held only resolve and determination. Her pace, though slow, was a steady and strong march. Her breathing was heavy, her hand shaking as she held my arm.

After she left, my father was shaken for weeks. He seldom spoke of anything else. He had hoped for forgiveness, but there had been none. He felt he was the laughingstock of the whole town. He could not understand why she had not gotten over it after all these twenty years since the divorce, why they could not be on friendly terms. I once asked my mother. Her answer took no pondering and was immediate and simple. "He has never said that he is sorry." My mother's refusal to see him during this first visit was an even stronger indictment against him than the divorce had been.

The second time she came back was for a family reunion, which was in '90. Her husband did not accompany her this time. It was my uncle's eightieth birthday party, a good opportunity to have a reunion. Edwin, my father's older and only brother, had always played an important role in our family. He had no children and was very generous with his money. However, it was not talked about openly that our clothing and Christmas gifts were often a result of his generosity. This generosity was also the source of much tension and many fights between my parents. My father felt that Edwin was buying our affection and that he and mother were plotting against him. Though he was a lot like my father, he was also able to show us the love and affection which my dad had difficulty doing.

This was the first occasion since the divorce that all eight of us kids would be together with mom and dad. Once again, this reunion was a type of gift from my uncle Edwin. No one else could have pulled it off. Because it was a public place, my mother was not too uncomfortable, though she kept one or two of us with her at all times. She visited freely with old friends and acquaintances, smiled, and was her charming public self, but she always kept a watchful eye out.

I called everyone together, taking a moment to separate ourselves from the public by drawing a foldable partition wall. I wanted for us to be alone together again, even if just for a moment. We all sat there in a circle, in silence, but it wasn't uncomfortable. It felt good, it felt like family. I looked around the room at my grown siblings and aging parents. Once we had shared a life together, depended on each other, lived in a log cabin together, played and worked and sang together. And, surely, my parents must have once loved one another; they certainly had shared many years.

My father and mother were now seventy-eight and seventy, respectively. She had traveled from Tennessee. There were eight children, ranging in age from forty-eight to thirty-three. One sister had come from the East Coast, one from Okinawa, another from Germany. The rest of us still lived near our dad in our hometown of Homer. We'd traveled far since those days on the homestead. We had gotten married and divorced, had children and grandchildren. We became machinists, schoolteachers, officers in the marines, tour guides, businesswomen, and construction workers. We were creative artists and musicians, poets and writers. We had a healthy respect for the earth and its creatures. We all were a small part of Yule and Ruth, and in some way, we were all carrying on what they had started.

During this second visit, I was able to talk my mother into letting me take her to the small fox cabin, where my parents and three older sisters first lived before building the log house. I only lived in this cabin for the first few months of my life. My mother told me she conceived me there, and that was why it had always been so special to me.

In 1948, when I was less than a year old, my father had taken a beautiful photograph of my mother carrying me on her back in an old military rucksack. It was taken just above that old cabin. It has always been my favorite photo of us. She is looking over her shoulder, smiling at me, a beautiful young mother in her twenties. I look at that warm, radiant, and loving face on that photograph today, and I still feel loved.

In the photo, I am holding a budding branch of spring alder, my curly blond hair standing out against a backdrop of glaciers and mountains. My eyes and face are crinkled at the glare of the spring sun on the melting snow.

I had that picture enlarged and framed. It hung in my classroom where I taught music, in a school only one mile from where that photo was taken. Just up the canyon a ways from those childhood meadows and forests where she sang me countless woodland rockabyes.

I had a strong desire to return and take another snapshot in the same place. To get there meant driving her for the first time through the yard, past the old log house, past the spot where her greenhouse once stood, past the old family garden plot and through those green hay meadows flowing gently down to Kachemak Bay and the beach below. It also meant risking running into dad. I could only imagine what she might feel driving past all those reminders of an unresolved and painful chapter of her life that she had walked away from. I felt very grateful that she agreed. I knew she was truly doing it out of love for me.

We arrived at the spot, with my brother-in-law Karl Luts and my sister from Germany, Wurtila, accompanying us and serving as photographers. We struck the same pose of almost fifty years earlier. This time there was a middle-aged man with thinning gray hair standing behind his now shorter gray-haired, aging mother. He holds a twig in his hand and the crinkled nose and eyes are recognizable, but the wrinkled forehead is new. This time, instead of studying the twig that was in his chubby little hand long ago, he returns her love-filled smiling gaze. The love in her eyes and smile hasn't changed, only her face has aged.

Since we were so close, we went on down to the fox cabin and took some more pictures there. I have other old favorites of my mother standing just inside the cabin, looking out the window. Some were taken through the window from the outside, others from behind her, showing her half-profile gazing out the window. She was pregnant with me, and my three older sisters were at her side.

I stood where my father must have stood in early '47 and took a picture of my forty-seven-year-old sister standing looking out the window next to her mama, as she had all those years ago. We also duplicated those taken from the back. The new photos show that same faraway look in her eyes as she gazes out the window to the blue mountains beyond. This time, I am also visible in the photo, fully grown and separate from her now, yet still deeply connected. This time, the old cabin has no roof, the door is gone, and the walls are beginning to rot and buckle.

As we drove back through the yard to take my mother back home, my father was in the garden beside the road. He saw us coming and approached the oncoming car. I asked my mother if she wanted to stop. She confidently said, "Sure, but just roll the vindow down." She inconspicuously reached over and took my hand. Wurtila, from the back seat, reached forward and reassuringly lay her hand on my mother's shoulder. There was something about this scene of running interference and playing the role of the reassuring protector that made me feel right at home.

"Hi there," my father said, "do you want to come in?"

"No, thank you," was her cool reply.

"Did you notice how tall the mountain ash has grown?"

It had grown from a small bush to a thirty-foot-tall tree between '69 and '90.

"Yaa," was her drawn-out answer trying to be polite.

"Would you like some potatoes?" he asked with a voice of a young Tom Sawyer trying to impress a disinterested Becky Thatcher.

"Sure," was her resigned reply.

He barely waited for the go-ahead; he was already busily digging an offering from the good land they had once tilled and toiled on side by side. These potatoes were the seed from those they had first sown in the Matanuska Valley and brought to Homer in '42. He was very proud of the fact that he continued the hill-selecting process all these years, even after she was gone.

He handed her some potatoes through the window. She thanked him in a quiet neutral tone and said goodbye. While he and I exchanged farewells, she squeezed my hand and looked away from him and up the road, that very same forest lane she had taken when she had left him over twenty years before. I knew it was my cue to let off the clutch and make our exit. I had never taken it out of gear. Somewhere up that old dirt road we all started breathing again.

Illness and age had taken their toll by the time of her third and last visit to Alaska. Osteoporosis and rheumatoid arthritis had left her fingers and hands gnarled, her neck and spine bent, and her legs taking slow and halting steps with the aid of a cane. During her previous visits, she still wore her waist-length hair piled neatly on her head, held in place with combs, Swiss style. It had only changed in color, from ripe wheat blond to pale honey silver. This time, however, it was closely cropped, thin and permed, and almost white. She looked like a little, bent-over old lady, like a different person. It was difficult for me not to stare.

Her face, swollen from the Prednisone, showed the pain that her mortal shell was experiencing. The only thing about her that had not changed were her eyes and her voice. To the very end, her voice was always the same. Being a writer and poet, she always took pride in her very clear, concise, and correct command of the English language, even though she spoke with the most beautiful and melodic Swiss accent. Her voice was as familiar, soothing, and comforting to me during this last visit as it had been all my life.

Her spirit had also changed. It had ripened and was stronger and brighter than ever. It was obvious the inner work she had been doing, the preparation for her next "plane of existence," as she called it, was shining through. She was still growing and pioneering new frontiers at age seventy-five, setting her course now toward her "bright shining star."

During this visit, she came to an outdoor potluck at the homestead. It was a momentous occasion. The passing of time, the presence of friends and family, as well as Uncle Edwin again, all made it easier for her to be there. She did not stay long, and did not go into the house. Nonetheless, we all felt good that we were able to spend some time with her on the soil she had put so much of herself into.

The night before she left Alaska, we had another family get-together at my sister Fay's house. My mother felt alright about having my father there so we invited him. This gathering would be close family only, much more intimate than the outdoor potluck. There was tension and apprehension in the air, yet also a sense of calm excitement.

My dad hung out mostly in the living room with the teenagers in front of the TV he always preached against. My mother stayed at the dining room table. People were eating everywhere, and the house was filled with the noise of four generations.

Suddenly, as if on cue, the noise subsided and the focus shifted to the dining room table. We all watched and listened with one eye and one ear only, trying not to be too obvious, with bodies half turned away, not to invade this private moment.

My father, now eighty-three, had come into the dining room unnoticed, and was standing beside my mother's chair. He was leaning down toward her to better hear; he refused to wear a hearing aid. He was wearing a handwoven tweed jacket and matching cap, worn and old, but well kept. He had a kindly look on his face, eager, yet not invasive as he sometimes tended to be. His desperation was replaced by a sort of genuineness and peaceful resignation, yet still seeking some reconciliation.

"I brought you some potatoes," he shouted down to her, much too loudly. "See here, some white, some red, and some banana potatoes. Remember? These are from the special seed we have been hill-selecting since Palmer." He looked so eager, so vulnerable.

Her gnarled hands reached up haltingly to receive the gift. Her face and eyes smiled as she caressed the potatoes and admiringly placed them on the table before her.

"Thank you," she said while looking down at the potatoes. And then again: "Thank you," this time with more feeling, looking up at him.

There was something different about the way she was looking at him, a pregnant look. We all felt the weight of it.

"I see you arr vering dat coat and cap I vove for you in Svitzerland." That had been in '57, almost forty years before.

"That's why I wore it, I was hoping you would notice," still loudly with a proud, almost embarrassed grin.

I wondered how he kept track of it all these years, what trouble and how many boxes he had gone through to dig it out for tonight.

"I noticed," she answered with affirmation. "I noticed."

We all noticed. We all felt the warmth of her handwoven coat on his back. We all tasted the sweet taste of his homegrown potatoes in her hands. And to seven adult children, also products of their weaving and cultivating, it made a small but important difference.

And for just a brief moment, the loom was once again humming, weaving freshly spun yarn, and the rich, dark virgin soil was being cultivated and planted. Two young immigrants in love were seeing the reflection of their unborn children as they gazed into each other's eyes.

Self-consciously, we relaxed our breathing and started moving and talking again. We cleared our throats, snuffled our noses, and wiped our eyes. We turned our backs and moved away slowly, out of respect for these two old veterans of ancient and half-forgotten battles, who with near-deaf ears and gnarled hands were slowly beginning to raise the flag of truce.

# CHAPTER 17

# *My Father's Hands*

Hands are amazing things. They are the instruments that carry out our minds' and our emotions' many requests, from replacing the tiniest screw in the frame of our glasses to wielding a sledgehammer.

Aside from our voice and facial expressions, our hands communicate more than any other body part. I'm not just talking about sign language. In many subtle and not-so-subtle ways, our hands express our feelings and emotion. Hands can express love and acceptance with a mere touch or gesture. Hands can express anger and rejection. Hands can make you feel warm and fuzzy, relaxed, cared for. Hands can make you cry, feel pain, humiliation. Hands can make you run toward or away from.

We all learn early the language of our parents' hands. As they spoon-feed us, stroke us, spank us, dismiss us.

Most of us who have either trained horses or dogs have been told not to discipline with our hands. Use a rolled-up magazine or newspaper when "spanking" our dog. When your horse nips you, give him an elbow in the mouth to teach him not to bite, not a slap with your hand. Why? You don't need to be an animal shrink to figure that one out. Smack that animal enough times with your open hand and he will start seeing it as a weapon to be feared and start flinching or running from it. We've all seen those flinching, cowering dogs, those head-shy horses.

You can untrain that response, or retrain them to see your hands as a source of sugar cubes and doggy biscuits. But believe me, it will take time. The more times that animal has been beaten, the longer it will take, and even then, he may only learn to trust one person's hands, while still fearing all others.

You don't train horses or hang around them without making many mistakes in this regard. I had a mare once who I trained to pick up her hooves with a snap of my finger. I was so proud of this trick. I did it with sugar cubes. I rewarded her at first for just the slightest movement of the hoof I was snapping my finger by, then slowly asked more and more of her. I had to pick it up with my hand a few times, rewarding her each time with sugar. Soon she was picking it up by herself to my finger snap. I have seen many owners of horses get their horses to pick up their hooves, never one by snapping. It was way cool.

Well, one day there was a new electric fence up and I did not show her where it was. It was dark and she walked into it and got zapped. When a horse gets shocked, it makes a loud snapping noise. I happened to be riding her bareback at the time. She snorted, reared up, and spun around. The fence did its job. Oh, yes, she dumped me on the hard, frozen ground.

Now, if you have any horse sense at all, I don't even need to finish this little snapping story. You guessed it! A few days later I had a neighbor over and was going to show off my finger-snapping hoof-raising trick. I walked up to the mare in the pasture, reached down to one of her front hooves and snapped. All hell broke loose! She reared and spun away from me and ran! My neighbor hooted and hollered. "Well, Kilcher, got any more cool tricks you wanna show me?"

Similar thing once happened when I was a teenager and was training one of my first horses to neck rein. Figured if I just whopped her on the side of the head with my coiled lariat rope she would figure out to turn. We were running at a full gallop, she did not want to turn, so I whopped her repeatedly, harder each time. I guess I showed her who was boss. Next time she saw that lariat in my hands she freaked out.

I've gotten a little smarter over the years, but I still make mistakes. I am currently riding a four-year-old colt. I've been bringing him up here to the head of the bay since he was a two-year-old, always with other older horses, only riding him for short stretches and working him a little.

One day I pulled the rifle out of its scabbard and did not notice his head was turned toward me. I jerked it out too fast and the butt of the rifle hit him hard right on his cheek. He jumped, causing the rifle to fly through the air, scaring him further. It's taken me almost two summers of gently and slowly putting that rifle in, and pulling it out, to get him to stand still, to trust me, to stay calm and relaxed.

I'm sure there must be research on this topic, but I know from experience it takes a whole lot of time, patience, and highly rewarding experiences to make up for one little mistake. Think how long it takes to reprogram a horse or dog that has been severely abused. There are folks who specialize in just that sort of thing. Sometimes the scars are too deep, the memories too strong. So, you have a scarred horse, head shy, a flinching cowering dog. Or, worse yet, they are aggressive and dangerous.

So just what in the hell does all this have to do with my father's hands? Patience, my horse-training friends. You wanna hang out with me and horses and my old man, you gotta have patience.

There was a big difference between my dad's voice and his hands. Some might say his words left deeper scars and bruises on my soul and mind than his hands did. One big difference.

Yes. His words and voice touched me in hurtful ways. They humiliated, belittled, embarrassed, made fun of, ridiculed, shamed. Yet there were many times his voice also affected me in positive ways. I was touched by his yodeling, his singing, his storytelling, his humor, his many foreign languages, his knowledge on many subjects, his curiosity, his dreaming—which, after all, brought him to this land. In other words, the good of his voice and words did much to counteract the bad.

His hands, on the other hand, only touched me when hurting.

No hugging, no gentle touching, rubbing, massaging, or tousling my hair. I am sure there was some of that early on, before I somehow became a threat and began to trigger his unresolved issues.

Yes. His voice and words and his hands were all a part of him, but somehow, I saw them as separate entities. With regards to the voice-and-words part of his self, I had a wait-and-see attitude. I did not fear that self unless he was screaming, cussing, or verbally abusing me. His hands, however, I constantly watched. They were either sleeping or awake. If sleeping, I watched them for the slightest twitch of awakening. If awake, I feared them. To survive, I had to learn all the tiny nuances, those many little steps from first awakening to stretching to twitching to moving to gesturing to grabbing, shaking, or slapping. To avoid pain, I had to learn how to quickly get away from, distract, soothe, cower, stoop, obey, admit, or agree. A lot of work for a kid.

\* \* \*

Because I spent my formative years in the wilderness, on trails, and on and around horses, it has shaped how I think about things. To me, talking, writing, storytelling is no different than going for a ride. There's getting ready, the start, the journey, and the end, maybe a little celebrating and hoorah-ing to unwind. Sometimes you come back relaxed, sometimes plumb tuckered out. There are many other useful analogies as well, but this one works for me. I haven't always understood all the trails I've been down, but they all taught me something, if nothing else than never to take that trail again. Sometimes they have taught me not to be hopeless; others traveled this same trail and made it, so I can too.

But no matter the trail, how long or easy or rough, when I get home, I always review. What went well? What went wrong, and why? I can't blame the horse or the trail I chose, or the weather. All I can do is learn from it all and try to pass it on.

I am taking you down this trail of my father's hands to show you how I made it home. So, in case you are lost on that trail, you can find your way by following my track. Maybe even take a few shortcuts. No matter how bad you're lost, take heart. Have hope. There is always a way out, or several ways. Mount up! Hang on! Let's ride!

Sorry I can't take you down the whole trail. Too long. Too hard. Too painful and personal. We'll just hit the high spots.

I had no clue how screwed up I was as a youth until I went to college and studied about kids that were raised like I was. Until I started working as a social worker and reading the labels they put on kids who stole cars, broke into homes, tortured animals, or cut themselves. These kids had some serious labels. Some of them had done some serious time in kiddie jails.

As I looked at some of the rap sheets of these most troubled youth in Alaska's foster homes and institutions, I wrote me up a rap sheet on young Atz. I was quite proud to say it was as long or longer than the worst. Big difference was, I did not go to jail or come under the scrutiny of state social workers. Avoiding the system made me less tough, kept me from a whole separate set of problems. My dysfunction, my scars, my healing journey was just as severe, however.

I had gotten into cutting myself. If you don't understand it, you should read up on it. I cut a cross in the center of my chest and put ashes in it. I read somewhere that the American Natives did it to make nice clean sterile scars. It did leave a nice scar cross. My little bit of adolescent chest hair and my shirt covered it pretty well.

So, I got bold and cut a big "ATZ" underlined on my left forearm. It was pretty nice work. Now I had me a nice cross and my name. I felt good. Had no clue why I was doing it or why it felt good. All I knew was that it felt good doing it and it felt good looking at it.

I was working with my dad in our tack room / shop / storage shed. He saw my name on my arm. I knew the minute he saw it. I always had my antennae out when working with my dad. "What the hell is that?" he screamed. It was the precursor to get his hand awake and mobile, ready for action. I don't remember my answer, I just said something. I knew he didn't really want to know, so I just said something to get it over with. "It" turned out to be a mighty hard slap.

Think about it. Not a little slap, not even a hard slap. This was a reach-way-down, come-off-the-floor, big-callused-hand, grown-strong-man-to-young-teenaged-boy slap.

*WHAP!!!*

I literally did a backward somersault when I hit the floor. My neck hurt for days. Thank goodness that was the last I heard about it. Simple. We worked through it nice and clean and quick in just a few seconds.

*Wonder what got him so worked up over my name on my arm,* I remember thinking at the time. Years, miles, relationships, therapy, and degrees later, I thought something else.

At first it was angry thoughts: *How in the hell could a father, an intelligent and educated father, not see the signs, not have some empathy, not see the open door of invitation into my bruised heart? What a fucking asshole!*

Not until much later, after screaming and dreaming him dead, nightmares of me straddling his body with him on the ground, thumping him with my finger in the middle of his chest, screaming spit in his face, did I begin to soften.

Only then did I wander down different trails: *I can't imagine what he must have been feeling.* His marriage slipping away. His dream of a community in the Alaskan wilderness slipping away. His kids slipping or running away. His oldest son acting out, flunking school. The accumulating pressure of providing for his family, having to leave them alone much of the time. No college degrees or real work skills that could land a steady job with benefits. A liberal, social, political animal on a wilderness homestead in a small, conservative community. A man who was often thought of as a socialist Nazi (even though he was from Switzerland) and a nudist (because we took saunas). A man who really did not fit in, socially or into the typical "homestead scene." He always felt the most himself, at his best, when he was the farthest from Homer, the homestead, his family.

His hands, the tools of his anger, sometimes actually held tools, or sticks, or belts. He seldom, if ever, took the time to plan his punishment, it was usually his hand or whatever he happened to have in it. No more than a reflex. A muscle spasm.

I remember one time he sent me to fetch a hammer from the huge, messy, who-knew-where-anything-was-and-if-it-was-out-of-place-it-was-the-kids'-fault toolshed.

I found myself immediately in that fear zone I had been in many times. Take too long, shit hits the fan. Come back without it, shit hits the fan. Ask for clarification of where it might be in the shop, big shit hits fan. Take a long time *and* bring the wrong tool ... *holy shit!*

All of these different "shit fans" were anything from getting screamed at to being made to run back and forth a few times, being made to clean up the shop, or getting slapped. On this particular holy-shit day, a first happened. That's why I remember it.

After handing him the wrong hammer—after taking way too long to find it—he hauls off and whomps me in the gut with it!

Hey, the bright side, first of all, was he hit me with the flat side instead of the claw part or the thumper part. It also could have been a sledgehammer. Or an ax. And he was thoughtful enough to wallop me in my stomach where no bones would break.

Now, don't feel sorry for me. I'm over it. I've sifted all the good out of it, and gave the rest back to him. I've forgiven him. He could have done better. He could have done worse. But I know he did the very best he could.

The older he got, the more his hands softened, or my image and memories of them did. I always felt guilt though at how I felt toward his hands. I always felt guilt when he asked me to rub his neck and shoulders, or give him a back rub and it was all I could do to not cringe inwardly at having to touch him, his flesh, which had caused me so much pain. After all my healing work, I should be over it. But just like that war veteran, sometimes you never get over the sound of machine guns or incoming mortars. You only learn not to jump or to tell yourself you are no longer there.

I finally let go of my father's fearsome hands on his deathbed. The first time he went to the hospital, near death, it obviously wasn't his time to go. He was very angry, sometimes swearing at the nurses and elbowing people who were trying to help him in and out of bed. He cussed the catheter, he cussed the IVs, he cussed the whole damn hospital. He wanted out. Several times he tried walking out of his room. He was often delirious, mumbling or speaking one of the many foreign languages he knew. The first thing visitors would ask was, "What's the language of the day?" It could be English, French, Italian, or Swiss. And much of it was curses.

When you could understand bits and pieces of his mumbling, it was obvious that he was reviewing his entire life. And it seemed that he didn't like what he was seeing. He finally got stronger, though his heart was still weak, and he went home. Home to the log house he had built in '47, the year I was born. We arranged for someone to stay with him around the clock to help him where needed.

The second time he went to the hospital, I could see his spirit was in an entirely different place. Perhaps that is why he was allowed to move on to the next realm. I was out of the state, and again I came back home to be with him. I was told his heart was failing, and the doctors weren't sure how long the medication would keep it beating. The picture I saw when I entered his room this time was very different. He was totally calm and peaceful. He spoke clearly and lucidly to all around him. He gave advice to his family and even the mayor of Homer. He was back in his rare sense of humor. On one day, the Alaska governor's office called to invite him to some sort of legislative reunion. He answered the phone and said, "Tell the governor that he caught me at a bad time. I'm croaking."

During my growing-up years, I seldom saw my father's tender side, maybe once in a while with my mother or a very young child. After leaving home, I only glimpsed this tenderness when he had a new girlfriend. I seldom, if ever, felt this outpouring of love and affection myself, though I'm sure he was able to show it to me when I was very young.

I remember once during that time, when I was a single dad living next to him on the homestead, I saw that playful tender side of my father. I walked into the open door of his cabin to find him sitting on the couch with his new girlfriend. One of his legs was thrown over hers. Both of his hands were holding both of hers. He was smiling. His usually serious and concerned face was calm and peaceful. Love was radiating from his eyes.

The whole house felt different. I wanted to tell him to sit right there and never move, to hold that pose for a few years while I ran and got my camera. Better yet, while I stayed there to watch. I usually felt jealous when I saw him being that way to others, yet I also felt uncomfortable. I wasn't sure I would know what to do with that love and tenderness if it ever came my way. I don't remember why I went to talk to him, or what about, but I have never forgotten what I felt seeing him looking at her.

When I walked into his hospital room, he looked at me and smiled in excitement. He looked as though he were greeting an old and dear friend. I thought he must be out of it again to be acting this way toward me, maybe he thought I was his girlfriend. As I walked closer to give him a hug and say hello, I could tell it was the real deal. He remained in that extremely loving and gentle place until he breathed his last, a couple days later.

One of the peculiar things he did during his last days was to hold his hands in the air and examine them. He would stare at one hand and then the other, slowly turning them and moving his fingers. Perhaps he was beginning to detach from his body. Perhaps he was thinking about his hands and all they had done. Perhaps he was reviewing the tenderness they had given and the anger they had expressed.

At one point, I was alone with him. He reached his hand out to me, not to shake hands, but more to give me something. It was a gesture that said, "Put your hand in mine." The old fear and apprehension visited for only a moment, then, realizing it was not needed, quickly left the room. My spirit knew this would be a profound moment long before I did.

I placed my hand in his. He pulled it to his face and began kissing it. Soft, tender kisses, and fast, small kisses. He started at the tip of every finger and worked his way up to the back of my hand. When the fingers were done, he kissed the back of my hand, maybe ten or fifteen kisses. Then he kissed the other one the same way, all the while looking into my eyes, as though I were his lover, exactly the way I had seen him look at his girlfriend that day in his cabin.

I never dreamed that forgiveness could be that easy. I felt a delicious warm shower bathing my soul. It washed away any remaining traces of anger, fear, and bitterness, leaving only pure love. Something I had never felt for my father, or from him.

My father was a man of few words when it came to the feelings department. He once told me that he would never say he loved me. That had been in response to my asking him if he did. His idea of showing affection was a tentative pat on the back, a hand on the shoulder, or that occasional hug, if I initiated it, with rapid nervous pats.

I don't know what he was thinking while he was kissing my hand. I do know that he was aware it was me. I also choose to believe that he was saying something to me, that he was passing something on to me, giving me a gift he had never been able to give me since those simple and innocent days I left his lap and somehow became a challenge to him.

I heard him say, "I am sorry, son. Please forgive me. I have always given you my very best, even though it was greatly lacking at times. Right now, this is my best. Please accept and receive it. I have always felt it, but today I feel it even more strongly, and today I am able to show you in a different way. Something has cleared, a blockage is gone. It never was you I was angry at, Son. It never was you who caused me not to be able to show you the tenderness I am showing you now.

"Let this moment be stronger than all the others. Let it wash away all the cold and dark memories once and for all. Add this to all the good inside you and do great things with it. Let go of all that which I piled onto your young shoulders. Give all of that back to me now and let me take it with me and put it where it belongs. Follow my example and take back the burdens you gave your children to carry. Show them the love they unconditionally deserve. Your best can be so much better than mine."

I heard all of that and more. It was a miracle, a rebirth. No born-again Christian ever felt more renewed, more cleansed than I did at that moment. I never would have thought it possible.

My children know some of the things I endured as a boy and young man, many of which I repeated and passed on to them. They know some of the feelings I have harbored and fought to shed. They know some of the challenges my childhood gave me. They know something of which I speak. They were there with me during part of my journey. So, when I say it was a miracle, they know what I am talking about.

The good part is I learned to read folks, observe, watch. Got me a degree in psychology and social work. Helped a lot of troubled youth and families during my career. The bad part is, I am way too sensitive, and I see danger where there is none.

I hear that electric fence snapping all the time. I see that coiled lariat and rifle butt coming at me. I jump and jerk a little less now, sometimes not at all. I have learned to control it. I have stopped blaming and become more accepting of that part of me. I have learned to tell those close to me why I jerk and jump, that it has little to do with them, and I share what they can do to help calm me.

Neither denial or blaming leads to healing. In my years working with troubled and institutionalized youth, I saw plenty of both extremes. Kids who worshiped their physically and sexually abusive parents, who couldn't wait to get back home to them, and kids who wanted to kill them. Believe me, I have spent years in both camps. It takes lots of time and therapy to quit blaming or to not be in denial, but to see things as they really were *and* to then accept yourself as you now are, to try to grieve and heal and move on. Forgiveness of self and others. Acceptance of self and others. Huge concept. Extremely difficult to achieve. But once there we are not finished yet. I believe the highest level we can achieve is then to even feel gratitude, for all that was, which brought us to that which is. Forgiveness. Acceptance.

Gratitude. Hard hard work. The kind of work pioneers and trailblazers of the soul were cut out for.

I have often said that I am closer to my dad now and understand him better, that I can clearly see what made him tick or explode. As I have learned to love and accept him, so have I learned to love and accept myself. The two seem to go hand in hand.

Thanks, Pop. You did a lot of things right. That last gift you gave me has not weakened, has not faded. It is permanent. A part of me forever. I will always be grateful. It is a kind, loving, smiling, and peaceful face I see and carry with me.

# CHAPTER 18

## *Elasticity of the Soul*

The big picture behind the meaning of "elasticity of the soul" is flexibility. To tie it to homesteading and my childhood, in particular, it means that the top quality you need to survive in that wilderness setting is adaptability. The ability to bend like a willow tree in the wind, to deal with whatever comes along, because things will surely come along that you can't prepare for.

One of the many important lessons of my youth was to take advantage of unforeseen opportunities, to trust that a less worn, more difficult path would indeed take you to the place you needed to go. It might seem unlikely, but taking the more difficult way was often worthwhile, and I learned to take an empty pack along with me. I never knew when I'd find something valuable to bring home.

So, in 2016 when my forty-year-old son, Atz Lee, fell off a forty-foot cliff and broke more than two dozen bones in his body, he unknowingly set off an avalanche, a plethora, a veritable smorgasbord of opportunities. But like most other times in my life, I didn't recognize it as an opportunity right away.

Being by his bedside in the hospital, and later his bed at home was only the beginning of this adventure I was to have with him for the next year. This was only the very first phase. This was my practice phase. Being in a situation such as that, you are expected to give without any thought of getting anything in return. It's easy—after all, the person is helpless and it is very one-sided. There are no expectations. But spending those hours and days with my helpless son helped to prepare me for that next phase of inner growth.

Now, I could just refer you to that place in the Bible where it says, "It is more blessed to give than to receive," or perhaps, "Do unto others ..." or another favorite, something about first pulling the log out of your own eye so you can more clearly see the splinter in your neighbor's. All of that is what I'm trying to say. But the old homesteader in me says that would be too easy. That picnic lunch always tastes so much better when you've walked a good distance to get to that beautiful spot.

Anytime we see something we don't like in someone else, it points to the same quality in ourselves. In those moments our first impulse is to change the other person. It is so much more difficult to change that quality in us instead. Once we do, though, it is much easier to become accepting of that other person's flaws, and sometimes as we work on ourselves, other people change too. Likewise, anytime we are longing for something from someone else, we can instead give it to them. I knew I had a chance to be with my son to help him while his broken body healed. I would also end up helping him build a cabin. But more importantly, I saw it as a chance to change myself.

Long ago, when my dad was still alive, I was pissing and moaning to yet another therapist about my relationship with my father. How all the things he had either done or not done, done too much or too little of, had caused all my problems in life.

He looked at me the way therapists tend to do when they're about to say something really profound that you don't really want to hear. "Have you ever tried doing for your father, or being toward your father, what you wish he'd have done and been for you?"

At first, I wanted to kill him. Then, I wanted to say something sarcastic, like, "I'm paying you how much an hour for this kind of BS advice?" Instead, I made the wise choice of letting that question sink in deep. It had never dawned on me! But a seed was planted, and soon, something new in me began to grow.

I tried my best to treat my father the way I always wished he would treat me. I saw him bask in the warmth of my new treatment of him, and he grew and changed right before my eyes. Sometimes it was as small as complimenting him. Sometimes it was dropping by to chat with him in the old log cabin. Sometimes it was going with him to play chess at one of his favorite cafés in town and just hanging out at the table and watching him for a half hour or so.

And sometimes the baby steps turned into adult steps. I might say something like, "Sounds like that really made you mad. I can see why." Or, "Boy, I was scared the other day when I got called on the carpet by my boss" (showing him my soft underbelly, my vulnerability). Or, "That was fun going skiing with you the other day. We'll have to do that again sometime." That was after having asked him to go skiing with me, the last time he ever put on his cross-country skis, in fact.

Whether real or only imagined, I noticed he started being nicer to me and we forged a new and better relationship. In fact, he even said to me one day, "You seem less stressed out than you usually are." I'm so glad I didn't kill that therapist after all.

As I sat by my son in his invalid state, I wondered if that same psychology would work with my son. If I did my best to treat Atz Lee more cheerfully, more patiently, would his cheerfulness and patience toward me increase?

I realized of course, that just the same as with my father, it would have to be genuine. I had to be doing it because it would make me a better person. I had to do it because I believed that it would improve the relationship. I could not do it merely as a devious means of getting the other person to change, to get something I wanted.

You see, as I'd learned, you have to believe you're doing it to change yourself. There can be no expectations of the other person changing. That's the beauty of it. That's why it works—and that's why it's so damn hard! Growing and stretching, I hate it. It hurts. But I told myself that if it was that hard, it must be good for me.

Call it an answer to a prayer, putting good intentions out into the universe, or whatever you want, but sooner than I felt ready, the unique opportunity arrived. Sort of right in my face. I couldn't pretend it wasn't there, so I figured this was as good a time to try it again as any.

A quick word about me: I would like to say I am fairly normal but I'm not sure about that. I definitely don't fit into that category of humans who always has a clear sense of what's best to do. For some people, weighing options and making hard choices of what's best for everybody involved comes easily, as second nature. Neither do I naturally consult with my many selves competing for attention and know clearly which one to listen to. I'm of a special subgroup of people, maybe the largest group, who have a painful struggle, a long and slow process of arriving at decisions. We struggle with knowing which direction to go and how to go about it. And most of us have devised special strategies to manage our weakness, becoming crafty and creative to navigate the emotions involved in making decisions.

I like to pretend I hear many voices advising me and helping me see all sides of an issue. I don't hear voices—I'm very clear about that. But I sometimes see pictures and scenarios playing out in my head. I don't make up those inner voices each arguing their position, I also put faces to their voices and choose a setting where the discussions take place—isn't that called a borderline personality something-or-other? Thank you for that, Mr. Inner Analytical Psychologist!

Actually, I must confess I stumbled upon this ingenious theory when I was quite young. Since then, of course, I have read books by noted authors who have fleshed this theory out for me greatly and added some impressive research. More on this later.

Back when I was on the high school cross-country ski team, living so far out in the sticks I often had to practice on my own, I was not always able to stay after school and practice with the team. Since there were no teammates to push me and encourage me and to compete with, I had to make up my own method of pushing myself. My favorite scenario was skiing in the Swiss Alps as fast as I could to save a remote village from an avalanche that only I could warn them about.

Along this entire trail through the Alps, every village turned out to cheer for me. You should have heard the roar of applause as I skied into that doomed village, just in time to warn and save them. While I was at it, I also saved a beautiful Swiss milkmaid in great distress. If I recall correctly, she may have been a Swiss Miss. Oh, the cherry brandy she put in my hot chocolate, I'll never forget it. You can laugh, but it worked!

I shared this highly effective and secret training strategy with a teammate of mine. He was four years younger so there was less chance of him laughing at me. He looked up at me and smiled sheepishly. "You know," he said, "I imagine things too, and it really works!" My point exactly. But us country boys did what we had to do to get by training on our own, on the snow and on the rough landscapes of our soul.

I still use this overactive imagination of mine today, and it's pretty much helped to make me who I am. Don't worry too much about it; I'll try to keep all the voices straight for you. They are entertaining, if nothing else, and often rather enlightening and helpful.

You see, I still remember the exact place I was standing when that first voice said to me, "Yo, dude! You got a real giving problem!" Of course, anytime you hear a voice for the first time, and then listen quietly for a bit, you recall all the other times that same voice tried to speak, only your hearing wasn't turned up real loud.

I was standing beside the refrigerator in our home in Hawaii, next to wife number four (neither Hawaii nor wife number four worked out). This discussion, or argument, was over the fact that I would not share the frozen raspberries I had brought from Alaska with my two preteen stepdaughters. Those two girls did not fully appreciate them! They saw no difference between those frozen raspberries from the sacred Kilcher homestead, and the many frozen berries their mother got from Costco.

After much accusing, blaming, denying, and defending, that still-small voice—or maybe it was a clear loud voice (or maybe it was my ex-wife)—said, "You have a real giving problem! You are a very stingy, selfish, and greedy person." (It must've been my wife, no inner voice would dare speak to me so bluntly and rudely!)

"Okay, thank you, Mr. Loud Clear Voice, whichever one of my many inner voices you are. I got it. You don't need to go on and on! It's not like my soul is all shriveled here. I've done lots of kind, generous, thoughtful things in my life." (A little defensive here, aren't we?)

Of course, you never improve if you are not willing to look at those areas that are holding you back. So, I allowed myself to listen and look. And I didn't like what I heard and saw.

Giving. Becoming a more selfless, generous person. I discovered over the last few years that it's about as hard to change that quality about myself as trying to grow my hair back. But thanks to the therapist a few years back and my dad letting me practice on him, I made some progress. And thanks to my son Atz Lee, my willing tutor and mentor, I made some more progress. With my dad, it was occasional weekend seminars. With my son, it was a yearlong intensive wilderness retreat.

Just in case there is any confusion here, let me be perfectly clear about one thing. There are many kinds of giving, and there are many kinds of selfishness. Not wanting to share my raspberries with my stepdaughters is one thing. Having difficulty being cheerful and kind to somebody who is being grouchy to you requires more of the inner emotional or spiritual realm. But of course, they are related. And I find that when I have trouble sharing things in the physical realm, it usually represents something for me in the inner realm.

If I had been taught from the time I was a baby that it is more blessed to give than to receive, and to listen to that small voice, well, it might've saved me a lot of work. There wouldn't have been any need to try to become a more giving person. There wouldn't have been any need to make up the many advisors in my head and strategies to keep me on a healthy path.

I was on my way to Colorado to spend some time visiting my daughter, Jewel, and my grandson Kase. I stopped off to visit some friends in Portland for a couple of days. It was in their home where I got the sad phone call that my son had had a serious accident. He had fallen off a forty-foot cliff and landed in the boulders below, at the upper edge of the beach and the high-tide line. After many hours, he had been taken by skiff and then helicopter to a nearby hospital where he was resting in stable condition.

One ankle, one hip, one shoulder, one shoulder blade, and twenty-one ribs fractured, broken, or shattered. Plates and screws and pins. His X-rays looked like a rough carpenter had gotten a little carried away with a cordless drill and some long screws and metal. The two punctured lungs, of course, were of most immediate concern and danger. I couldn't talk to him. I knew there wouldn't be anything I could do by his bedside, so I continued to Colorado.

When I arrived in Colorado, I realized I was in a state of distress and anxiety. I did not know what I should do. What should a father who had a son in the hospital do? I did not know who to ask or where to go for that answer. After Colorado, I was going on to upstate New York to meet my wife where we were going to celebrate her mother's ninety-first birthday.

A special birthday, an important event. Visiting my grandson and daughter who I hadn't seen in a while was also important. My son was not dying, and he would still be in the hospital when I got back in a few days.

But that logic did not help. I was in a high state of stress. I remember feeling so angry that this should be so damn hard for me. I found myself envious of those people for whom a similar decision would be so easy. I decided the best place to start was just to admit that I didn't know where to start. That I didn't know what to do. So, I decided to talk to my daughter.

Once I had committed myself it was too late to back out. Before I knew it, I was talking to my daughter. Go figure, the person I choose to admit to that I don't have a clue what a father in my position should do was my daughter! I heard a voice coming out of my mouth saying, "I'm so ashamed and so embarrassed that I don't know what a father should do in a situation like this." There. It was out. My voice started out strong, but by the end of that short sentence I was crying. Hearing myself saying that, I was ashamed and embarrassed. It brought up such old and deep emotions, long locked away.

As always, the details of what we talked about are forgotten, but they don't matter. What has lingered are the feelings and ideas and beliefs we talked about. And the healing that occurred, as it always does, when vulnerability and true intentions are present.

What would a *normal* father do in a situation like this? What should *I* do in this situation? What does my son want me to do? Why is this so hard? Why can't I be normal? What would I have wanted my father to do in the same situation?

Jewel did a great job. At times, she was a sounding board; other times, she responded as a child of mine. Sometimes, she responded as a parent. At the end of the process, the discussion, which was indubitably the best and most productive therapy session I've ever had, I booked a return flight to Homer.

I told Bonnie I wouldn't be joining her up in the Adirondacks for her mother's birthday party. She and her mother understood, of course. I'm sure I was the only one struggling with making that decision. Who would want to admit to the world, "Yeah, I had a tough time deciding whether to go to a birthday party, go play with my daughter and grandson, or go help my son who just damn near died?"

So, I returned and sat by his hospital bed. I helped to drive him back to Homer and helped him up the wheelchair ramp and into his hospital bed in his living room. I helped him with his medications and his water and his food and going to the bathroom. Sometimes I cooked for him. Sometimes we talked. Much of the time I just hung out. Much of the time I watched him sleep. But one thing guaranteed, as the days turned to weeks, every moment that I was there with him, I was growing. Thinking, reflecting, feeling, evaluating, and pondering. Mostly about the nature of being a parent, of being a human, of sacrificing, of giving, of expecting nothing in return.

From wheelchair to walker, from walker to crutches, then one crutch, then no crutches, baby steps turned to therapy as bones, ligaments, muscles, and memories slowly healed, finding their way back, returning to their places. It was a long, slow journey of patience and pain and determination, but all along the way, I held the deep abiding belief that all would again be well.

* * *

Atz Lee chose one of the most strenuous and time-consuming activities to heal. The cabin we built together out in the wilderness began with dead branches with surveyor tape tied to the ends, sticking in the snow to mark the dimensions. A broken healing body and a dream marked by dead branches sticking in the snow. Four feet below was the frozen ground. Into that frozen ground we would sink a new foundation. That's called starting from scratch. But we had a pioneering spirit and lots of experience on our side. The roof would be on before the heavy snows of the next winter fell. The body would heal and strengthen.

Nobody put a gun to Atz Lee's head. But he couldn't have chosen a more perfect activity and setting for his therapy program. There would be countless opportunities on a physical, emotional, and mental level to strengthen him, to challenge him, to push and pull and test him. Whatever concept you have of a building project like this, well, multiply it by ten or twenty.

There were miles of boardwalk to build across boggy swamps just to be able to get there with our four-wheelers. There was a sawmill to pull into place across the frozen snow with snow machines. And all of this needed doing before the freeze broke up, of course. There were countless dead trees to fell with chainsaws and then pull into the sawmill with four-wheelers. Each round log had to be milled flat on three sides. Other logs had to be milled into dimensional lumber to be used for framing. Countless supplies had to be hauled in over the snow before the breakup, or through the mud after.

If you are not walking through deep snow or deep mud or deep grass or deep swamps, you are clambering over dead blown-down trees with sharp broken branches sticking out like quills on a porcupine.

You are walking along the trunks of skinny trees five or six feet off the ground, like tightropes. You fall off. You climb back on. It is easier to climb on a trunk and walk along it as you would a skinny bridge than it is to climb over countless logs three to five feet off the ground. No, there isn't any crawling under it—it's too overgrown, or undergrown.

Hours of time are spent with a chainsaw in your hand. Clearing trails, cutting through logs, cutting through brush, just so you can pull two or three logs to the sawmill. A rope tied to one end of the log, the other end tied to your four-wheeler. You spin out. You try again. You back up and hit it harder. Your front end comes off the ground and you almost flip over backward. Your hands hurt from tying and untying countless knots. Your knuckles are bruised. Your left foot is screaming with pain from running the gear-shift lever up and down all day.

Every part of my body ached at the end of every day. I can only guess how his body felt. Those unbroken parts now trying to get strong again. Those broken parts trying to mend and heal. All those plates and screws trying to integrate themselves. Hips, ankles, shoulders, ribs. Pain! I asked him as often as I thought it was helpful, "How are you doing?" And he was always good about giving me a report. An honest assessment.

But how many young soldiers returning from the trauma of war, if even one or two battles, eventually heal their wounds but never their hearts and minds? How many return with no physical wounds to heal yet still are deeply wounded?

Many things triggered my son, caused him to relive the trauma of that fall off that cliff that night. Many things caused his PTSD to kick in. He described his PTSD kicking in as a "shutdown" or "meltdown." Sometimes, it might be related to a loud sound associated with danger such as a sharp band-saw blade snapping and breaking on the sawmill. Other times, it might be a sudden movement that caused intense pain in his body. Other times, it might be something as simple as being thirty feet off the ground on the peak of the roof and looking down.

Believe me, and take it from a Vietnam veteran who knows, there were countless opportunities for him to confront the traumas of his past. Countless opportunities to work through them, to tell himself that was then and this is now. Countless opportunities to sit and breathe deep and allow himself to tremble a while, slowly regather his inner strength and continue what he was doing.

Sitting by his bed watching him as he lay helpless had its challenges and difficulties for me. Watching him struggling to regain the full use of his body, to do slowly and with difficulty that which he used to do fast and easily, and to watch him push himself to his limit was harder for me yet.

But being at the bedside and watching him trying to get his broken body to work again was nothing compared to watching him when he hit that wall. Watching him get back up and being willing to get another run at it and smack it again. Watching him believing and having faith that each time the wall would get smaller and weaker, would hurt less, would have less power over him. Watching him learning to avoid situations that he could, and bravely confront those he could not. That's courage. That's bravery. Whether coming back from a war in which you were never wounded, whether coming home with a limb missing, whether falling off a cliff, it all leaves a mark somewhere, it all needs to be dealt with. It's all bravery! It's all courage!

The more time I spent out there helping my son build his cabin, the more I was able to fine-tune my therapy program. It started out, shall we say, simple. If I wanted my son to thank me more frequently, or notice small things I had done, I would do it to him. I thanked him more. I let him know I noticed small things he had done. That soon led to my trying to be more observant and aware of my reactions to him. For once you have a conscious awareness, you are able to make conscious choices.

As I became more observant I noticed that he and I reacted similarly to situations and had similar stressors. Of course, it was easier to notice his reaction to a stressor first. It was also easy for me to blame him for my reaction to his reaction. That would quickly lead me to trying to change his reaction, which I did not like. Like most good old human reactions, the change-the-other-guy's-problem game doesn't often work. Most of us have been there and done that.

Instead, I began talking to him about how I dealt with stress in unhealthy ways, and that freed him up to talk about himself, which led to talking about how the tension wasn't really between us, but in how we both reacted to stress. We saw how we were misdirecting our anger and taking it out on those closest to us. And that was only adding to our stress.

One morning we were loading up our four-wheelers and trailers to head up the beach to the cabin-building site. We had to leave at a certain time to beat the high tide. There is always tension in the air when you're trying to tie down and secure many items for a long trip and beat the tide. Even when you have plenty of time, there is tension. When you're traveling with an outgoing tide it's much more relaxing. This morning however, the tide was coming in.

I arrived with a lot of anxieties. My biggest one was that I would speak or act rudely or impatiently to my son because of my stress. When I arrived, I could see by his face that he was also feeling stressed. He looked up and said in a sort of joking, disguising-his-stress kind of voice, "Hey you're late. We got to get moving; the tide's coming in!" I could've responded in many different ways. Prior to my wilderness therapy training program, I would have responded differently. Or I would not have responded and sulked for three or four hours instead.

"Good morning, Son!" I walked to him, trying to put on my friendly face. "Man, I've been stressing all morning about how hard it's going to be to pack all these lengths of chimney. That, plus both of us pulling a trailer up the beach and trying to beat the tide. I could have used a 'Good morning, Pop. How you doing?'"

It may not have been the perfect opening. It was a bit critical of him. I could have guessed he was stressed and asked him how he was doing. Regardless, I let him know what I was going through, what I was feeling, and took a risk to tell him what would feel good to me.

"I've been feeling stressed out too," he said. And then he told me what would make him feel better. So, we started over by saying good morning. We hadn't even gone anywhere and already it was a good day.

I think of that old expression, "Killing two birds with one stone." Except here it was more like killing three birds with one stone. I believe it helped him, it helped our relationship, and it helped me. I tried to be an example for him, I tried to be a role model. I tried to let him know what I was feeling and going through and how I was dealing with it, however imperfect it may have been. I told him I saw how my reactions, ways of dealing with my stress, were often stressful for him.

Throughout our time together out there, building this cabin, instead of just reacting to him, or trying to change him, to tell him there was something I did not like about the way he was handling a situation, I tried instead to merely let him know *I* tended to react. Many times, it was simply a matter of my having to learn to accept how he dealt with stress. And for me to accept my reaction to that. There were times nothing really changed, except our acceptance of each other. And as it always does, that took a lot of the charge out of the situation.

My biggest challenge during this entire wilderness therapy retreat seems to be the hardest to describe, to wrap words around. It has something to do with allowing another person their experience, accepting it, and not being affected by it, not taking it on. It is a difficult enough concept with a nonrelated person you are having a relationship with. It becomes more challenging with a spouse. Most challenging yet with a parent or a child. It is so much easier in those close relationships, to feel personally responsible. To feel self-judgment and self-blame or to want to blame the other person for your pain.

I had a college professor forty years ago who taught me something I have never forgotten. He taught me that you forget most of what you learn, especially details and specifics. He went on to explain that only the broad concepts and the general feeling of what you learn remain years later. His point was, why teach all those details if they are forgotten? Why not just teach general beliefs and values? Similarly, sometimes one detail or one small story can represent or serve as a metaphor for a much larger concept.

We were freezing cold. We had just set up our wall tent and it was getting dark. Some of the work had been difficult to do with our gloves on. We were both in a work frenzy to get the fire going and our sleeping bags laid out on top of the spruce bows we had laid on top of the snow. We both knew we had to get warm in a hurry.

Atz Lee was trying to start the fire with some bits of dry birch bark and spruce branches. I was trying to help him. My intention was to be helpful, which, of course, included not only handing him bits of kindling but also giving him my most excellent and expert advice, my much more experienced, "elder" advice.

That didn't work at all. The words he chose, the tone of voice which carried those words, and the look on his face, all told me in no uncertain terms, that I was not welcome or needed there right at that moment. He was irritable. He was snappy. He was impatient. He was scowling. He didn't tell me directly. Indirectness. I hate that. It drives me crazy.

Keep in mind that this was at the beginning of my wilderness therapy program. At this point, I still wanted to stuff him inside the stove and light it on fire. I didn't do that, however. Instead, I just withdrew and sulked for a while. Tried not to make it obvious, but hoped it was. Hoped he would feel as miserable for hurting me as I was feeling. All good, normal human stuff. All good grist for the emotional mill.

That was just one incident of many. But the lesson was always the same. My son is feeling something. He is expressing it as best he can, probably the way he grew up watching me express my frustrations. What is he feeling? What can I do to help him right now? How can I, at some point, possibly role model for him a more appropriate way to express *myself*? Over and over again these lessons came to me. And as with anything, the more I practiced, the better I got at it.

My tried-and-true method of dealing with anxiety, fear of the unknown, fear of the future, is to plan it out, talk it out, think it out, wear it out. It often drives anyone around me crazy, but this is my strategy. I developed it out of necessity and self-preservation. Yes, it mostly has to do with how I was raised. For some reason, the way my dear old daddy ran his life, we were often unprepared, had to get by on a shoestring, in a rush and a panic, in total survival mode. That is predictably when the feathers hit the fan. The lesson was simple: a lack of planning caused pain.

I ran a good part of my life in similar fashion. Putting off, avoiding, postponing anything that smells of anxiety, which, of course, only increased it. So, I learned that even though I hated doing it, I had to plan, I had to prepare, I had to get a grip on just what it was I was afraid of so that it would lose its hold on me. Most people around me now agree I'm more of a prepared, think-ahead kind of person.

I don't know why my son's style bothers me so much, but it drives me absolutely crazy. I should be very familiar with it. I used to do it myself. His way of dealing with the unknowns of the future which stress him out is *not* to deal with them. And when he gets there and has to pay the price of not having the proper tools or supplies with him or not having thought about the tide and getting caught by it or not being able to do what we planned because it wasn't planned, he seems to roll with it and not get upset about it all. I believe that's the way he's developed, so he can stay in a stress-free mode where he's comfortable. For him, I believe, it's less stressful to leave some details unplanned, even if it means paying a price at the other end. And I hate that.

When I see somebody heading into a complicated or potentially dangerous situation unprepared, I see nothing but feathers hitting the fan. I go into my old fearful-child mode. It was never a matter of, "Gee, I wonder how it will go this time?" As children, we all knew exactly what would happen, because it always did.

Now, for some unknown reason, my planning ahead, going over every little detail of things that might never happen and taking along extra tools and supplies, planning alternatives and four different ways we could put on a roof covered with thick frost, and then presenting my son with all of it first thing in the morning before he was awake drove him completely crazy.

So, the way we dealt with it without killing each other was this: I did all my planning and preparing and packing by myself. I did not drag him through it. When we got where we were going, I was prepared and had everything with me I needed. That way, my own need did not affect him. He went along preparing as much as he felt comfortable doing. And if his lack of preparedness only affected him, like not having an extra pair of gloves or enough food, I could usually cover because I had extra. If there was something we did not have with us, or plan ahead for that affected the trip or the job, I held myself responsible because I did not have the expectation for him to think of it, therefore I wasn't disappointed in him.

Eventually, we got better at going over the more important items and deciding who would make sure they got done ahead of time. We got better at checking each other. Me planning less, him planning more. But overall, to prevent the stress and anxiety of not being prepared, I still had a higher need to think things through more thoroughly. I believe Atz Lee will always have less need to spend a lot of time thinking and planning ahead. He'll always be more relaxed about dealing with the unexpected and accepting what wasn't planned for. He is an adult. He knows when he has planned well enough, and has learned to deal with the consequences. And who is to say his method is any worse than mine? He certainly isn't as stressed out and as anxious as I am most of the time.

But we have talked about how it is a different side of the same coin. We are both trying to minimize our stress and anxiety to the best of our ability. As long as our individual styles work for us, we'll keep doing it. We also realize that our way of dealing with the unknowns of the future tends to bring up even more anxiety for the other. And that's a biggie. Realizing all of that is a biggie.

How much did my efforts, years ago, change my dad or myself or our relationship? How did my much more recent efforts affect or change my son or myself or our relationship? Things were affected. Things *did* change. Things were set into motion. Wherever there is good intention and effort and a willing heart, it will bear fruit. Like my daughter is fond of saying, "Sometimes you just have to be willing to show up."

Even if those annoying qualities in my dad or my son didn't all disappear, I noticed them much less because I was busy working on my own. It seems to be one of those great truths that if we try to be the change we want to see in others, there are great ripple effects. Maybe their problems go away because ours do. I tried it. And poof, it worked!

Change is slow. Sometimes glacier slow. There won't be loudspeakers blaring or crowds cheering for some of the hardest inner battles we fight, for the many small victories throughout our lives. That is our job. It is a big job. To notice those small milestones and pause a moment to let it soak in and to celebrate. If we do a good job with that, we keep going, we keep trying, we keep struggling. If we fail on the job, we give up, we quit.

Recently, Atz Lee and I were in a tense situation. Shane was there, as well as three or four other people. Shane was explaining something he had made that he was very proud of. He had it covered with a big quilt to protect it and was waiting for the right moment to unveil it. In the middle of his talking, I reached down to grab a corner of the quilt so that when the time was right I could help him with the big surprise. Atz Lee, being the ever-thoughtful and considerate brother that he is, looking out for his older brother, interpreted my move as taking attention away from Shane, trying to rush him along, or possibly even revealing the surprise myself.

It quite understandably brought up some feelings for Atz Lee, and he said, "Hey, don't get in a rush," or something to that effect. The exact words don't matter, it's what those words triggered.

I felt publicly shamed, humiliated, embarrassed, and scolded. I reacted as though I had done something terribly wrong. Those feelings of embarrassment I felt in front of my sons and their friends standing around took hold of me so fast that all I could do was turn and walk away.

After pulling myself together I came back and Shane had a chance to finish telling about what he had made and show it off to everybody just the way he had planned. Even though I was faking it fairly well, I wanted to crawl into a hole. Now I was feeling ashamed and embarrassed for walking off and making an ass of myself in front of everybody. Oh, yes, I wanted to get very mad at that person who had so humiliated me.

I motioned for Atz Lee to follow me and we walked off a little ways to be alone. I asked him if he could listen and he said, "Sure, I figured you'd have something to say." Fortunately, at this point, my inner cowboy had pretty well sorted out what was going on, "back at the ranch." Way back, at the childhood homestead ranch long ago. I explained in a few simple words how feeling ashamed, embarrassed, and humiliated in public was one of my biggest scars, which still got bumped occasionally. I told him that to this day, I still didn't know what it was my dad was feeling at those times he felt the need to humiliate me. My son nodded and said something to let me know he really got what I was saying.

Then he told me what had come up for him when he thought I was cutting his brother short, not giving Shane his moment in the spotlight. "Yep," one of us said, "looks like some heavy stuff came up for both of us and it collided."

I gave him a hug. I felt very soft and emotional—almost like crying. Yep, that's what happens when I asked tough, crusty old cowboys to find that soft, vulnerable place deep within instead of hiding behind anger. Later that evening I called him and said, "Son, I want to thank you for a great gift you gave me today. First, you said something that brought up age-old emotions; that was part of the gift. Next, you let me tell you why I reacted the way that I did, which was another big part of the gift. And then, you very clearly told me what had come up for you. We did a good job of sorting it out, putting everything back where it belonged, of moving forward stronger and healthier."

That's when the loudspeakers blared and the crowd went wild! That's when the bands began to play! That's when I was asked to walk onstage in the glare of the bright lights and the television cameras! This was the mother lode of all celebrations! Accomplishment! Recognition!

You said, very simply, "Thank you for the elasticity of your soul."

So, thank you, my son, my namesake, Atz Lee. For showing up day after day. With courage. With determination. Striving to make yourself and the world a better place. I'm proud of you. I love you. You've been a patient teacher.

# CHAPTER 19

## *The Fox Cabin*

I went yesterday to my very favorite place on our entire seven-hundred-acre homestead, the fox cabin meadow. The fox-farmer's cabin where I took my mother to be photographed on one of her visits once stood at the edge of that meadow. It stands no more, existing only in memory, a photograph, and a story. In my mind, it will stand forever. Let me tell you why.

The history there is as rich as dark, fertile soil. It had been homesteaded by a man named Harry White in the late 1920s, and like many others of that era, he was a fox farmer. The abundance of forest animals, marine mammals, and fish provided the food to raise foxes.

When my father first found that piece of land in the late 1930s, it was already a patented homestead but had been abandoned. He located the owner and bought his first piece of Alaskan real estate. He and my mother, as well as my three older sisters, lived there for several years while they homesteaded the adjoining 160 acres. This was a luxury. Most homesteaders had to camp out in a temporary shelter until they built a habitable structure.

I have no memory of living in that cabin. We left there when I was not quite one year old, in 1947. Though he broke his back building it, my father completed our longhouse and we moved in.

Before moving in, however, my parents took their first journey back to Switzerland with their three oldest daughters. I was always told mother wanted to go and give birth to me in a "real" hospital. I was born in a hospital in Basel, Switzerland, the same one my mother was born in, back in 1920. When I was older, I found out that she'd wanted to leave my father at that point and he thought taking her back to the old country would help change her mind. It did. She came back to Alaska with my father shortly after I was born and had three more children. In 1956, seven children now in tow, we returned to Switzerland for almost two years, and my younger sister was born there in 1957.

My father successfully lectured and showed his homesteading movie all across Europe. He bought a brand-new VW bus in Germany, and except for the ocean crossing, mom, dad, and eight children drove that bus all the way to our homestead cabin. I remember only parts of that trip, and there are other parts I try hard to forget. How their marriage survived it, I will never know.

Even as a young toddler, I remember going with my older sisters down through the meadows to visit that fox cabin. It was tiny, perhaps ten by twelve, just two small windows, and it was always a little dark in there. It had a door made out of gray boards with leather hinges and a homemade wooden latch. In the center of the door at about eye-height, there was a small opening you could see out of by moving a sliding piece of wood. This was always helpful to know whether it was a friend knocking or a black bear.

There was a small cookstove that served to heat it, a small kitchen table, a bed just wide enough for Mom and Dad, and a wide bunk bed above for three sisters. I had a crib. There was a handmade ladder going to the upper bed that my father made. He carved a foot at the top of the ladder and painted the toenails red.

In the center of the floor was a trapdoor. Beneath that door was the root cellar, which fascinated me as a kid.

The log house I grew up in was ordinary, but that fox cabin was special. It was magical. Part castle, part haunted house, part tree fort. It was a getaway from noise and confusion. It was my earliest harbor for solitude, healing, feeling my sadness, and for trying to figure out who I was.

As soon as I was old enough, I would run down through the hay meadows, through the hillsides of wild roses, geraniums, and Jacob's ladders and run inside. After spending some time there, I would go out and climb up on the shed in the back. I would sit on the hot black tar paper, burning my rear, and lean back against the moss and clay-chinked logs which were already more than thirty years old. I felt safe. I could dry out my tear-soaked soul in the Alaskan sun. Sometimes I would just sit in the strawberry patch behind the cabin and gorge myself into sweet fructose bliss.

During those visits, I did much the same as when we all lived there, I spent most of my time out of doors. From what my parents tell me and from what I can see in old photos, the small cabin was mostly used for sleeping and getting out of the weather. There was an outdoor table where my mama did most of her preparing, preserving, and cleaning of food. I am sure she even sewed and knitted outside. Certainly, a big part of the day for both my parents included caring for the garden, looking after the animals, gathering wood, hauling water, and hunting, gathering, and foraging.

On rainy days, I would stay in. I loved climbing up and down that ladder, admiring that hand-carved foot with the red toenails, and playing on the bunk beds. Although I only lived there for a few months as a baby, it always seemed so familiar.

Sometimes I stood and gazed out the southern window and tried to see the world as my mother saw it in those early years. Meadows rolled gently to the steep bluff and the beach below. The five-mile-wide bay with her many moods, from gray to turquoise, from angry autumn swells to late-evening summer glass. The mountains and glaciers rose from the far side of the bay. Even at a distance, they made everything seem small. I grew up thinking those towering, spruce-covered, snow-capped mountains and glaciers were the edge of the world. A safe and strong border.

But knowing my mama, she also surely spent time being far more nearsighted. There were wild roses, plus raspberries and elderberries from which she made juice, jellies, and jams. There were the fields of dandelions for fresh spring salads. My father also planted crab apple trees and chokecherry trees on the sunny south slope in front of the cabin.

I also played in the fox pens. The frames were spruce poles covered with chicken wire. Some of the larger pens had smaller pens within, possibly to separate the young from the adults. There were also hallways going from one panel to another. It was like a giant labyrinth and sort of an open-air condominium for me, a perfect playground for a young boy. An old cabin, a bunch of old fox pens, a hillside full of wild roses, and a strawberry patch.

Later, when I was older, those fox pens served a very different purpose. When there wasn't enough work for us kids to do, or my father just happened to think of it, he would send us down to pull out staples from the chicken wire. They were big and rusty and hard to pull out, but recycled staples were good for stapling up barbed wire for the cow and horse fences. It was not easy work, but being down by the old fox cabin and able to work at my own pace—and play a bit—made the work bearable.

I also learned to value recycling and hard work. And staples. I only found out years later that you could buy brand-new staples at the general store for cheap. As an adult, I still hoard old rusty staples like they're gold, until I go on a purge and throw them away and buy new ones. Even now I do it with a twinge of guilt, but I must say it feels good. This holds true for many aspects of my personality—saving, recycling, using *all* you can and using it up before ever considering throwing it away or buying something new. It's the homestead mentality.

My father discovered the old fox cabin when he first came to this country. He was on his way from Seward to Homer, traveling the hundred-plus miles by foot.

With no trail and only a map to guide him, he set the straightest course possible. In the early days, with only distant neighbors, a radio, and a wind-up phonograph, we were to hear those stories of that historic journey over and over. As we huddled away long winter nights around the kitchen stove or around our living room table, our father and his stories were our main entertainment. I hear his voice now, always to the steady pulse and hiss of the Coleman lantern. When I light a Coleman today, it is never without a vivid flood of such warm memories. How he almost fell through the snow into a deep glacial crevasse, only to be saved by the skis tied across his pack.

Of all the stories my father used to tell, my favorite was of how he found the fox cabin. After giving up trying to cross the Harding Icefield, he went back to Seward. This time he took a less direct route through a mountain pass. This more circuitous route took him through Moose Pass, then down the Kenai River to the coast. From there it was only a little over a hundred miles down the beach to Homer.

But it was the land east of Homer where he was interested in looking for a homestead. One can only guess his excitement as he neared the land he'd heard so much about. An area where coal was lying in big chunks on the beaches, just waiting to be gathered for fuel. Where forests were thick with spruce ideal for building. Moose, bear, and fish were plentiful; the soil was rich and fertile. He was close to his dream, close to the land he planned to stake and homestead as his own.

Some fifteen miles past Homer, he saw a small trail going up McNeil Canyon. His curiosity called. He followed the steep foot trail up to the first meadow scattered with alder, birch, and elderberry. The native grass was over six feet high. As he looked up the slope, he saw a cabin peeking out from behind an alder patch. He walked up the trail and for the first time, saw the fox cabin.

It was probably only ten or fifteen years old at that point. Gray, weathered logs chinked with moss and grass mixed with beach clay. It was small. One door and two windows. He went inside and looked up at the roof. It was still in good shape. The cabin was cozy—tight and warm. He liked it. It felt good. If he was anything like I am, I think he must've known right then. This was the place.

\* \* \*

The older I become, the more amazed I am at all that my new-to-the-wilderness immigrant parents did. Each was required to do many things completely new and foreign to them in their own realms of responsibilities.

For my mother, whose own mother had been a seamstress, sewing and knitting were no big deal. Sharing some of the hunting and gathering chores was totally new. Preserving foods by drying, canning, pickling, and salting were things she had only read about. Making the most delicious dark ale for miles around soon become second nature. Doctoring your children at home from either store-bought or homemade remedies had to be learned quickly. Though home births were more common in those days, I nonetheless admire anyone that attempts it. My mother had only one sort of home birth. She was en route to a small local airport, where a bush plane was to take her to the closest hospital, when my sister Sunrise decided to enter the world. She was born instead at a friend's house that had a stable, where my father could leave his team of horses after traveling the beach to Homer.

I have heard numerous stories regarding my father's strengths and stamina from various old-timers over the years, fellow pioneers who were not easily impressed.

Along with his strength, intelligence, and love of the outdoors, he also had to his advantage one winter of logging and cabin-building in Sweden. This experience must have left a lasting impression on my father, who, at the time, was barely twenty years old. He told us countless stories of that cold winter logging period of his life. Skiing thirty or forty kilometers to a dance in the village after working a twelve-hour day felling trees with the crosscut saw and an ax.

All that aside, much was new for him in Alaska. Logging for a winter was a short haul when compared to homesteading in the remote wilderness year after long year. He learned how to hunt moose, black bears, spruce hens, ptarmigan, geese, and ducks, and he learned how to set a net and catch the silver salmon on their last journey along the shore to spawn in the mountain streams.

He acquired horses and cows, learned to use them for work, for transportation, and as a source of meat. He learned to butcher in the barnyard and in the wild. He became an expert on which coal strewn along the beach burned the hottest and left the least ash. He learned to navigate the beach highway to town until icebergs forced him to use his sleigh on the overland route through swamps, gullies, and ancient dense spruce forests. Both parents became local authorities on common edible plants, berries, and mushrooms.

Both my mother and father had to learn the many subtle nuances of wilderness living: home entertainment, arts and crafts, hobbies, and passing their old-country culture down to their kids through music and storytelling.

Looking back, I see that my father was ill-suited in one major regard to wilderness living. He was basically a social creature. From some of my mother's earliest diary entries, it was obvious that my father had a strong need to spend much time with other people, and this of course meant leaving my mother alone to tend to the kids, livestock, farm, and garden. In short, holding down the whole damn fort. All of this, fifteen long remote miles away from anyone, in the wilderness.

Many of her early entries said such things as, "Left alone with the three young children again. They all are sick. I had to help the milk cow give birth to her calf. The garden needs tending. I am tired. Where is Yule? He stayed the night in town again."

He was not a bad or neglectful husband, but I believe strongly that the pull toward intellectual stimulation and social interaction was my father's drug of choice. He seemed to have little control over it. Yet paradoxically, the more romantic and philosophical aspects of wilderness-subsistence-living also appealed to him. You've heard the term, "gentleman farmer"? Well, my dad was a "gentleman homesteader."

I experienced him back and forth, home and gone, pioneer and social creature, including Mr. Politician. His physical work on the homestead, like his presence, was sporadic. Sometimes I believe his frenzied work pace and how he tended to drive those around him, was in part to make up for how he felt about the time he spent away, the many things he was not getting to—in short, his guilt. He spent many years in Anchorage, a five-hour drive from Homer, constructing homes. And just as he tended to stay in Homer longer than needed back in the horse-and-wagon and old-Ford-tractor days, likewise he spent way more time in Anchorage than his work required. Yet, of course, what wife or family can argue with a man who says, "I need to go sell coal in Homer," or, "I need to go build houses in Anchorage." We needed the money.

There's no mistaking all he did accomplish, all the hard work he did do, the seven-hundred-acre legacy he left behind—the roads, fences, buildings, forests cleared, hay meadows planted, lives impacted. It's all relative, I suppose. And what is also true is he was a driven, unhappy man. Sadly, he died feeling he didn't accomplish his dream. In the end, it's our self-assessment we live and die by.

I recall once, in my early twenties, when I was just home from Vietnam. I was not much younger than my father was when he homesteaded. We got into one of our many arguments and I said something to him about his not having any dreams or ambitions. If I recall correctly, this was in response to his criticizing what I wanted to do with my life now that I was back from the war. I will never forget his response—not just the words but the emotion behind them. "You think I have never had any dreams?" he shouted. His voice began to quiver and he began crying. It was the first and only time I saw my father cry. He continued, still shouting, crying, and there was a deep pain in his voice, though I would only come to recognize it years later. "You think I had no dreams down there in that little fox cabin, with my little family around me? You think I had no dreams coming home alone from the beach late at night and seeing your mother waiting high on the bluffs above waving the lantern? You think I had no dreams …?" He was becoming angry, but I knew it was not at me. "I had dreams," he whispered, sobbing quietly, "I had plenty of dreams."

*Oh, that you could've spent more time there, my dear papa. No, not in your dreams, but in your feelings, your softer feelings. In that place of vulnerability. Because what you gave me that day was a gift, a gift of who you really were. Or, at least, a gift of a side of you I never got to know near well enough. A glimpse of that place where we never spent time together. But we did get there at the end, my dear papa. That's where we ended up being together.*

He dreamed of orchards that would thrive in the northern clime—many fruit trees did well in similar climates elsewhere in the world. He dreamed of rolling meadows, with hay crops growing tall and gardens thriving in the long summer days of the midnight sun. He dreamed of log houses and water-generated electricity. He dreamed of many children, playing and working on the land. He dreamed of a simple life close to the earth, with minimal dependency on civilization. He dreamed of communal living, people helping each other, contributing their talents for the good of the community. He dreamed of artists and craftsmen living in harmony with the land and each other.

I am sure he dreamed of far less important things, such as carving his giant birch and spruce burl bowls by the warmth of the woodstove. Telling his stories to the hiss of the Coleman lantern. Teaching his children how to not only survive, but to thrive and live as part of nature. Playing his many hand-carved flutes on cold winter nights. Dried kelp, dried pushki (cow parsnip), garden hose, or copper pipe—oh, how he could play them. I am sure he dreamed of caring for and providing for his young Swiss bride, maybe even making love to her in the meadow of wild roses.

*I know you had dreams, Papa. You had many dreams and good ones. Maybe too many. You never could celebrate those many dreams you did accomplish, but instead dwelled sadly on those you left unfulfilled. Perhaps that is why, when asked on your deathbed what you wanted us to do, you left us with a couple of dreams you were never quite able to accomplish.*

*"There needs to be more love," you told us with fading breath. "Get organized and get along. Oh yes, plant an orchard."*

You see, even though my father loved trees, he only dabbled. He planted a few chokecherry and mountain ash, and one maple. He also had some gooseberries and currants. He did quite a bit of communicating with government agencies regarding importing various varieties of trees. He planted one crab apple tree right over the edge of the hill in front of the fox cabin. That was the extent of his orchard. As with other aspects of my father's life, his talk and his dreams were far bigger than his actions and accomplishments. He was a dreamer, an idea person, the queen bee. He was never quite able to gather those worker bees around him. But never let it be forgotten that it was his dream that brought his branch of the Kilcher family tree to Alaska.

So, this year, some sixty years after he planted that first choke-cherry tree and crab apple tree there below the old fox cabin, Fay, my very efficient and organized green-thumb sister, planted the very first bona fide orchard on the homestead. Where? You guessed it! Down by the fox cabin, closer to the beach, just that little bit warmer in the winter, just that little bit earlier in the spring. Down there by her daddy's trees. Down there where a whole lot of dreaming had gone on so long ago.

That's why I went down there yesterday, to gather some of the crab apples from that old tree. I also went to gather and taste old memories and dreams, be with the spirits of my mother and father.

I used to have some outrageous flying dreams. The majority of them took place down by the fox cabin. I usually took off from the ridge just above the cabin. Once airborne, I would circle above the cabin, catching the updrafts from the bluffs coming off the water. I was always amazed in the morning after awakening, at the vividness and clarity of my aerial view of the cabin and surrounding area. Those flying dreams always seemed so real.

I once asked my mother, who was into all sorts of mystic stuff, from astrology to numerology, mythology, and dream interpretations, what she took my dreams to mean, why they were always over the fox cabin. Her reply was short and sweet. "Vell, my son, it is really very simple. You ver conceived in that cabin. That is ver your papa and I made you. Ven you arrr sleeping, yur spirit returns to the place it vas given a body, ver it entered this realm."

I believed her then and I believe her still. Though born in Basel on a trip back to the old country, I always considered myself

Alaskan-born. You might think that's too much information, but hey, because I'm so connected to that exact spot, I think it's pretty cool.

*　*　*

Yesterday I had little seven-year-old Maya with me. She's my ex-wife Beth's youngest daughter, but I love her as though she were my own. I must confess she is very easy to love. She's a forest fairy, or maybe an angel. She was only three pounds when she was born and has a rare growth disorder called Russell-Silver syndrome, which affects her growth and ability to gain weight both before and after birth. But her spirit is strong and undaunted. She touches all she meets. It doesn't take Freud to figure out why she came into my life. I need to tell you a couple things about her so you can better understand why that trip to the old fox cabin was so special.

When she was about four, she had a birthday party. Two of her little friends, who happened to be brothers, could not come until the party had already ended. She quickly ran to her bedroom and came out with a bag of party favors for each boy. Then she gave them each her two most special presents she had just gotten, things she had always wanted. After the boys had left, her mother asked her why she had given away her two most treasured items. Her reply was pure and simple, right from her little spirit. "Love isn't love till you give it away." I am convinced she had never heard that saying. Somewhere she had learned that lesson and was passing it on.

Another time we were walking back to our car from the beach in Hawaii. It was quite a long walk, maybe three-quarters of a mile. I was amazed at how quickly she was walking; she was staying ahead of me. Her legs were like little toothpicks, she was no taller than an average two-year-old, but the Russell-Silver syndrome causes her body to be asymmetrical. One side is a little larger than the other. As a result, one of her legs is longer. You can barely tell, and she's learned to compensate quite cleverly. Somehow, she slightly bends her longer leg to make them the same length. It doesn't slow her down a bit when she runs, climbs, or plays soccer. It certainly wasn't slowing her down on that walk from the beach. When I asked her how she could walk so fast, her answer left me breathless and reaching for my little notebook that I like to carry with me in case inspiration strikes. "I can see the air all around me and it is moving, I walk with the wind." I swear to God, that is exactly what she said. I wrote it down on the spot!

As I showed little Maya around, it brought back fond memories of the times I took Jewel, Shane, and Atz Lee down there. I wonder now if I told them how dearly I loved that place. I have a sense that back then, I wasn't able to fully access all of my memories and feelings, or share them intimately. Those days prior to the divorce in Anchorage and single-parenting at the homestead are mostly a big blur.

Jewel, do you remember the times I took you there to take all those pictures? Those slides and a song I wrote about the old fox cabin were the centerpiece of the Alaska dinner show our family did in Anchorage. The song talked a little about the history of the cabin, and how even though it was decaying and sinking into the earth, it would never fade from my mind.

*It won't be standing long, it's been there a*
*long, long time,*
*but it will stand forever in my mind.*

I have these neat old photos of the cabin when I lived there as a baby that my mother sent me. They would have been taken in the late forties; the cabin still looked so new. I love seeing my parents as they looked back then, smiling and in love. They must have been around thirty. My three older sisters were usually wearing little dresses and I was in diapers, usually a mess. In one photo, I am playing in the doghouse with a bone.

I put those old slides together with the ones I took showing me visiting the cabin with you and your brothers. I was about the same age as my father had been in the earlier slides. You kids were also close to the same age as my sisters had been.

It was quite amazing and emotional to see the comparisons. One slide showed my parents and their children in front of a fairly new cabin in good repair, standing tall in the middle of that lovely wild grass meadow. The next showed an almost fallen-over cabin with most of the roof gone, nearly forty years later. The baby in the doghouse was now fortyish, with children of his own.[1]

Those slides of you kids and me were taken in the mideighties. When I went there with Maya, another fifteen or more years had gone by. The cabin is now just a hole in the earth, with a few old rotten logs laying around. I had salvaged the good logs for milling and using on my new log house.

I showed Maya the barely visible remains of the old stable. You have to know where to look to find the rich earth that took back the stable logs. A slight mound, maybe a few inches high, in the shape of a rectangle is all that remains of the old log structure.

We walked down to the crab apple tree. I was in no hurry. We had all the time in the world. Sometimes it was little Maya beside me, other times it was little Jewel. It felt good to be taking my time with you, being patient with you. Not feeling rushed or pressured.

Maya has no idea how cathartic she has been for me. And you, Jewel, can't know unless I tell you, how often I have redone parts of my parenting of you through her. It is like a second chance to go back and do it right; gentler, better. I always believe at those times that you can feel it all those many miles away, and that it is making a difference for you as well.

Little Maya and I finally got to that crab apple tree. I held her tiny hand to help her down the steep slope. Although the tree is old, it is not very big. It is perhaps twenty-five feet tall, with slender branches which break easily from heavy snows and hungry late-autumn black bears looking for that last feast before hibernating. An adult can only climb to the first crotch, about five feet off the ground. First, we picked the good apples off the ground. Next, we picked those we could reach. Now it was time to get in the tree. That's when the magic began for

1. See photos in insert.

me. As I picked Maya up to carefully lift her into the tree, I was lifted as well, carried back to another time.

You were not much older than little Maya. You came inside, very excitedly telling me that you and Grampa Yule had grafted a regular-sized apple into the crab apple tree. I remember you explaining how Grampa had slit the bark of the crab apple tree, inserted the small branch of the grafting apple, and then bound it with something. I remember listening but not hearing, not feeling or pouring myself into your little skin.

But I got a rare second chance that most parents never get. I looked up at Maya and saw you, my little seven-year-old Jewel, up there in that tree instead, and I let you tell me that story all over again. I could hear Grampa's excited, animated voice as he told you, his young and eager captivated audience, all about what he was doing. Oh, how your grampa loved an audience. He was always at his best having someone watch him and listen to him as he talked, explained, and pontificated his way through something he loved doing. Up there in that apple tree with you, he would have been in his element.

When he got really excited, he spit when he talked; you never wanted to be standing too close to him at times like that. I'll bet he was spitting that day.

I am sure you must have gotten a history lesson on how he first found that cabin, and how that apple tree came to be. You must have learned a fair bit about agronomy around the world, and of course a PhD-level lecture on grafting.

You told me again in great detail, with such excitement, how the grafting actually grows into and becomes a part of the parent tree. You told me how you and your grampa were going back in the spring to be the first to see whether or not the graft took. I could feel your anticipation of the pending miracle to be unfolded later that summer.

I recalled vividly how you did go down there with your grampa when the blooms were on. You returned to tell me there was no blossom, that the graft hadn't taken. You seemed fine with it, quite accepting and mature. I let it go at that point, but there under that tree, hearing the story again through new ears and new heart, I heard so much more. I heard the rest of the story.

So much did come from that grafting; so much did blossom and bear fruit. You and your grampa bonded up there in the tree that day. He grafted a part of you into his past, into his passion, into his heart. Up there in that tree, you saw him at his very best, as few people did. You were the new tender branch and he was the old tree, and you two became entwined. The time he spent with you that day so long ago helped nurture all your tender blossoms and the rare fruit they would bear someday: a compassionate, caring woman who loves nature, respects and recognizes the sanctity of all life—even a small branch— who feels and understands the connectedness of all things, who knows that even though all blossoms may not open and some experiments may fail, spring always comes carrying new hope and strength.

You looked so radiant up there telling me that story, knowing and feeling that I heard even more than your words were saying. Even a child knows when they are being truly seen, deeply heard. The moment felt good. It felt right. No matter how it went the first time, this moment was what counted.

The apples little Maya was raining down on the ground around me finally awakened me from my visit with the long-ago you.

"What are you looking at?" she asked.

"I was just thinking about my girl Jewel when she was little like you."

That satisfied her. I said, "Thank you, Maya."

She smiled down at me, feeling appreciated for her hard work up in the tree. Indeed, she was appreciated at that moment. Not just for the tiny apples and the annual ceremonial pie they would make, but for the sweet fruit of long ago that I was finally ready to taste.

The next time you come to visit, would you go there with me? It's never too late. I believe we could both fit up there. I'd love to hear that story one more time, or any other story you may want to tell, for the first or second time. Better yet, I'll get an apple branch from your Aunt Fay's awesome apple tree, and you can show me how to graft it, just the way my dad showed you.

# CHAPTER 20

# *Kase's Town*

Love and patience—I've never had a good grasp on these two concepts.

I understand the words well enough. But to get right down to it, it might be more accurate to say I've never been a calm and patient person, and I don't know that I've ever felt deep, pure love for someone and felt it in return.

Take the easier of those two concepts: patience. Because of my unique and special childhood, I was given a rare seventh sense: the ability to detect even the slightest impatience in others. Unfortunately, this gift came with the severe disability of not being able to recognize impatience in myself, especially as it begins to sneak up on me and take over.

One of my ex-wives once asked me in exasperation how it was that I could be so sensitive to impatience in others and yet be such an impatient person myself. Apparently, she'd never met anybody or experienced herself the very sad truth that often we do the very things we hate to see in others. In one moment, I could be the quivering child, and the next I could be a raging, out-of-control adult.

Regardless of how anyone else may see me, I'm the only one who can ultimately say what I see on my inner landscape. Whether I'm mildly annoyed or ready to chew and spit nails, I've learned to hide it well. Those closest to me or around me a lot know better, of course.

At this point in my life, I would dearly love to believe I've made great strides in showing patience and love. But I fear I'm still only a beginner.

The other day my wife and I were visiting with another couple. Somehow the subject of patience came up. For some reason beyond my grasp, I asked my wife if she did not think I'd become much more patient in the eight years we'd been together. Oh, what a seemingly innocent question! Right there in front of our friends, God, and the whole world, she shattered the fragile illusion I had been living under.

She stopped. "Um, not really."

Somehow, I was able to quickly gain control of my impatience and anger. Wearing my best happy face, I calmly asked, "Really? You've got to be kidding."

She amended her answer a bit and said that at times, instead of being impatient, I may just walk away, muttering under my breath.

*Well, okay*, I thought, shoving food in my mouth to keep from proving her right. I tried to continue with dinner.

Later, after our friends had gone and I'd ranted and raved a while more, she did admit that maybe I was a bit more patient. I guess it's all relative. In the end, I couldn't blame her. I see who I am now compared with that monstrously impatient younger me. And my dear Bonnie is comparing me to the calm tribe she was from.

As for the subject of love, that requires just a *little* bit more elaboration. The research is clear that children raised in an abusive or neglectful environment, where little or no love existed, are likely to be severely impaired in the love and relationships department.

While I was earning my master's degree in social work, I did as much research in this area as I could. I may have been a dysfunctional hick from the sticks of Alaska, but thank God I was smart enough to know where to look to find out what my chances were at navigating marriage and life in general. I wanted a realistic idea of how successful I could be at becoming a patient and loving father. On an unconscious, instinctual level, I was looking for what kind of emotional crutches or prosthetics I'd need. Even back then, before I had children, I had doubts and fears about how well I'd be able to manage in the love department.

Of course, knowing what lies ahead and what needs to be done, and then actually being able to do it are two vastly different things. Blaming your parents or life or anything external for your emotional impairments is pointless. Being angry that you only have one leg solves nothing. Your only solution is buying that prosthesis and learning how to use it. This is called taking responsibility for your life: you play the best hand with the cards you've been dealt.

I can say that today I increasingly feel love from and for the people around me. Even my patience with people is growing, though I'm not going to ask Bonnie to confirm that anytime soon. Especially if we're with friends.

What really made it a big deal was the fact that I believed deeply I was a real failure at being a father. There are still times I marvel that my children love me and want anything to do with me. We have had many good talks about this over the years, and sometimes they still have to reassure me. Each one, in their own way, has told me that they are thankful for who they are and for the childhood they had. And most of the time I believe that. Yet while parenting had never been my strongest role, I found grandparenting even more of a stretch.

I think it's safe to say I failed at being more than just a distant relative to my two sons' kids. I can think of many excuses for this, from them living in another state to my going through many divorces. Nonetheless, I never pulled off being what I consider a good grandfather. I regret that and I hope for the chance to get things right by all of them. But when my little girl had a boy, something told me this was my last chance to get something right and I knew the pressure was on. Things are different when your only daughter tells you she's expecting. I'd had no role models, since both my grandparents lived in Switzerland. But I strongly suspect I'd still have challenges if both sets had lived next door. Being a marginal dad doesn't set one up for wild success as a grandparent.

I deeply wanted to make an effort to do better with Kase, and not that my chances with the others were shot, but I had a fresh slate here. I knew there were some hard feelings in the way with my sons and stepchildren's families, but so far, I hadn't screwed up too badly with this one. Maybe somewhere down deep I sensed a success with him could carry over into better confidence with the others.

Jewel knew I'd felt like a failure as a grandfather and that I wanted to do better. We agreed early on that he should call me "Opa," the German name for grandpa I'd always hoped to be called. And because we are a family of yodelers, I also suggested what I thought was a brilliant idea: I would yodel over the phone while Jewel held the receiver to her belly. With such early imprinting, my unborn grandson would have a special connection with me from the start. Jewel wasn't convinced of my brilliance right away, but ultimately, she obliged.

She held the phone up to her stomach, I yodeled, and then she returned. "Bonding commenced," she said.

Sure, it was corny. But I believe it worked, let me tell you.

Given my record as a grandfather, when I'd visit Kase, I tried to spend a lot of time with him, on his level and in his world. Jewel always made big efforts to give us time together and to think of ways to include me in their life. She'd say I was a good Opa, that she appreciated all I did, and that Kase loved me and missed me when I wasn't there. She salved that "bad grandfather" wound many a time. Whether or not my inner critic felt I deserve it, I soaked it in deeply.

So, when she called and we began planning what would be her first time returning to her homeland in many years and Kase's first official visit, all my anxieties and fears about not being the Opa I wanted to be were fighting for attention. But I was struck dumb for several moments when in the midst of telling me how excited Kase was, Jewel said, "Actually, Kase asked if you were *handy*."

Immediately, my skin prickled up. In the lingo of Kase's father, Ty, a world-famous cowboy, being handy was all that matters about a man.

I cringed inside thinking about all I had to live up to with that. And I'm not ashamed to tell you I felt pretty small considering what

Jewel might think about me, the father she had known. I had serious doubts I was or ever would be handy in that little boy's eyes.

Once, while visiting Ty's ranch in Texas, he took me to the graveyard of some retired bucking horses. With us was his Hispanic ranch foreman whose English was minimal. I noticed one of the headstones had an interesting name.

"'Good Old Bastard,'" I read. "What's the story there?"

Ty chuckled and told me that when he buried the horse, it had no name. His foreman suggested it because when he'd do something particularly praiseworthy, that was what Ty would call him. It was a high cowboy complement.

Now, cowboys seldom, if ever, offer help. If asked, they'll go to great lengths—but not until it's asked for. Get on a horse with a loose cinch and a cowboy will say nothing, even though any cowboy knows that saddle will twist off the horse as soon as he steps into the stirrup. Better to let the man fall and learn a lesson than offer a hand unsolicited. It may seem rude not to correct someone who hasn't asked for it, but this unspoken policy assumedly makes for strong, dependable hands. Cowboys seldom compliment or praise, but when they do it's minimal and easy to miss. And on those rare occasions, you can be assured it's something special.

To Ty, *handy* is a word that, on many levels, meant that a man was admirably proficient. Such a man is unique among hundreds, something of a cowboy Olympian. A fellow cowboy might say, "He'd do to ride the river with," suggesting that in the complicated, treacherous dangers ahead he'd trust him with his life. *Handy* carries something of that deeper meaning.

So, when little Kase asked his mother if his Opa was handy, he was asking a whole lot. He knew the extremely high standard that came with that title. The real kicker was when he asked his mother, "Is Opa as handy as Dad?" My fear of not measuring up was so strong I didn't hear Jewel's reply. I was so beyond panic, I went numb, fighting the urge to cut and run. I think she said something reassuring so as not to disappoint him.

But another jolt of anxiety came when their plane developed mechanical problems and the trip was canceled. She called and told me Kase wouldn't stop crying and asked if she thought Opa would be sad too.

Hell, I couldn't admit it to him, but a big part of me considered it a relief that they might never arrive.

In Kase's mind, I knew he thought he was headed for endless adventure in a mythical wilderness, the place where long ago his mother had come from, and where his sepia-toned great-grandparents cleared the land with a team of horses and a crosscut saw, just like in the old photos. And now he wasn't going to get to visit his patient, loving, and perfectly handy Opa, who, in his mind, was racked with sobs at the disappointment.

However, the mechanical problems were soon resolved, and the trip was back on. And my anxiety returned just as quickly.

Fortunately, I had been learning to listen to myself better. I once read a series of books by Hal and Sidra Stone, husband-and-wife psychiatrists, about our many inner selves, and something about it resonated deeply. Whenever I've had conflicting emotions, I've thought about how those different selves within me can control me and cause me to react to life very differently. Sometimes this idea allows me to gain some control and respond a little better, a little more lovingly.

We've all said things like, "Part of me wanted to (do something bold), but the other part was too afraid." As the theory goes, our "aware ego," is in charge of those inner selves, and it is that ego who decides which selves are best suited for any of life's demands, like a carpenter might choose which tool to use for a particular job. Problems always come when a strong inner self overpowers the aware ego and takes off with the body, making us say and do things we don't want to.

Never in my life have I wanted to succeed as badly as I did on the day of my grandson's arrival. Never in my life have I wanted so much for my very best qualities and inner selves to be with me. And never had I more desperately hoped even a trace of those dysfunctional, scarred selves wouldn't be anywhere nearby.

When the day arrived, I paced the pavement at the small airport like a new father expecting his first child. The plane landed, and I headed out on the tarmac to meet them.

Today, I could not let that child down.

When he came into view from behind the plane his face lit up with excitement. "Opa!"

I crouched down and held out my arms and he ran to me, launching himself through the air into my arms. He almost knocked me flat, but I battled to stay upright as I battled my anxiety and doubts.

And that's where the magic began. Now don't get me wrong. It wasn't an out-of-body experience—at least I don't think it was. I've only ever heard about such experiences, so what do I really know? But a part of me was observing all of this in a detached, separate sort of way.

Down there on the tarmac, on my grandson's level, is where the magic began seeping into my old soul. It was seeping in from that young, innocent body, with small arms wrapped tightly around my neck as his soft cheek nestled against my grisly one. It seeped in until it consumed my whole being. It was a new feeling, but it was one I had been preparing for as hard as I had prepared for anything in my life.

I had not been preparing for this particular situation. I had not been preparing to be a better grandfather, or to be more loving and patient with him. But I had been preparing essential tools, tools that would help me in many situations, tools that would help me be more aware, more mindful, a more enlightened and spiritual person.

Perhaps it is my homestead upbringing that often has me comparing the journey through life as having a backpack full of essential tools, and knowing when and how to use them. Back on the homestead, whether clearing an obstacle with the ax, or removing a mudslide from the trail with a shovel, it was all about having the right tools along. You bring home a rabbit or a spruce hen, it's because you had the right tool along and knew how to use it effectively.

The tools I had along to prepare for my grandson's visit were tools I'd picked up years before to help me better understand my inner landscape, what made me tick. Specifically, how could I become more loving and patient, while still accepting and trying to understand my impatient and sometimes unloving nature?

I'd condensed the aware ego theory greatly to fit my own uniquely shaped brain, and then given it my own twist. We have many inner selves, some stronger, some weaker. Sometimes we choose carefully which self we want to be, other times one of our dominant selves takes over, and before we know it, we're simply reacting. We use a sharp ax to cut a bouquet of flowers, smashing half of them. We use our .22-caliber rifle to try to bring down a moose.

Think of a wise, experienced father telling his children when to use which tool, and those obedient, well-trained children who check in with their father on which tool would be best. That vigilant homestead father, because of his unique wilderness and survival training, is always acutely aware of all tools and all situations, and knows how to match them up.

That father, that person inside us who is in charge, is not one of our primary or secondary selves, it is a higher or stronger self, an all-knowing self. I hope to become so in tune with that aware ego that I will be continually guided to the best choices. The more tuned in I become, the sooner I will notice when an uninvited self tries to take over, much like noticing when an uninvited stranger tries to break into your house.

To me, my aware ego is a wise old cowboy in charge of a huge range with many cowboys under him. They all know he's the boss, the foreman, but they just call him "the old cowboy." It works for me really well. And I might add, he works for me really hard. No easy job being in charge of Atz Kilcher's mob of inner ranch hands. This image best suits my wilderness range-riding mentality, although the homestead father with the kids and the tools works well also.

Now you have a better picture of the magic that is about to happen there on the tarmac holding my grandson. This is by far the toughest job this old cowboy has had yet. He has to take drastic measures, basically start from scratch, and do something he's never had to do before. It's going to be like building a brand-new self with only the best materials.

He starts by clearing all the selves out of Atz's mind and soul. Strong, weak, good, bad, stubborn, brave, loving, impatient. He calls them all up against the chain-link fence surrounding the tarmac. He then positions himself between them and Atz, kneeling with his grandson. His long, well-worn duster is flapping in the gentle breeze, his old range-rider hat pulled low, but not so low that they can't see the seriousness in his eyes. Those negative selves who are sure that Atz will fail—Doubt, Skepticism, Impatience, Anger, and all of their friends—are waiting for that chance to rush by the old cowboy and go back to their usual tricks. But the big six-gun on his hip also makes quite an impression.

One by one, the old cowboy points to certain selves and lets them get by his careful scrutiny. Patience and Love lead the way with confident strides. Kindness, Understanding, and Gentle Firmness round out the crew the old cowboy has chosen for this job. Many selves, many ingredients for success. The cowboy ponders. Now he's got to roll up this special combination of selves into one brand-new self and give him a new name. But what should that self be called?

As that crew of his very best cowboys merges with that grandfather on the tarmac holding his grandson, it comes to him: "Of course! That's a no-brainer. I will call him Opa!"

A powerful self. No unwelcome ranch hands will enter his realm without his invitation under any circumstances.

The old cowboy quickly turns back to the fence to make sure all are still in their place. Atz raises his head from where it was nestled next to his grandson and looks over his shoulder. He nods lovingly and approvingly at the old cowboy, silently thanking him, and then adds his don't-even-think-about-it glare to the unruly mob by the fence.

Kneeling with Kase, I feel the love supporting me. Gone are the fears and memories of past failures, the pressure of the limited time to introduce him to his Alaskan heritage. Only love and peace remain in the outstretched protective arms of the old cowboy. The big pistol he wore on his hip, the rifle in his saddle scabbard told those many selves they would not bully their way in this time.

Hand in hand, we walked to his mother coming to greet us. And her smile told me she saw the change in me too. Somehow her dad had transformed into an "Opa" right before her eyes. I felt the new me, a brand-new, loving, and patient Opa, born again in the magic.

It was an amazing feeling.

* * *

We met "Oma Bonnie" at the car and rode to our house together for our first adventure.

"There's a big surprise waiting for you," I said.

"What is it?" he asked.

I smiled. "You'll just have to wait."

Alaska is a big place. He'd heard big stories. His mother, his grandparents, even his grandparents' parents had carved out their homesteads and settled the wilderness. He'd seen some of it on TV, so it was even bigger than life! My surprise would have to be a big one. The idea finally came to me when I went back to ask my inner five-year-old to lead the way. He took me back to the homestead and showed me the little pretend houses we built in the dense alder thickets. The trunks of the alders lying almost horizontal to the ground formed the imaginary walls. The higher branches and leaves where the roof. A few simple boards and rounds of wood were our furnishings. Each of us kids had private residences in that magical alder patch.

Then, my little former self took me to the steep canyon right beside our house where we'd pretended to be cave dwellers. At the time, it didn't feel like pretend. Some caves were dug in four or five feet and were at least that wide. A couple had two or three levels. These caves were a different world where we couldn't hear our parents calling us to work.

We'd had countless trees we'd escape into. We climbed trunks or knotted ropes to get up and built simple platforms as high as we could. In one giant birch, all eight of us had separate branches, a special space for each of us. These spaces were our private escapes from that crowded one-room cabin. The only limit to our fantasy was our creativity.

But most special of all, we had trails—horse trails, cow trails, bear trails. We made trails with our feet and an ax. And each led to adventures in a different world. Some led to mushroom-filled forests or swamps of low-bush cranberries. Others led to fertile meadows of imagination. And it was on these trails and the many destinations they took us where the songs, the stories, the poetry, and the paintings were conceived. It was on these trails where we recovered the sustenance of our soul, picking it like low-hanging fruit. My small former self reminded me that this is where I'd found myself. Nature filled the holes left by the aunts and uncles and grandparents back in the old country.

When we pulled up, everything was ready. I'd spent the week creating a whole town for Kase. I knew he understood that a town was roads and houses, and I wanted him to have the permanent feeling that there was a whole town built just for him, not simply a few trails somewhere in the remote Alaskan wilderness. I was even going to name it after him. It would be "Kase Town"—especially perfect since his middle name is Townes.

I went crazy out there on my five acres with the old John Deere and the scraper on the back. I made trails with intersections and junctions and even a couple of parks. There was a large pond that would be our lake and a small creek we could build a bridge over. But I saved the best part, choosing a spot for his cabin, for him to pick out. I placed signs and bridge-building material in place and left the trails merely roughed in. We could choose names for roads and intersections to put on the signs later. I wasn't interested so much in building a town as building a young homesteader. I wanted him to feel connected but also to learn you have to work for what you get, to make him a responsible young man.

We opened the doors and Kase popped out. "Where's my surprise?" he asked.

"Kase Townes Murray, welcome to your town!"

With a five-year-old's total honesty, he looked around puzzled. Clearly this was not his idea of a town with roads and houses and stores.

His mother stepped in to help me. "Actually, Kase, this is the beginning of a town. This is how all towns start and you get to help build it. It will be your very own town!"

"I've already built some roads with our tractor," I said, "and you can help me finish them. You can drive the tractor! I built a couple of parks and some tree houses in the alders. I've already gotten some things done ahead of time, and I'll show you everything else that still needs to be done. Your Opa still needs a lot of help. But you get to choose where we're gonna put your cabin. And you can name every road in your town!"

Slowly, I saw the light in his eyes come on. And seeing that was worth all the effort and more!

Kase rode the tractor with me. He helped run the scraper blade. He used a shovel and a rake and picked up sticks. I told him that picking up sticks and clearing land was at the very top of being a good homesteader. He helped me decide where the bridge should go and then we built it. He named the roads, and the bridges, and the lake. And he gave his town a beautiful name: "Townesville." I already had the sign.

Finally, it was time to make those magical alder houses. I had already built a trail into the center of a dense alder thicket and cleared a space. I had set up a short section of a log standing on end with a piece of gray board on top of it serving as a table. I told him it was time to go and have an early birthday party in his special house. His eyes lit up like a dream come true. This old-school Opa had made the grade.

I told him I had to go ahead to make sure everything was ready. I wanted to be sure I could see his face as he entered our fantasy realm, the realm of my own childhood. The walls, the roof, and the door were all made of flexible alders and branches I had woven together.

Light came in through the center and I had my little guitar by the table, which was set with cupcakes and ice cream. All was prepared.

I have performed on many stages in my life. I have seen enthralled audiences as they breathlessly watched and listened to my daughter and I yodel in harmony. I used to teach elementary music, I know what little excited expectant faces look like.

But Kase's face as he came around that last alder and in the branch door with his mom, his huge eyes, and his open mouth, took me right back. This was it. We'd made it. We were in the magic zone.

We had a party there, each of us sitting on a round of wood around our gray wood table. And beneath the green roof of leaves, we ended the day with a song about a hermit thrush who lived in the alders that my oldest sister Mossy wrote when she was thirteen, playing in her own alder house in the canyon. She taught it to me, I taught it to my daughter, and she taught it to Kase. Three generations, still in the alders, still singing about the hermit thrush.

It was getting late. They'd traveled far that day and were tired. When Jewel asked Kase if he wanted to stay with Opa, I was sure he'd have had his fill of this unfamiliar place and these grandparents he didn't know well. But he said yes, as though it were the most natural thing in the world. And we all slept well that night.

I went to sleep picturing the old cowboy smiling, bundled up in his sheepskin jacket as he stood guard at the gate to Townesville.

When I woke, he was standing beside the bed.

"Opa, can we go down to my alder house?"

I'm one of these grouchy wakers. At least until I've had several cups of coffee. But I didn't have time for the usual morning funk to settle down on me. Before I knew it, I had my guitar in one hand and my grandson in the other, and we headed back down to the magic zone.

We talked, we sang, and then out of the corner of my eye I saw a fluttering, a bird. It had landed just a few feet above our head in an alder branch. It's rust-colored back and speckled breast told me right off it was a hermit thrush. I pointed without a word and he whispered, "Is that the hermit thrush?"

"Yes." I could hardly believe it.

"He must have heard us. That's why he came."

There was only one way to respond to that. "Yes, that's why he came."

We worked. We played. It was easy. All I had to do was remember how old I was. When I practiced shooting my bow at the silhouette of a bear he got so excited. It's like he'd suddenly morphed into a little hunting-gathering-survivalist caveman man-cub. No sooner did I shoot an arrow than he had to race to the target to tell me how close I was to the bull's-eye, shouting the results like a referee from the field. I shot till I could no longer draw the bow.

We spent hours in my shop looking at old bones and claws and teeth and skulls. We looked at piles of roots and interestingly shaped pieces of driftwood. I showed him the jewelry I made from these objects. I showed him the baskets I made. It was like leading a duck to water. He soaked it all up as though he had some dehydrated DNA strands that had been waiting for this moment.

It was easy for me to understand how he would love those same things I had loved at his age. But he loved doing different kinds of work with me! Hard work! In small doses, of course. But it amazed me that he loved the many ways I like to spend free time, the way I like to express myself through my art.

We rode horses. We chased cows. We visited a family quite a ways out in the wilderness that had a lot of young kids close to his own age. He watched his mom and me help with some of the ranch work. Ranch work, of course, was nothing new to him, but it was the first time he had seen his mother and his Opa working cows together. After the work was done, we went inside for refreshments and to sing a few songs for our friends and some of their neighbors. After all, it's not every day that Jewel just happens to drop by. And there in that living room, surrounded by a group of strange adults and children of varying ages, some more magic dust was sprinkled. Kase chose that moment to sing with his mother for the first time! Now tell me, how cool is that?

Later that day, his mother heard him yodeling for the first time. A short while after that, while riding behind me on a four-wheeler, he yodeled again. This was big! This was huge! A long-standing Swiss family tradition was handed down to yet another generation. Obviously, something was shifting in him. Could've been having his own town. Could've been that house in the alders and the visiting hermit thrush. Could've been the songs and the stories. Could've been Alaska. Could've been being close to his roots, or possibly rediscovering his own, long lying dormant.

Countless opportunities he gave me every day to practice love, practice patience. Countless opportunities for me to bask in the warmth of his love and adoration. Countless opportunities he gave me to feel and believe myself worthy. Countless tests I passed. Countless causes for celebration. The newness, the clumsiness, and the awkwardness was fading. I was growing brand-new heart muscles.

We are in the car ready to leave. It's not just as simple anymore as running out to the truck and jumping in and somewhere down the road putting on my seatbelt. Now it's getting him ready, getting all his gear ready, getting them in the truck, and then buckling him in. Oh, yes, his snacks and his drink. And oh, yes, all the things he forgot.

"Opa, could you go get Froggy?"

Froggy. I go get Froggy. Well worn, but still well loved.

"Opa," he said again in his sweetest voice, not a clue on his horizon that he's taunting the monster, "would you go get Fluff-Fluff?"

Of course. Fluff-Fluff. He has to have Fluff-Fluff. He's been with Kase since he was born. Little does my grandson know there are three or four identical Fluff-Fluffs in case one gets left behind. But Fluff-Fluff can't be left behind. I go get Fluff-Fluff.

Now, it's a long way from the truck back to the living room where all the toys are. I go around the truck again, walk the twenty steps to the stairs, up five steps and another twenty to the living room. I'm not a young man anymore, so I take my time. There's no hurry, nothing else to do but to practice being Opa.

Not until I return from my third trip back and forth, this time with "sippy cup," do I hear the clamoring at the gate. It sounds like a blood-frenzied pack of hounds held back by a prison guard. The noise tells me they've been trained to be that angry and impatient. They want to storm Townesville and eat my forgetful little grandson. They want to tear me limb from limb. But the noise is not outside of me. It is inhabiting my body. I only pause long enough to make sure the old cowboy is still on duty. Yep, he's got it covered! I see he's called on some of the tougher ranch hands to help him out. The hounds don't stand a chance.

Way too soon the three-day visit has ended. But boy, did we ever pack in some good adventures. Just before I take him back to the airport to meet his mom, I take them out to my shop of treasures. I give him a small pouch he can wear around his waist. It's otter fur and the flap snaps down to hold everything inside. I give him the three treasures to put inside this gift I've made, and I make a small ceremony out of it.

*A horse tooth for speed. A beaver tooth for hard work. And a bear tooth for strength.*

I tell him he will think of me when he sees those treasures, and I will think of him when I look at mine. He cries when I tell him I can't send any bullets home with him, but I promise to send him some when I can get the firing pin removed. He tries hard to understand but doesn't.

On the way to the airport we pass the coffee shop and he looks at me in a very adult, conspiratorial way. *Opa, are you thinking what I'm thinking?* I pull in and get him a hot chocolate with whipped cream and marshmallows. His mom will never know.

Then, I take him to the airport and we hug goodbye. We hold onto each other tightly for a moment. I'm so sad to see him go. I believe I've fallen in love with him. It wasn't hard.

The plane taxis down the runway. I wave. I'm not sure if he sees me. But it doesn't really matter. I'm good. We're both good. Really good. I think about love and patience. Maybe I'm getting more used to the feeling.

I've been a people-pleaser all my life. Trying to impress people with anything I thought might impress them, even if I had to make it up, even if it wasn't really me. I've been looking for validation all my life, many times and in all of the wrong places. But there's no one to tell you where to look, so you just keep looking and giving it your best shot. Making mistakes. Wiping off the dust and getting back on the horse. Maybe you get tired after a while, quit trying as hard, maybe you slowly just start accepting who you are and trust that those who matter will see you.

We go through life looking for those special recognitions, those certificates, those degrees. We long for the awards and banquets held in our honor. It's natural. We're born with that longing, and we all deserve to know we're flawless children of God. We all deserve to rediscover ourselves, to finally find ourselves.

Thank you, Kase, for trusting with the faith of a child. And thank you, Jewel, for the second chance. Or perhaps a first chance. Or perhaps it wasn't chance at all.

\* \* \*

As I'm putting the finishing touches on this chapter, the phone rings and it's Jewel saying she has something to ask me about Kase.

And in less than the space of a heartbeat I travel light-years, ponder profound mysteries and commune deeply with what I call my higher power, even contemplating possibly changing my definition of him. Because partner, no matter what kind of a sorry, crusty buckaroo you've been on that big ranch of life, a coincidence like this makes you look at just what you do believe about who's running things.

"You will never believe it," I say to her, "but I was just writing about Kase. It's my favorite chapter so I think I will end my book with it."

"Why is it your favorite chapter?"

"First, it's a feel-good story," I explain. "The perfect place to end. Seeing everything through his five-year-old eyes for the first time and through my long-ago five-year-old eyes again was pretty powerful, my daughter. To be looked at with such innocent, adoring eyes as though you were God, or at least a child of God, or at the very least a darn handy human being. I couldn't ask for a more perfect ending. It may just be my best act, the only stretch of pure white on the long canvas of my life."

We chat a while, and then she says, "The reason I called is, I wanted to plant a seed. Don't feel you have to answer right now and please don't feel any pressure. It's just a seed."

"I love seeds," I say. "Plant away."

"I'd like Kase to spend more time with you."

Big goose bumps on my vocal cords prevent me from answering right away. But when my voice returns I say, "I'd be honored."

I am fortunate to have been honored many times in my life. I have felt that flood of warmth many times. But never had that word taken on its full meaning for me like it did in that moment.

And then she softly said, "*I'd* be so honored, Dad."

This is the daughter who once said to Shane when I was taking care of his young boys for a few days, "You can't be trusting your young boys with our dad." She was younger then. So was I.

She's read the latest books and consulted with the top authorities on how to properly raise her son. She's carried the scars caused by falling off horses I had her ride way before they were ready. And she's known scars on her soul from my screaming, shaming, and blaming.

But now, my daughter was confirming that a miracle had happened.

And she didn't expect me to merely be Opa in town. She was asking me to take them to the head of the bay where the bears and wolves live. With deadly guns and sharp knives, where glacial rivers and quicksand lurk, and into the heart of the great wilderness his great Opa Yule had settled.

She explained briefly and clearly what she felt he needed to learn, what he'd gain from time with me. She explained why I was the perfect person to do this and then she listed my qualifications like I'd never heard from anyone. But mostly, she talked about watching the two of us together and what it brings out in him. I guess I hadn't noticed any of that and didn't know I was bringing anything out in him. I was too busy experiencing what he was bringing out in me.

I reflected on all the self-doubt I went through before he came to visit, that inner self who was afraid to trust that he could do it as he knelt there on the tarmac. I'd hoped I could make it through the next three days without blowing it too badly and having him leave hating me.

I stood there with the phone in my hand and an unbelievable joy in my heart, looking at newly fallen snow and the sunrise coming over the glaciers and mountains. No hesitation this time.

*I'd be honored.*

Later, I drive out toward the Kilcher homestead. I'm going cross-country skiing at McNeil Canyon Elementary School where I taught music and PE until I retired. I get a text, a photo of Kase skiing in Telluride. I know he must be next to his ski instructor, Lara, and her phone, so I call them back. By now, they've finished carving and tearing up the slopes, and he's at swim lessons.

"Way to go, Grandson! Skiing and swimming in one day! I'm really proud of you!"

"Tell him about the jump you went over," I hear Lara saying.

"Opa, I went over a big jump today and went at least three feet off the ground!"

"Wow! Way to go!" I shout into the phone. From the noise and splashing I think he may already be in the pool.

"Guess what, Kase? Opa went swimming this morning and now I'm going cross-country skiing. It's a swim and ski day for both of us!"

"Say goodbye to your Opa," I hear his coach saying.

"Goodbye, Opa." More splashing and he's off! He's got treasures to retrieve from the bottom of the pool, underwater tea parties to attend with Lara, and hot chocolate and marshmallows and many other goodies to savor. I thank Lara for thinking to text me and hang up.

I ski around the loop. It's bitter cold. The skis barely slide. The trees are covered with snow and the sky is bright blue. The view of Kachemak Bay, with large floating ice flows, and the mountains and glaciers beyond is more breathtaking than the subzero air I am breathing. An absolutely perfect ending to a perfect day.

This is the very same view I knew growing up, the very same view my parents chose. The Kilcher homestead lies just down the canyon about a mile from here. I feel very close to them at the moment. I feel their presence. I think about all they gave us. Beautiful surroundings, many wonderful qualities and talents, limitless opportunities, and yes, some hardships too. At this point in my life, I can see that it's mostly good stuff that my parents gave me, but I had to take the bad stuff and make it into something I could use—skills and knowledge that continue for generations, courage, bravery, and a stick-to-it mentality. It was only when I grew up and went to college and read self-help books that I realized my ability to do all these things to improve my life came from that courage and bravery and perseverance. My parents unknowingly gave me both the disease and the antidote. They gave us these wonderful tools, though I didn't know it for years. These tools I had only seen as useful in the physical pioneering realm, for homesteading, hard work. It took me into middle age to stop blaming them, and only when I finally saw through the bad did I see that those hidden tools they left behind, something I could only access once I forgave, that those tools could be used in all realms of life.

I push myself forward through the snow, past the encrusted trees. I feel the warmth from inside rising up to meet the cold air. And all of those thoughts and my busy mind go to a quiet place where only feelings are allowed to dwell. I close my eyes and simply *feel*.

# ACKNOWLEDGMENTS

I recall vividly the first time I earned twenty-five cents for selling a bunch of radishes. Of much more value than the money, however, was the lesson and realization of everything and everyone involved in transforming that small reddish seed into a shiny silver quarter in my pocket. Finding the land, tilling the garden, buying the seeds, buying that old Jeep that took the radishes to town, the store owner who bought my radishes, and the customer who came later and bought those radishes and took them home. A long chain of events. A big team. Every element integral to reaching the final outcome, much like the production of a book.

Without my agent, Sandra Bishop, the many editors who worked on this project, including Marie Prys, Mick Silva, and Courtney Vatis, and all the other folks at Blackstone Publishing, this book would still be just a radish seed.

A special thank you to Vikki Warner, acquisitions editor at Blackstone, a kindred soul, who first read my manuscript and said yes. You believed in my first bunch of radishes and bought them. I am deeply touched.

And a special thank you to Mr. Black, founder of Blackstone Publishing, who, like my father, is a dreamer and a pioneer.

I am most grateful to my wife, Bonnie, the first reader of all my rough drafts and first listener to my stories. Thank you for believing in me.

Thank you, my children, Shane, Jewel, Atz Lee, and Nikos—you know me well and still love me.

And finally, a big homestead Alaskan thank you to the many fans of the dream of my pioneering parents. Each and every step, every insight and ounce of support from the seed of my first draft to the fully grown radish of a book that you hold in your hands today, was an integral part in making this book come to fruition. I couldn't have done it without you all, and for that I will always be grateful.